Home Was the Land of Morning Calm

△
▼▼ ADDISON-WESLEY PUBLISHING COMPANY

Home Was the Land
of Morning Calm

A SAGA OF A

KOREAN-AMERICAN FAMILY

K. Connie Kang

Reading, Massachusetts   Menlo Park, California   New York

Don Mills, Ontario   Wokingham, England   Amsterdam   Bonn

Sydney   Singapore   Tokyo   Madrid   San Juan

Paris   Seoul   Milan   Mexico City   Taipei

Many of the designations used by manufacturers and sellers to distinguish their products are claimed as trademarks. Where those designations appear in this book and Addison-Wesley was aware of a trademark claim, the designations have been printed in initial capital letters.

Library of Congress Cataloging-in-Publication Data
Kang, K. Connie.
    Home was the Land of Morning Calm : A saga of a Korean-American family / K. Connie Kang.
      p.   cm.
    ISBN 0-201-62684-5 (hardcover)
    1. Kang, K. Connie. 2. Women journalists—United States—Biography. 3. Korean-American journalists—Biography. 4. Korea—History—20th century. I. Title.
PN4872.K36   1995
070'.92—dc20
[B]   94-49532
                                                        CIP

Jacket design by David High
Text design by Linda Koegel
Set in 11-point Bembo by Jackson Typesetting

1 2 3 4 5 6 7 8 9-MA-9998979695
First printing, June 1995

To my parents,

With love and gratitude

CONTENTS

PROLOGUE

By nature all men are so alike.

It's by their habits they become so different.

—Confucius, *Analects*

On a cold January night in 1951, when North Korean troops were about to invade Seoul, I rode on the rooftop of the last train bound for Pusan with my mother to escape the oncoming Communists. Bone-chilling wind from Siberia whipped across the "freedom train," which was jampacked with soldiers, the sick, and the injured. There was no room inside for able-bodied civilians—not even children.

"I don't want to go up there, Mommy," I protested. "It's too scary."

"We will be all right," Mother assured me, even though I could tell she was scared herself. "See those fellows on the train? They will secure us," she said, pointing to the men on top of the train with a big wad of straw rope in their hands. "If we don't take this train, we will surely die in the hands of Communists. This is the last train to Pusan."

Over our layers of heavy underwear and sweaters, Mother and

I wore pants and coats made of U.S. Army green blankets purchased on the black market. We looked fat from all the clothing, and it was hard to move quickly because of the bulk. Mother had spent several days sewing the appropriate clothing while we prepared to leave Seoul. We were luckier than most; not everybody could afford the warm American blankets that were much in demand that winter.

The noisy, smelly train station was packed with people, many of whom called out the names of relatives. Hungry babies cried for their mothers' milk. An exasperated mother, so emaciated she looked like she might collapse any moment, gave her baby a piece of dried squid for a pacifier, but the baby spit it out and continued bawling. Many women had crying children strapped to their backs while they also carried a load on their heads. There were not many men around because most had been drafted into the military or other wartime duties. After a while the cries of children became indistinguishable in the commotion, as the mob of people bustled about.

In the dim, flickering light of oil lamps, I saw a long row of refugees seated atop the train, their belongings stacked beside them. From a distance, the elongated mound of people and their possessions looked like odd-shaped chimneys on the train that stretched so far back, I could not see its end. And when I opened my eyes wide and looked up at the top of the train from the platform where I stood, and thought about what it would be like to be up there while the train moved, I felt dizzy and nauseous.

"You better get on the train now, or there won't be any place left," a stern, tired-looking middle-aged man told my mother. He sounded irritated. "Let's go. Let's hurry."

"Yes, yes," my mother said, still hesitating. He and several younger men, who we learned later were seminary students from the North Korean capital of Pyongyang, were helping families like ours who were not accompanied by males. The men looked like they had been on the road for several days. Their dark Western-style trousers and coats looked worn, and their woolen caps had holes. As if to make up Mother's mind for her, the stern-looking man came toward me with a rope. He tied it around my middle and threw the other end up to a man standing on top of the train, who lifted me up, his left and right hands alternating on the rope, as if he were drawing a bucket of water from a deep well.

Mother climbed very slowly up a small staircase at the back of the coach with the help of the young man who had pulled me up. When I got up on the top of the train, I was surprised to see how roomy it was. Looking up from below, I had imagined a narrow strip of space barely enough for Mother and me to sit, but there was plenty of room for the two of us and all our belongings. With the help of the man who pulled me up, Mother arranged our allotted space efficiently, as if it were a family room. An eighty-pound sack of rice was placed about three-quarters of the way toward one side of the train, as one would place a couch. A bundle containing kitchenware and clothing was put along each side of the rice. I sat on a straw mat in the middle so I could lean back on the sack of rice. The straw sack was secured to the train with a rope clear across the width of the rooftop. My mother sat beside me and held me by the cord tied around my middle with one hand to make sure I didn't fall off the train. The "freedom train" traveled all through the night, chugging away, sometimes whistling and passing what seemed like interminable expanses of farmlands and mountains.

Not everyone was as fortunate as I on that fateful night when Mother put her life and mine on the line by taking to the roof of the train. That night several youngsters fell accidentally to their death. Life was cheap. I could have been one of them, had my mother not secured me and grasped the rope tied to my waist throughout the long trip, her hand nearly frozen under her mittens from the exposure to the biting wind. Whenever my mother caught me dozing off, she pinched me. "Don't fall asleep. Don't fall asleep," she said. "You'll fall off the train if you do," she said, all the while not once letting go of the rope around my waist.

The journey from the upturned eaves of my ancestral home in North Korea to that of an immigrant's life in America has been a meandering one. It has included many stops along the way: Seoul, Pusan, Fukuoka, Tokyo, and Okinawa. From the littered streets of

Pusan, where homeless urchins in tattered clothes wandered with cans to collect food, and lepers with only a hole for a nose and inch-long stumps for fingers panhandled menacingly, my mother and I escaped to Japan on a small fishing boat on a moonlit October night in 1952. We hoped to reunite with my father, who had come to Tokyo from New York, soon after the Korean War broke out on June 25, 1950.

"Go safely, Kyonshill-ra," I heard my uncle Suk-Hoon Choi calling my name, from ashore, as fishermen pushed the boat away from the shore. With the full moon shining so brightly, grownups worried that we might be detected even before we got out to sea.

I wondered when I would see my uncle again. He was my mother's only brother. "Take care of yourself, too, Uncle," I said from the boat. Men on the boat helped me slip down to our tiny compartment under the deck. It felt damp and smelled of mildew. I lay over a thin quilt and wondered how I could stand to be cooped up inside that small space through the long journey on the sea. But when I put my ears to the wall and heard the sound of the motor, I felt good. It assured me that it was not just any boat we were taking to Japan but a special, motorized boat that would withstand big waves and whales in the sea. When I was four years old, I had seen the skeleton of a whale during a visit to my uncle's medical school, and I had feared whales ever since. When Mother said we were taking a boat to Japan, the possibility of whales capsizing the boat frightened me more than anything else.

Mother and I each had a bundle containing a change of clothing and a small bag of food for the trip—rice seasoned with marinated beef and vegetables, made into seaweed rolls. We wore old clothes intentionally because we would be discarding them and changing into new clothes once we reached Japan.

The trip took twenty-four hours. When we arrived, we were arrested almost immediately for illegally entering the country. Our boat docked at the wrong place, and the Japan-born Korean college student my mother had hired as our guide had gotten us lost. Two months later, after brief stays in jail, a detention center, and a hospital, we were released on bail and reunited with my father. Our journey on the train from Fukuoka to Tokyo was like a dream. The Japanese train traveled along miles of magnificent tangerine groves. "Look at those tangerine trees," I said excitedly to my father. Citrus fruits were so precious in Korea, only the rich could afford them on the black market. If you were lucky, you got one or two tangerines or oranges from Santa Claus for Christmas. But in Japan, there were mountains of tangerines!

It was so pleasing to be inside a coach with clean dark-green velvet seats with white lace covers. What a contrast from my train ride to Pusan. And how I savored the taste of the box lunches we bought from vendors in uniforms who came aboard during stops and bowed before and after each transaction. Garnishes of sliced tanger-ines with their green leaves and thin slices of pale pink ginger inside the lunchbox looked so pretty and luscious. I was sure I was going to like my new home. For my mother, the train ride to Tokyo brought back memories of her student days in Japan fifteen years earlier when she was training to be a schoolteacher and lived in a dormitory with Japanese roommates. "The Japanese are just as I remembered them," she said. "You have to hand it to them—they're so good at pleasing their customers."

☯

Our six happy years in Tokyo came to an abrupt end just before my junior year in high school when my father's work took us to Okinawa, which was then under U.S. jurisdiction. I did not like the heat and humidity of this semitropical island, which, in the 1950s and 1960s, was dominated by U.S. military installations. Except for the raging typhoons during which we boarded up windows and lived inside with kerosene lamps, my three years in Okinawa were unmem-orable and ended, thankfully, when I started my university education in the fall of 1961.

Shivering in my blue and white sleeveless seersucker dress and white sweater, I landed at San Francisco International Airport in

September 1961. During the bus ride from the airport to my hotel in downtown San Francisco, I felt excited and scared. I had never seen a more beautiful city. The white buildings on hilltops seemed precariously stacked on top of each other, yet they dazzled like jewels in the sun. Flowers and plants dangled from window boxes. And the people looked so chic in dark clothing. I was the only one in a summer dress and white shoes. Little did I know then that San Francisco would one day become my adoptive home. After one night, however, I continued on to Kansas City, then to Columbia, Missouri, to begin my American education at the University of Missouri.

My encounter with the United States changed my life. It opened my eyes to a world where people made choices based on their individual preferences. In America, individualism reigned, not family consensus. America provided me with a new set of eyes to judge my own culture and value systems, and my contact with America sparked an internal revolution that continues to this day, challenging the assumptions I inherited from the East. Ideas that Americans take for granted, such as egalitarianism, justice, and fairness, gradually became part of my own value system. I have come to believe as strongly as anyone else in the inherent equality of all people—a concept foreign in my Confucian-steeped culture. I have come to believe in fairness, the rule of law, and the importance of rules and process—all alien concepts where I came from. But the encounter with America has been a mixed blessing: I have been enriched by it, and I have suffered because of it.

In 1967, after six years in America, I returned to Asia, but America had changed me irrevocably. I was no longer totally comfortable there. After only three years, I returned to the United States—this time as an immigrant. I did not realize it then, but when I arrived at New York's John F. Kennedy International Airport in January 1970, I was part of the second wave of Korean immigration, seven decades after the first wave. Over the next twenty years this second wave would increase the population of ethnic Koreans in the United States from seventy thousand to one million and help change the face of urban America.

Because I had learned English from an American tutor when I was in primary school, I did not have the language handicap that most Korean immigrants struggled with when they arrived, and from which many still suffer. I managed to find interesting work as a newspaperwoman while so many other immigrants opened grocery stores and pursued jobs that were so completely at odds with their plans for life in America. Koreans did not come to America to open liquor stores and laundries. They aspired to much more, but they quickly found out that their professional training in Korea was not recognized here, and that their limited English consigned them to jobs that did not require language proficiency, such as cleaning or opening one's own business.

Since I am among a handful of Korean American writers working on major American newspapers, I receive telephone calls and letters from Koreans from all over the country. Some want just to make an acquaintance. Others ask me to write stories they would like to see in print. Their suggestions often have little bearing on the reality of mainstream journalism, however. Could I do a story about a meeting of Korean senior citizens in Hollywood? Since an important South Korean politician has arrived, could I interview him? A Korean American woman in San Jose asks me to help her fight a lawyer who she says took $40,000 and has not done anything for her. She has complained to the State Bar of California, but she is getting nowhere, she says. After three decades of working in newsrooms of metropolitan newspapers, I know these stories are low priority to American editors. So I explain. Still, they contact me, by phone, fax, and letters, with more of the same kind of stories they want me to write. I sometimes think that they just want to talk in Korean to someone in the mainstream to air what bothers them about American society.

However assimilated I might feel at times, and however much my profession and my acculturation pull me into American society, I identify with immigrants because I am one of them; we share the same fate. We have brought to America memories of our ancestral land, memories not only of the clear rivers and breathtaking mountains but also of poverty. We have the indelible scars in our psyches of the Japanese occupation, the Korean War, the partition that still keeps eleven million Korean families separated, and the three decades of South Korean military rule during which we were unable to speak our minds even from here for fear of retribution to loved ones back home. We have many stories to tell, but we have been reticent. Where do we begin? How do we begin to explain who we are, why we are here?

Though we are not as well known as the Chinese and Japanese, Koreans have been in the United States since the dawn of the twentieth century—working in the sugarcane fields in Hawaii, growing rice in the Sacramento Valley, and picking oranges in southern California. Often mistaken for Chinese or Japanese, Koreans have worked hard, dreaming of the day they would return to their country when it would be free from foreign domination. Many have given half of every dollar they earned toward the end, the Korean independence movement.

The Korean diaspora began with critical decisions President Theodore Roosevelt made in 1905. In a secret treaty with Japan, he agreed to give Japan control over Korea and Manchuria in exchange for Japan's promise not to interfere with the U.S. presence in the Philippines. Continuing foreign intervention over the next five decades has inextricably altered not only the course of my life and that of my family, but the lives of seventy-five million ethnic Koreans everywhere.

It was a direct result of Roosevelt's decision that prompted one of my ancestors, Tong-Hwi Yi, to leave home to help wage the Korean independence movement in Manchuria, China, and Russia. A brilliant soldier and an orator, General Yi, my grandmother's cousin, became the premier in the Korean Provisional Government in Shanghai and devoted his life to regaining his country. My grandfather, Myong-Hwan Kang, followed Yi to work in the resistance, leaving Tanchon, our family town by the East Sea. For six hundred years my ancestors had lived and died in that rugged and picturesque country where even in the twentieth century tigers, leopards, and wolves roamed at night. My parents went to sleep at night hearing wolves howling near their home—a long way in miles and years from San Francisco, where they now go to sleep listening to foghorns by the Golden Gate Bridge.

This, then, is a story of the Korean diaspora. It is a story of my native place, a rabbit-shaped country we call the Land of Morning Calm. This is also a story about my family and how we lived through the turbulent changes of the twentieth century, and my own journey to America, my adopted home, which began when my great-grandfather Bong-Ho Kang embraced Christianity and set the Kang clan on the road to Westernization.

March 1995
LOS ANGELES

ACKNOWLEDGMENTS

This book would not have been possible without the guidance of my parents, who instilled in my brother and me our Koreanness—knowledge of our roots that was even more important because we grew up away from our ancestral land. My father's contribution to this project has been enormous.

I am indebted to Joo-Han Kang and Dexter Waugh for reading several versions of the manuscript and offering many helpful suggestions during the more than four years it took me to write this book. I am grateful to Don Fehr, my editor at Addison-Wesley, who gave his meticulous attention to the manuscript and helped me keep the focus on the bigger story. I also want to express my appreciation to Henning Gutmann, my present editor at Addison-Wesley, and Lynne Reed for their contributions. Reed and her production team have been a joy to work with. I thank Barbara Lowenstein and Madeleine Morel for seeing me though the project. Last, but not least, I cannot thank enough K.W. Lee, who has nurtured me and hundreds of other Korean Americans with his generous heart and spirit. Thank you all.

AUTHOR'S NOTE ABOUT KOREAN NAMES

A word about Korean names: The traditional Korean style is to use the family name first, followed by personal names. This is a statement that the family is more important than the individual. But Koreans who live in the United States and other Western countries have adopted the Western style of using their personal names first. This is a challenge to the traditional behavior pattern as much as a concession to convenience.

In my book, I made the decision to use the personal name first, followed by the surname. Inasmuch as this is a story about a Korean-American passage, I feel comfortable doing that.

1. LOSING THE COUNTRY

(1900–1910)

Into this land no more our own,
Does spring come also to these stolen fields?

Bathed in sunlight shower,
I go, as if in dreams, along a lane
That cuts the fields like parted hair,
To where the blue sky and the green earth meet.
—Sang-Hwa Yi (1900–1941), *Korean Verses**

MAIN CHARACTERS:
Soo-Il Kang, my paternal great-great-grandfather
Bong-Ho Kang, my paternal great-grandfather
Bong-Keum Kim, my paternal great-grandmother
Myong-Hwan Kang, my paternal grandfather
Myong-Hwa Yi, my paternal grandmother
Tong-Hwi Yi, my paternal grandmother's cousin

*Translated by In-Soo Lee (1916–1950)

My Uncommon Ancestors

There were no lawyers or judges in our county, but when people had disputes, they came to see my great-great-grandfather, Soo-Il Kang. Because of his enormous physical strength and unusual rise to power and wealth from a rather humble background, he was a folk hero more than a century ago in Tanchon, in what today is North Korea. By the time my great-great-grandfather was in his middle years, he had been a respected man-about-town for many years, admired as much for his oratory, bravery, and wit as for his physical prowess. He was a top-class amateur wrestler of *ssirum*, the Korean-style wrestling, an expert at head butting, and a champion at hand wrestling. His articulateness and his power of persuasion had become legendary.

In those complacent years before Korea was swallowed up by Japan following the Russo-Japanese War of 1904–1905, and before my great-grandfather converted to Christianity, my great-great-grandfather led a privileged life that gave him much satisfaction and respect. Impeccably dressed in voluminous light gray or blue Korean silk trousers, a satin jacket, and a deep-blue topcoat with buttons of jade or amber, and a stern horsehair hat tied at the chin with black strings, Soo-Il would sit cross-legged on a satin cushion in his parlor behind sliding paper screen doors, listening to both sides of a dispute, while periodically puffing on his two-foot-long bamboo pipe. Then he would tap his pipe on a low lacquer table in front of him, as a modern-day judge would pound his gavel, and would confidently issue his rulings. The disputants went away accepting his decisions as a fair resolution of their problems. This was his volunteer work, for he enjoyed solving peoples' problems.

Soo-Il Kang was the second most powerful man in the county of Tanchon. When he made his rounds on a light-gray donkey, people bowed their heads and dared not look at his face. At the peak of his career, Soo-Il lived in a big, slate-colored, tile-roofed house with many rooms that opened onto an inner courtyard, and his ample storehouse was filled with sacks of rice, beans, dried and pickled fish, and fruits that would last until the next harvest season. He had no one to envy, for life had been good to him, especially considering his humble beginnings.

The story of how my great-great-grandfather made good was often rendered like a fable by people in our hometown. When Soo-Il was a lad, he lived on the banks of Big South River, a main waterway to Tanchon City, then the capital of our county. It was shallow, except during the rainy season. Soo-Il often went to the river to fish. One summer day in the 1860s while he was sitting on a rock with a bamboo pole in his hand, the county chief approached him. "Give me your back, young man," the county chief ordered.

It was customary for high-ranking officials to demand that they be carried across the river on the back of any man who happened to be around. Soo-Il knew he had to carry the old chief, but he was a proud fellow and he did not like doing it. Reluctantly he offered his back to the county chief and proceeded to wade into the river. When Soo-Il had crossed halfway and reached the deepest point, where the water reached his thighs, he suddenly stopped. "What shall I do with you, sir? What shall I do with you, sir?" he asked, acting as if he were going to drop the official into the water.

Sitting on Soo-Il's back in the middle of the river, the county chief was incredulous. In nineteenth-century Korea the county chief had great power; he could sentence a man to death, or at least see that he be given a good flogging. After a minute, though, his surprise changed to admiration. The official was impressed with Soo-Il's nerve. He had never seen a lad so daring. "My good young man, how can you leave an old man in the middle of a river?" he said. "Your back is strong enough to carry ten old men like me," he cajoled. Soo-Il took the chief across the river and returned to his spot on the rock and continued fishing. On the next day, the county chief summoned Soo-Il to his office, where he offered him a job as a low-level clerk to run errands. Soo-Il learned quickly and within several years was named civilian deputy chief, while he was still in his twenties. Because Soo-Il had grown up poor, he was not sent to a private school to learn the Chinese classics. He had a photographic memory, though, and while he ran errands for the county chief, he learned Chinese characters by committing to memory the nameplates of the homes to which his boss sent him. That is how he learned thousands of Chinese characters and how he could tell when men who worked for him made a mistake.

As he rose in the county bureaucracy, rich people brought him gifts to stay on his good side. People brought to his home many bolts of silk, satin, cotton, and ramie, plus countless bushels of the choicest harvest crops of every kind, including rice. Though Koreans had money (the currency was called yang) rice was the real currency. Everything was measured against the price of rice—which was more precious than gold. In this way, Soo-Il's wealth accrued during his long years in office, and by the time he was in his thirties, the Kangs led a privileged life. They had a home in town and a mountain estate of orchards and millet fields in the village. They had more than 1,000 yang—the equivalent at the time of $100. That was a lot of money in Tanchon of the 1860s, when people said, "Even the heavens know about it when you have 1,000 yang."

His first son, Bong-Ho, born in the Year of the Dragon in 1868 when Soo-Il was nineteen, was the pride and joy of his father. Sons born in the year of the Dragon in the Asian zodiac are destined to greatness and power, and the boy seemed headed to something spectacular. His teacher at the private school was astounded by his quick mind. He quickly learned the Chinese classics, which were to Koreans what Latin or Greek was to Europeans. By his thirteenth birthday, he had finished all the Chinese classics, and a promising future awaited him. Generous and gregarious, Bong-Ho showed promise as a leader. Soo-Il wanted the most beautiful girl in town for his son's bride, and he dreamed of the many grandchildren who would keep him company in his old age.

Besides being a judge, Soo-Il was also a talented matchmaker. He had helped tie so many knots that people came even from the most remote corners of the county to seek his assistance. Bearing

gifts, families with marriageable youngsters came to him, expressing
an interest in so-and-so's son or daughter. Taking a long drag on his
bamboo pipe, Soo-Il would think about the request for a bit. Then
he would get on his donkey, visit the other party, and successfully
talk that family into agreeing to the marriage.

When Bong-Ho was twelve, Soo-Il Kang began to think about a
bride for his son. For many generations as far back as he could remember, the Kangs had been endowed with good, strong physiques and
quick minds, but not many offspring. There were usually only one or
two sons born in each generation. Soo-Il wanted many grandsons, and
he could think of no one better for Bong-Ho than the eldest daughter
of a wealthy man named Kim. Bong-Keum Kim—the Beautiful One,
as she was known—was reared like a princess on the purest glutinous
rice, the sweet rice used in delicacies. Her father, one of the richest men
in town, had married late in life to a beautiful young woman, and Bong-
Keum had come along when her father was quite old. He considered
his daughter more precious than ten sons. Her skin was peach colored,
her nose was delicate, and her almond eyes were bright like star sap-
phires. To Soo-Il, the mere thought of bringing the Beautiful One into
the Kang home was immensely pleasing.

Soo-Il Kang visited old man Kim to talk marriage. "Ah, but
my dear honorable chief, my daughter is just a child. She is too
young to marry," Kim said, trying his best to disguise his shock and
fear at such a proposal. The very idea of giving away his beautiful
child seemed unthinkable to him. "All right," Soo-Il said, trying to
hide his disappointment, "but I will be back." For a year Soo-Il
Kang visited Kim frequently. Finally, Kim went to the private school
where Soo-Il's son was a student to inquire about him, and was told
by his teacher that Bong-Ho was the smartest boy in all Tanchon
and that already he had mastered all four books of the Chinese classics. Pleased with what he heard from the teacher, old Kim accepted
Soo-Il Kang's proposal, and Bong-Ho and the Beautiful One were
married. They were each fourteen years old.

Like his father before him, Bong-Ho worked as a civil servant.
But unlike his father, who had come from a humble background,

Bong-Ho indulged the role of a rich man's son to the hilt. He went to work every day at the county office. But civil servants in the Korea of my great-grandfather's day did little more than process an occasional document and meet with people who came to see them. There was no clear demarcation between work and play—or public and private business. There was always the gameboard for *tujon,* a Korean version of a card game, in the office, and Bong-Ho and his colleagues enjoyed playing the game, while talking and smoking their long bamboo pipes.

Lunch was a leisurely affair. A male servant brought Bong-Ho's midday meal with a large bowl of steamy rice, soup and half a dozen side dishes on a small portable table. After lunch he pushed a few more papers and, more often than not, spent the rest of the afternoon talking with colleagues or visitors. On hot summer afternoons, Bong-Ho, wearing a loose-fitting traditional jacket and trousers made of starched ramie that kept the skin cool, dozed off, seated cross-legged, a paper fan still in his hand. The pace of life in our hometown was unrushed, moving with the quiet rhythm of nature.

After work, as was customary for the males of his class, Bong-Ho and his friends went to a *kisaeng* house, a fancy restaurant, to be served by pretty women trained in the art of entertaining men with songs, music, and small talk. Seated beside each male guest, a *kisaeng* often fed her guest by putting tidbits of food into his mouth. A *kisaeng* was nothing like a prostitute, but more like a Japanese geisha—trained since childhood for the profession of entertaining men. A *kisaeng* was mostly a good listener, who also sang and often played the *kayakum,* the Korean zither, and knew when to be flirtatious and when to withdraw. Thus, my great-grandfather whiled away his evenings in the company of a pretty *kisaeng,* smoking, drinking, and gambling, accepted and expected for Korean men of his day and social class. Korean men believed that their wives should be treated honorably, because their most important role was to bear children to carry on the family lineage. Wives were not playthings. To play, married men went elsewhere.

At night Bong-Ho frequently returned home drunk and boisterous, picking fights. But no matter how late he came home, his wife had his dinner ready, kept warm in brass bowls covered with silk. She reminded herself that no one could be kinder than her husband when he was sober. Bong-Ho's bouts of nightly drinking and gambling may explain why it took so long for my great-grand-parents to have their first child. My great-great-grandfather Soo-Il waited night and day for a grandson. And, my great-grandmother hired shamans and prepared feasts to appease the spirits and prayed for a son. It was almost six years after Bong-Ho's marriage before he heard the happy news that the Beautiful One was expecting.

In 1887, the Year of the Pig, Soo-Il's first and only grandchild, Myong-Hwan, was born. The zodiac sign would give him a long life and happiness. Servants slaughtered a fattened cow and a pig, and cooked pheasants and chickens to celebrate the baby's 100th day, a milestone because so many children did not live that long. Soo-Il invited hundreds of people to share in his joy.

Myong-Hwan had the good looks from his mother's side and the physical strength and intelligence from his father's side. Early on, his father took him to a teacher in town for tutoring. By the time he was thirteen, Myong-Hwan had become the top student at the private school and had attracted the attention of a scholar named Min-Kyo Yi, the uncle of General Yi. Myong-Hwan's intelligence and good looks caught Yi's eyes immediately. Min-Kyo, whose name meant "Teach the People," was a noted scholar who had spent much time in Seoul even though his family lived in Tanchon, four hundred miles away. He wanted the boy for his son-in-law. His daughter, eighteen-year-old Myong-Hwa Yi, was his only child. Min-Kyo Yi spoke with the teacher and inquired about the boy's family. Satisfied with what he heard, he asked the teacher to be an intermediary between himself and the Kangs. When great-great-grandfather Soo-Il and great-grandfather Bong-Ho heard that the prospective bride was a member of Tong-Hwi Yi's family, they were delighted.

The boy and the girl were married in the time-honored Korean way. The wedding had been arranged by their families. The first time they laid eyes on each other was at their wedding ceremony.

The traditional Korean bride was several years older than her husband because she was expected to be an older sister to him—and to be mature enough to do housework at her in-laws' place. The newly-weds, as was the custom, first went to live with the bride's parents briefly, then took up residence in the Kang household. Myong-Hwan and Myong-Hwa had little in common except that they came from good families in the same hometown and had similar given names. Since both were only children, perhaps neither knew how to make compromises, and there were inevitable personality conflicts. Myong-Hwa, who had a sharp and inquisitive mind, was not a typical daughter-in-law who obeyed without question. She asked many questions. Myong-Hwa, after all, was born in the Year of the Horse, a favorable astrological sign for males, but not females. Girls born under the horse sign are said to be exceptionally bright, but strong-willed. She was both. Myong-Hwa's independence brought a new dimension to the Kang family, which until then had known only women who uncomplainingly catered to their men.

Even after his son's marriage, Bong-Ho kept up his leisurely life of drinking and gambling. He had a concubine, too, but since most men of his position did, it was not an issue. His voice was hoarse from too much tobacco and liquor, and doctors said he would not live past forty. One night when he was returning home after being out on the town, his steps unsteady from too much rice wine, he swore that he saw a goblin. The mischievous spirit crept up to him and asked, "Where are you going sir, Honorable Scholar Kang?" When Bong-Ho told him he was going home, the goblin told him he was headed the wrong way. Side by side, my great-grandfather and the phantom walked. In the nick of time, Bong-Ho awoke from his stupor and found himself on the banks of the Big South River, and the goblin was no longer there. One more step and he would have drowned. (I neither believe nor disbelieve in goblins. I have never met or had a conversation with a mischievous spirit, but that does not mean that others have not.) My great-grandfather swore that he really had seen the ghost, and he was embarrassed about it when he told the story later in his life after he had become a Christian.

By the time Bong-Ho was in his thirties, he had squandered much of the family's money. His gambling debts had become so large that the family had to sell one of the houses in town. Bong-Ho and his wife moved to Boshigol, the Kang family's estate. Great-grandfather Bong-Ho had named it Boshigol, which means the "Village of the Pheasant on Its Stomach," because he thought a slope of a hill alongside our ancestral house was shaped like a crouched pheasant. Boshigol, the name of both our estate and the village, was an idyllic place, just outside Tanchon City in the northeastern part of the Korean peninsula, about 150 miles from the Chinese border and 450 miles from the Russian seaport of Vladivostok. Every spring azaleas, forsythias, white aspens, and apple, pear, and apricot trees turned Boshigol into a flowering forest. My ancestors had settled there in the fourteenth century, having come from Chinju, a seaside town in the southeastern tip of the Korean peninsula that is the original home of the Kang clan. Since then they had called these valleys, hills, and mountains their home.

My forebears hardly knew what went on outside their small feudal society. Their knowledge of the world was limited to tales from Buddhist monks and scholars returning from visits to China and Japan. Our hometown was far away from Seoul, and local officials generally were left alone as long as they provided their share of contributions to the tax office at harvest. An occasional trip to the capital and warm hospitality extended to visiting officials from Seoul had been sufficient to continue their complacent lifestyle. They were content with their land and their families; as long as they could tend their ancestors' graves, and as long as tenant farmers produced sufficient food, what more could they want? What went on outside Korea was of no consequence to them.

☯

But my family's placid life ended when Japan declared war on Russia in 1904. The war between Japan and Russia was over control of Korea and Manchuria. Because of its location at a crossroad of regional power politics, Korea had long been, according to a popular Korean proverb, a shrimp in a sea of whales—Russia, China, and Japan. When the whales fought, it was inevitably the shrimp that got hurt.

Historically, Koreans were xenophobic; this was understandable, as nothing good had ever come from their contact with foreigners. Thus, since the Japanese invasion of Korea at the end of the sixteenth century, when enemy forces looted the country and set fire to count-less buildings—even palaces in the capital—isolationism had been its policy, except toward China. The Middle Kingdom, as China was then known, was Korea's suzerain to which court officials, bearing gifts, paid a yearly tribute. Korea's ruling class considered all foreign-ers barbarians except the Chinese, whom they looked up to as their cultural mentor and the only civilized people in the world.

But by the mid-nineteenth century, after Western powers pried open the doors of China and then Japan with gunboat diplomacy, Korea, too, was forced to adjust to a changing world. Though the peninsula was not on the main trade route, foreign ships appeared from time to time on its shores and demanded trade. Koreans re-buffed them, but they returned—Japanese, Russians, Americans, French, Germans, and Dutch. Finally, in 1876, after four years of haranguing, Korea opened its ports to Japan, whose warships had come knocking on Korea's gate. In the so-called Treaty of Friendship that resulted, Japan foisted on an ignorant Korea provisions that were anything but friendly. With the treaty, Japanese merchants and offi-cials swiftly moved in, enjoying extraterritoriality. The very thought of this valuable piece of property, which Japan had coveted for centu-ries, being within its grasp must have had Tokyo officials salivating. Korea would link Japan to the Asian continent. It would be a military base from which to launch other conquests, a rich source of raw materials, and of course, a market for its products.

After concluding the treaty with Japan, Korea also established ties with the United States, Russia, Great Britain, Germany, and France. China, which had its own motives for checking Japan's in-road into Korea, played a midwife's role in some of these other relations. China's role notwithstanding, Japan's penetration into Korea was swift and widespread. By the 1890s, the Japanese had been involved in banking and shipping in Korea. They started a postal service and operated many other businesses. Kimono-clad Japanese lived in numerous settlements, mostly in the southern part of the peninsula, where Koreans soon became accustomed to the peculiar sounds of their wooden clogs slapping on the streets.

During this time, an indigenous peasant movement called Tonghak, meaning "Eastern Learning," erupted in the southwestern section of the country in Cholla Province and began to spread. Under the feudal class system in Korea, the lower-class tenant farmers supported the idle landed gentry on whose lands they worked. Life was hard for the peasants, especially in the conservative south, where class distinctions were pronounced. Disgusted with corrupt officials and high taxes that broke their backs no matter how hard they worked, peasants in the movement began periodic attacks on government offices. Tonghak was both a peasant rebellion against society's corrupt rule and injustice, and a religion that proclaimed the equality of all humans—a radical notion in nineteenth-century Korea. Followers of Tonghak opposed foreigners, especially the Japanese. The movement had an enormous appeal and caught on throughout the agrarian south.

It took the cruelty of one corrupt county magistrate to light the flame that brought Japan and China to loggerheads in a conflict that would be the precursor to the Sino-Japanese War of 1884–85. Since his appointment in 1882, the magistrate in Cholla, Pyong-Gap Cho, had bled his subjects by extorting money for personal use, such as collecting taxes in rice to improve his father's burial site. But the final straw for the peasants was the enormous rice tax he levied on irrigation water from the reservoir they had built. Their repeated petition for redress got nowhere. In February 1884, led by a local Tonghak leader, peasants occupied the county office, seized weapons, distributed the illegally collected rice to the poor, and then destroyed the reservoir. The investigator dispatched to probe the incident blamed the Tonghaks for the trouble. Local members were arrested, and some were even executed. This injustice enraged the peasants even more. Ten thousand men, armed mostly with bamboo swords and amulets, which they believed protected them, converged on the provincial capital. The eight hundred men sent by the government were no match. Before the central government could dispatch reinforcements, the ranks of the rebels had swelled to twenty thousand, and the rebellion erupted like wildfire throughout the southern part of the country. A frightened Korean king, against the advice of many, appealed to China for help. China, delighted at the chance to enhance its influence in Korea, said it would send troops right away. When Japan learned of this development, it, too, dispatched soldiers to Korea under the pretext that it had to protect its citizens living there. The arrival of Japanese soldiers angered China.

The Tonghak rebellion having been suppressed, the Korean government said there was no more need for foreign troops. China proposed withdrawing all troops, but Japan balked and continued to send troops. On July 25, Japan made an unprovoked attack on Chinese ships in the Yellow Sea. Simultaneously, Japanese troops marched north to attack Chinese units. The first Sino-Japanese War lasted six months, with Japan the victor.

With China gone, Korea, whose own forces were helpless, was now forced to sign a series of agreements that virtually placed her under Japanese rule. The Japanese obtained rights to build railroads and telegraph systems. All ports on the southwest coast, which had been previously closed, were opened to Japan. Under a new treaty of military alliance, Korea became, in effect, a source for Japanese military supplies. All Chinese residents were to be deported.

With China's fall, the rivalry for power now came down to Russia and Japan. Inside the Korean court, a power struggle ensued between pro-Japan and pro-Russia factions. As the rivalry between Russia and Japan continued to intensify, the survival game became even more critical for Korea, which historically had played one power off the other to survive.

After the Sino-Japanese War, Russia and Japan made an agreement that neither country would interfere in Korea's internal administration, or send military instructors or financial advisors without prior mutual agreement. But by the turn of the century, Russia had tried to lease land in Masan, in the southeastern part of Korea, to build a naval base. The Russian plan was frustrated by Japanese opposition, but Russia's goals were clear. Had Russia obtained the site, it would have been a halfway point in a sea link between two crucial harbors, Vladivostok and Port Arthur in Manchuria.

Around this time, in 1900, the Boxer Rebellion, a mass movement against foreigners, broke out in China. Numerous foreign nationals were killed, and the diplomatic corps in the legation quarter of Peking was besieged. An allied expeditionary force, which included troops from Russia, England, Germany, France, the United States, Austria, Italy, and Japan, was sent to put down the rebels and rescue the diplomats. The largest contingent in this force was the Japanese. The Russians, however, in addition to their contribution to the allied force, sent a separate expedition to occupy Manchuria on the pretext of protecting Russian railways there.

Getting ready for what now seemed an inevitable clash with Russia, Japan in 1902 made an alliance with Britain, a foe of Russian expansionism, while Russia befriended the French. In the following year, Russians crossed the northern Korean border to Yongampo at the mouth of the Yalu River and began acquiring land and putting up buildings and telegraph lines. Russia's attempt to get a lease on the region was blocked by Japan and Britain, but the area was nonetheless opened to trade.

With Britain on its side, and a well-equipped and -trained army of two hundred thousand troops, Japan was now ready to push the Russians either to back down or to fight in Manchuria. Japan made its demands. The Russians responded by offering to withdraw their troops from Manchuria and to recognize Japan's interest in Korea so long as the country was not used for military purposes. But they argued that Manchuria lay outside the Japanese sphere and that the presence of Russian troops there was not a Japanese concern. They even proposed to divide Korea into a Russian and a Japanese sphere roughly at the middle of the country at the thirty-ninth parallel.

When it became clear that the Russians were not going to back down, the Japanese struck without warning, just as they had attacked China ten years earlier. On February 8, 1904, Japanese ships opened fire on Russian installations at Port Arthur. Two days later, war was officially declared. Japanese troops landed in the port of Inchon near Seoul and immediately marched into Seoul. The Korean government was forced to sign a Japanese proposal, which among other things promised to protect the Korean monarch, should his life be in danger, and allowed the Japanese to use any part of the Korean peninsula for military operations in securing the king's safety. This was Japan's ruse to turn Korea into a military base in the war with Russia.

Koreans suffered as the armies of Japan and Russia moved through their peninsula, using it as a land bridge. Along the main dirt highway that ran from Seoul to the Yalu River on the border with China, Japanese soldiers enlisted the service of Koreans to feed the troops and take care of their horses and equipment. Those who dared to resist were beaten. They enlisted Korean women to draw water from wells; the Japanese army's demand for water was so great, many wells went dry. Women had to travel to remote mountains and carry water jars home on their heads.

Russian soldiers did not recruit Koreans to work for them; instead, they pillaged farms, where they set up encampments. Rampaging through the countryside, they stole calves, pigs, and chickens. Having their livestock stolen devastated Korean farmers, who were so poor that their daily diet consisted of rice mixed with barley, and vegetable stew and pickles. Eggs and meat were so precious that the average farmer ate them only a few times a year, on birthdays and holidays. Worse, Russian soldiers raped Korean women. Frightened people sent their daughters to stay with relatives in places far away from the invasion route. Girls who stayed were hidden in large pickle urns. Many dressed like boys and wore a farmer's big straw hat. Koreans say that undisciplined armies lose wars; the Russian forces lasted just a little more than a year. In July 1905, Russia admitted defeat. Japan was now the most powerful whale in Asia.

The Settlement

The settlement of the Russo-Japanese War affected my family profoundly. The president of the United States, Theodore Roosevelt, whom my ancestors had not even heard of, was a key player in the geopolitical decisions that forever changed the Kangs' lives.

On July 6, 1905, two young Koreans sat awkwardly in their rented formal suits and silk hats as they rode in a carriage to Sagamore Hill, Theodore Roosevelt's summerhouse in Oyster Bay on Long Island. The Koreans were on a mission of vital importance to their country. Syngman Rhee, a slight man of twenty-nine, with fair skin and a high forehead, sat on one side of the carriage. His traveling companion was Pyong-Ku Yun, thirty, a tanned and vigorous-looking Methodist minister from Hawaii who doubled as an interpreter for Korean immigrants. They had been classmates some years earlier at Paejae, an American mission school in Seoul that was a hotbed of liberal ideas. The men looked pensive as the carriage approached the final leg of the trip to the big house on the hill.

Rhee had been a student radical whose protests against the conservative Korean king in the 1890s had twice landed him in prison. But in a decision fraught with irony, he was freed from jail in August 1904 and, after being allowed to recover his health and regain weight, was dispatched to America to persuade Roosevelt to save Korea from Japan's encroachment. Rhee had been selected by reform-minded members of the king's palace guards because he was thought at the time to be the only one who both spoke English and had American connections. Officially, Rhee was traveling on a student passport to study in the United States, but unofficially, he carried messages from a king's aide to the Korean legation in Washington, D.C., hidden in the fake bottom of his luggage. The king was in no position to issue an official appointment because he was under Japanese surveillance.

On his way, Rhee spent a few days in Hawaii to visit with members of the island's large Korean community, firing them up with news of the grave situation back home in order to raise money for his mission. Staying in Yun's home, the old classmates discussed how they might persuade Roosevelt to honor Korea's sovereignty. It was their understanding that Roosevelt was to mediate a settlement of the Russo-Japanese War in the fall in Portsmouth, New Hampshire, and was therefore a key player in their country's destiny. What they did not know, however, was that a good part of the negotiating had already been done.

Arriving in Oyster Bay on the morning of July 5, Rhee and Yun checked into the Octagon Hotel and promptly submitted their request for an audience with the president, along with letters of introduction from Secretary of State John Hay and Secretary of War William Howard Taft. Rhee had obtained a letter of introduction from Hay during an earlier meeting with him, and Yun had gotten Taft's letter through the superintendent of the Methodist Church in Hawaii when Taft traveled through there on his way to Japan a month earlier. In addition, Yun had brought from Hawaii a petition bearing four thousand signatures of Koreans urging Roosevelt to protect Korean independence.

As they sat in the waiting room of Roosevelt's summer home, the two Koreans felt the heavy weight of their compatriots' and their country's fate. They were at once excited and scared. Roosevelt, wearing his U.S. Volunteer Cavalry Rough Rider's uniform, strode into the room and greeted them warmly. "Gentlemen, I am very happy to receive you. What can I do for you and your country?"

The imposing figure made them so nervous that they forgot to recite the statements they had carefully rehearsed the night before. Rhee was to have argued that under the 1882 Treaty of Peace and Amity establishing diplomatic relations between the two nations, the United States was obligated to come to the aid of Korea when it was under threat from a third country. And, Yun was to have talked about the petition signed by four thousand Koreans in Hawaii. Instead, Rhee mumbled a few phrases that he could hardly recall later, and Yun handed Roosevelt the petition and a letter urging him to safeguard Korean sovereignty.

Roosevelt gave the document a quick glance. "I am glad you have come to me," he said. "I would be glad to do anything I can in behalf of your country, but unless this comes through official channels, I can't do anything with it." Handing the petition back, he promised to present the documents at the September peace conference in Portsmouth, if they would have it sent to him through the Korean legation in Washington. "You see, gentlemen, my position is simply to invite the two nations to come together to make peace. I have no power to interfere," Roosevelt said, bidding good-bye. Elated by the meeting, the Koreans told American reporters assigned to the summer White House what the president had said.

They returned to their hotel, packed their bags, and left for Penn Station to catch a train for Washington. When, upon their arrival in the capital the following morning, they saw a story in the *Washington Post* about their meeting with the president, they became heady with excitement and a sense of accomplishment.

But Rhee and Yun were in for a surprise. The Korean minister, Yun-Jong Kim, turned down their request to submit the petition to the State Department. "I cannot send it without instructions from the home government," Kim said. The response was unexpected, and they were stunned. For three hours Rhee and Yun tried to persuade Kim, but the longer they talked, the clearer it became that Korea's representative in Washington was not the man they thought he was. After his arrival in Washington earlier that year, where he enrolled at George Washington University, Rhee had visited Kim many times and, believing Kim to be a faithful ally, he had confided in him about his plans. Angered by the betrayal, Rhee and Yun stormed out of the building. After a sleepless night, the pair returned the following morning and tried once again to talk to Kim, but this time the minister ordered them to leave and threatened to call the police.

What Roosevelt had not told his Korean visitors at Sagamore Hill was that his administration had already made a deal with Japan. Even as the three were meeting under his roof, Roosevelt's secretary of war was on his way to Tokyo to sign a secret agreement—the

Taft-Katsura Treaty. This pact, whose content was not declassified until 1922, gave the United States free rein over the Philippines in return for Japanese control of Korea and Manchuria. Roosevelt knew that the pro-Japanese minister at the Korean legation in Washington would not do anything to upset Washington's arrangement with Japan. Not knowing this, Rhee and Yun had taken Roosevelt at his word. Such was their initiation to the deceptive intrigues of early twentieth-century geopolitics. The Treaty of Portsmouth, signed on September 5, 1905, under Roosevelt's aegis, gave Japan de facto control of Korea and set the stage for annexation and Japan's thirty-five-year colonial rule.

A month after the Portsmouth Treaty was signed, Korea's King Kojong convinced an American educator, Homer Hulbert, whom he had known for almost two decades, to act as his emissary to Roosevelt. Hulbert, a member of a prominent New England family that had founded Dartmouth College, had come to Korea in 1886, after responding to the king's request to the U.S. State Department for Americans to teach English to his noblemen. Hulbert had won the respect and confidence of the king for his work on behalf of Koreans. Kojong had hoped Hulbert could meet with Roosevelt before the Tokyo government had a chance to implement the Portsmouth Treaty's provisions in Korea, since the king wanted a treaty that would enable him to at least retain control of foreign policy.

But Japan was in a hurry. The ink was barely dry on the treaty when the Tokyo government dispatched Marquis Hirobumi Ito, a former Japanese prime minister and an elder statesman, to Seoul. King Kojong and Prime Minister Kyu-Sol Han put off Ito for almost a month while they waited for Hulbert to reach Washington. But on the evening of November 17, the same day Hulbert arrived in Washington, Ito, escorted by a general and the Japanese minister in Korea, entered the quiet grounds of Changdok Palace. The Japanese troops surrounded the building where Kojong's cabinet met. Japanese officials went inside, showed a draft of the protectorate treaty to Prime Minister Han, and urged him and the seven ministers in the room to accept the proposal. Prime Minister Han refused. Getting up from his seat, he said he was going to consult the king. He did not get far. Japanese gendarmes grabbed him and held him in a side room while Ito and his men intimidated the remaining ministers into endorsing the Japanese scheme. Ito then went to see Han to try to persuade him once more, but when that failed, the former Japanese prime minister told the Korean prime minister the treaty was valid because a majority of the cabinet had approved it. Then, like bandits in the night, Ito's men took the foreign minister's seal and affixed it to the pact.

The treaty, turning over Korea's foreign affairs to Japan, was effected by 1:00 A.M., November 18, 1905, Seoul time, within an hour of Hulbert's arrival in Washington. The Japanese government promptly established the office of residency-general, and Ito became its first resident-general, "answerable" only to the Korean king. On November 22, the Tokyo government announced to the world that the Korean government had "voluntarily" accepted a treaty placing its foreign affairs in the hands of a Japanese resident-general.

In Washington, Hulbert tried in vain to deliver Kojong's message to Roosevelt and his new secretary of state, Elihu Root, who had replaced the recently deceased Hay. U.S. officials had Hulbert pacing the floor for more than a week, while they waited for official word from Tokyo. Finally, on November 25, a day after a dispatch arrived from Tokyo, Root saw Hulbert. The secretary of state told Hulbert the Korean government's "voluntary" acceptance of the protectorate treaty on November 17 made the king's letter moot.

With the signing of the 1905 treaty, my great-great-grandfather Soo-Il's job as the civilian deputy county chief in Tanchon County was eliminated. A lesser position was created and given to a pro-Japanese collaborator. Other unforeseen events also occurred in my family. Soo-Il's young and pretty second wife, whom he had married after his first wife had died, left him. His son went further into debt from gambling losses. And now that Soo-Il no longer enjoyed the power of his office, creditors were not afraid to hound him. To reduce his expenses, Soo-Il sold his house in town and moved to Boshigol to live with his son Bong-Ho and his daughter-in-law.

Then, in an action that would do more to change the course of my family than perhaps any other single decision, my great-grandfather converted to Christianity. This happened soon after General Tong-Hwi Yi, my grandmother's first cousin, had been relieved of his command when the Japanese dissolved the Korean Royal Army following the Protectorate Treaty. Yi, who had become a Christian in 1904 while he was the chief of the Kwangwha-do Garrison in the Korean Royal Army, visited Tanchon with a Canadian missionary friend in early 1907. Yi was now actively teaching and working with missionaries to convert Koreans not only to Christianity but to modern Western ideas. Yi urged my great-grandfather to become a Christian. My great-grandfather had only the highest respect for Yi, a colorful general known for his clean living, who never touched tobacco or liquor. In earlier times, Bong-Ho had not gone near the revival meetings that Yi conducted, even when they were held across the street from his home, but now he seemed open to listening. Bong-Ho had lived much as he wanted and had come to realize that there had to be more to life than wine, women, and money. Stirring inside him was a yearning for some other way of living.

So he asked General Yi what one had to do to become a Christian.

"It's very simple, my honorable scholar Kang," Yi replied. "To become a Christian, you simply abandon liquor, tobacco, gambling, and women—and, accept Jesus Christ as your savior."

Bong-Ho, who was thirty-nine, was astonished by how little was required of him to become a Christian. "Is that all you need to do?" asked Bong-Ho.

"It's that simple," Yi assured him, to which my great-grandfather replied, "I can do that."

If giving up his bad habits and accepting Jesus Christ would transform him into the kind of man he much admired, like General Yi, he wanted to do it. Bong-Ho was baptized by the Reverend Robert Grierson, the missionary doctor with whom Yi had traveled widely. From that moment on, Bong-Ho Kang became a new man. He cut off his topknot, wore his hair in the short Western style, and grew a trim mustache. He stopped drinking, smoking, gambling, and womanizing.

People in Tanchon said Bong-Ho had gone mad, that he had been bewitched by a foreign religion. But Bong-Ho began to study his new religion with the devotion of a scholar studying the Chinese classics. Working with missionaries, he went wherever he was needed, any time of the day or night. The transformation that had come over his life was so remarkable that people became Christians by his example. If this foreign religion had the power to change a man as it had Bong-Ho Kang—a man who had squandered his family's fortune on drinking, gambling, and women—it had to be good for them, too. So, men and women, old and young, came to him. My great-grandfather established seventeen churches throughout North Korea. A born raconteur who was gregarious like his father, Bong-Ho enjoyed preaching. His own testimony of what Christianity had done for him was the best evidence. He would dedicate his remaining years to spreading the Gospel of Jesus Christ. And, like the story of his father, Soo-Il, the country boy who had made good because of guts, wits, and physique, Bong-Ho's conversion became folklore in our region.

Korean King's Emissaries to the Hague

Meanwhile, in Seoul, the beleaguered King Kojong looked to one more international forum to try to arouse the world community to his nation's predicament. The Second International Peace Conference was scheduled for June 1907 in the Netherlands, and the king wanted to send his representative there, even though Korea had not been invited. Kojong asked Hulbert to be his emissary to the Hague. Hulbert suggested that Kojong appoint Koreans as his envoys, explaining that as an American he might be more effective as an advisor. The Korean king took the suggestion and appointed three distinguished men whose family names were all Yi. They were Sang-Sol Yi, a former vice prime minister; Chun Yi, a former judge of the

Korean Supreme Court; and Wi-Jong Yi, a former secretary of the Korean legation at St. Petersburg.

Hulbert arrived several months ahead of the official delegation to do advance work. He became acquainted with the respected British journalist William Thomas Stead, the editor of the *Courrier*, a journal devoted to the activities of the Second Hague Conference. Stead was a valuable ally to have. Kojong's emissaries arrived in the Hague on June 24, 1907. Three days later the Koreans circulated to all the delegations, except Japan, a summary of Korea's case. Stead published the entire document in the *Courrier*, with an editor's note that said the king's envoys deserved a hearing, even though their country had not been invited to the conference. But Ambassador M. Nelidov, the chief Russian delegate and the president of the conference, said that he could not admit the Korean delegation unless the government of the Netherlands issued an invitation. The Korean delegation visited the Dutch foreign minister, who told them his government was not in a position to question the validity of the protectorate treaty. The heads of all the other delegations said the same thing. The king's emissaries were not given a hearing.

Korea's cause did, however, get some favorable publicity in the world press. Wi-Jong Yi's address to a gathering of journalists, of which Stead was the president, generated wide interest. Yi told the journalists that unless Japan's aggression was checked by an international body, his country would be taken over. He explained the events leading up to the protectorate treaty—how Ito, escorted by troops, had forced it upon Korean officials. And he reminded the journalists that the foreign ministry's seal had been forcibly affixed to the Japanese proposal at 1 A.M., while the Korean prime minister was held captive by Japanese gendarmes. Yi's plea generated numerous news dispatches, but these did not change the minds of the delegates at the Hague. Chun Yi became distraught and committed suicide in the Hague.

Kojong's appeal to the international community not only angered the Tokyo government but accelerated its timetable for a total takeover of Korea. In the early hours of July 19, 1907, while Hulbert and the Korean emissaries were preparing to leave Europe, Japanese officials forced Kojong to abdicate to his thirty-three-year-old retarded son, Crown Prince Sunjong.

Koreans reacted to the forced abdication of Kojong with massive public protests, but Japanese soldiers quashed them, beating down the protestors with bayonets. The spilling of Korean blood aroused no reaction in the international community. For three years, while Sunjong held the Korean throne, Japan extracted "agreement" after "agreement," raising Korean anger to new heights. Outrage at the injustices erupted in violent acts. In Manchuria, a young Korean resistance fighter named Chung-Gun An assassinated Ito, the mastermind of the Japanese takeover and the first resident-general, on the platform of a Harbin railroad station where he had arrived on an official visit. In Seoul, another assassin stabbed Wan-Yong Yi, the collaborator who had helped Ito seize power and was premier under him. And in San Francisco, two Korean expatriots shot and killed Durham W. Stevens, an American and a friend of Theodore Roosevelt's who had been employed by the Japanese to prop up the resident-general's government in Seoul. During his visits to the United States, Stevens had spoken and written glowingly of Japan's interference in Korea, saying that Koreans favored it.

In Seoul, Japanese officials now forced Sunjong to sign a new agreement giving the Japanese resident-general authority to control Korea's internal affairs: the only foreigners the government could employ had to be Japanese nationals, and the post of the vice minister in every ministry had to be filled by a Japanese. By 1909, about two thousand officials in the Korean government were Japanese. With that, the resident-general transferred judicial powers to Japanese courts and on August 22, 1910, made Korea its colony. A week later, Sunjong, only three years after his enthronement, was ordered to issue a proclamation giving up not only his throne but his country as well.

My grandfather, Myong-Hwan Kang, saw the notice posted in front of Seoul Train Station. He was twenty-three, and a student at a Christian boarding school in Pyongyang called Taesong Academy, which was patterned after a Western school. Since he had enrolled at Taesong Academy at the suggestion of his in-law, General Tong-Hwi Yi, he had become imbued with many new ideas. Taesong was an exclusive school for Korea's new leaders. It was founded by Chang-Ho Ahn, a Christian convert and a patriot who had gone to the United States to study Western thought, and who had returned home to work for his people, leaving his family in Los Angeles. Ahn, a few years younger than Yi, was a friend of the general, and Yi lectured at the academy whenever he was in Pyongyang.

My grandfather had made a stopover in Seoul on his way home, to spend a day or two taking in the sights of the capital before heading for a summer break in the tranquility of his Boshigol home. As he walked out of the station, he saw a small crowd gathered in front of a public notice—the announcement of Sunjong's abdication. He felt his heart drop. Since the turn of the century his country had become increasingly entangled in international power struggles in which Koreans themselves had no voice, and their rulers, it now appeared, were completely ineffective in preventing the Japanese takeover. But all the bad news could not have prepared him for the moment when he saw the notice that stated in plain words that the king had abdicated.

His eyes blurry from tears, Myong-Hwan walked slowly past Namdaemun, the magnificent south gate to the city with its multicolored beams topped by an upswept Korean-style roof, then beyond the Toksu Palace on his left. He was simply overwhelmed with a feeling of abandonment. Did Korea not have a friend anywhere? Was Korea just a pawn in the power struggle of big nations? He paused a moment to gaze at Pukhan Mountain, towering behind the Changdok Palace, past the Gate of Flowering Culture. This mountain, which on his previous trips to the capital had made him feel peaceful, gave him no solace now. He could barely muster the energy to walk another quarter of a mile to an inn near the old American legation in Jo-dong. On the following morning, instead of lingering in Seoul, he took a train to Pusan, then a steamer to Yohaejin, a small port town six miles from Tanchon, and walked home.

Homecoming had always been a joyful occasion for my grandfather because the Kang family estate, surrounded by towering trees and flowering shrubberies and brooks along both sides of the houses, was like paradise on earth to him. There was a magical quality to Boshigol. It seemed impervious to bad news from the world outside.

But this time the public notice he had seen at Seoul Train Station tugged at him, like a personal summons for him to work toward regaining his country's independence. Grandfather wanted to leave for Manchuria and join the resistance movement. General Yi, who was my grandfather's mentor and also his in-law, had already gone there. So had Ahn and some of his Taesong classmates. After the Japanese had disbanded the Korean Royal Army in 1907, Yi traveled throughout Korea, espousing modern-style education by making passionate speeches in cities and towns and establishing schools. Then, shortly before the annexation, Yi moved to China with his family. Operating out of Manchuria, he organized a military academy and trained soldiers to fight the Japanese, and founded schools for the children of Korean exiles and independence fighters.

Grandfather, who belonged to a secret student society for independence fighters, wanted to slip out of the country and join the resistance. He had become even more convinced of what his teachers Tong-Hwi Yi and Chang-Ho Ahn had said—that Korea needed new leaders. Without a new generation with new ideas and skills, Korea would not be able to free itself from Japan's yoke. As he thought, my grandfather recalled the many talks General Yi had given, urging Koreans to shed their old ways and embrace new education to prepare themselves for a modern age. And he remembered the night he and Yi had traveled together in a snowstorm, composing poems as they walked, trying to keep their minds off the bitterly cold weather. To my grandfather, Yi was the bravest, most honest, and most principled man in all of Korea—more than worthy of his devotion. He felt compelled to follow Yi wherever he went and help him achieve his dream of an independent Korea.

But the situation was not that simple. He was the heir to the Kang clan, the only male of his generation, and thus the one who should remain and guard the family estate. What if he were killed before he had a son to carry on the family lineage? His wife had given birth to two daughters, both of whom had fallen ill, and only one had survived. The high fever from the illness and the strong herbal medication that was used had made the surviving child retarded. Myong-Hwan felt torn by his duty to his family and the other duty to himself and to the cause of Korea.

He bemoaned his fate and that of Korea, and the backwardness of his country and its rulers. While the outside world was changing rapidly, the Korean upper class had continued its idle life of complacency. The men of the upper class spent their entire lives doing little more than pursuing the Chinese classics, studying genealogy, and worshiping their ancestors, because of the traditional prohibition against working with one's hands. Japan, having come to realize how far behind the West it had been in technology, had mobilized a national campaign to modernize. But in Korea, the elite had continued to lead their ritualized lives of leisure, leaving Korea to fall prey to Japan. In the end, Myong-Hwan decided that he must do his part for Korea. He made his preparations quietly. In the autumn of 1910, my grandfather left his weeping mother and wife to join the resistance in Manchuria.

2. THE RESISTANCE

Lashed by the bitter season's scourge,
I'm driven at length to this north.

Where numb circuit and plateau merge,
I stand upon the swordblade frost.

I know not where to bend my knees,
Nor where to lay my galled steps,

Naught but to close my eyes and think
Of winter as a steel rainbow.

—Yook-Sa Yi, 1904–1944, *Korean Verses*★

MAIN CHARACTERS:

Myong-Hwan Kang, my paternal grandfather
Myong-Hwa Yi, my paternal grandmother
Bong-Ho Kang, my paternal great-grandfather
Bong-Keum Kim, my paternal great-grandmother
Tong-Hwi Yi, my paternal grandmother's cousin

★Translated by In-Soo Lee

My Grandfather Joins the Movement

Manchuria was a familiar place to Koreans, for they had lived for centuries on those windswept plains, which had once belonged to them. Stretching northwestward across the Yalu River at the northern border of Korea, this vast territory, nearly three times the size of the Korean peninsula, had been part of Korea's Koguryo Kingdom for most of the first century B.C. until the seventh century. In its glory days in the fifth century, the powerful Koguryo people, known for their horsemanship and hunting, had ruled from what is today Seoul in the south all the way to Manchuria in the north. In the excavated tombs there, the legacy of Koguryo lives in the murals depicting warriors on horseback.

Even after the Chinese takeover in the eighth century, the sparsely populated but rich terrains of Manchuria continued to lure impoverished Korean peasants, whose unending poverty and subjugation to their landlords and corrupt government officials made their lot no better than that of oxen. Korean settlers put up with bitter Manchurian winters and mounted brigands who periodically hounded them because life there was still preferable to the one they had left behind. The growing season was shorter than in Korea, but they plowed deep into the soil, fertilized well, and rotated crops. What they grew was theirs. That was a lot more than what they could say about life in Korea.

But the Korean population in Manchuria began to change at the turn of the twentieth century, following the Russo-Japanese War in 1905. With the Japanese takeover of Korea imminent, Manchuria now became an important base for independence fighters, along with Siberia in the Russian Far East. In the midst of Manchuria's uneducated peasants, now came celebrated leaders such as General Tong-Hwi Yi and Chang-Ho Ahn. Intellectuals, students, and soldiers all poured in, lending a sense of purpose and excitement to the Korean settlements. It was into this setting that my grandfather arrived after he left Boshigol to follow the stirrings of his heart.

For ten days, my grandfather, Myong-Hwan, walked northward to Manchuria on dirt roads that sometimes were just wide enough to accommodate a peasant's oxcart. Along the way he took lodging in farmhouses, where for a small sum he could get meals and rest for the night, usually sleeping next to children in thatched-roof houses with mud walls. In some houses, he could not even stretch out his tired body because the rooms were too small for his long frame. Myong-Hwan traveled light, carrying only a pair of blue-gray winter silk trousers, a jacket, and socks—all padded with cotton for the approaching bitter Manchurian winter—and two pairs of straw shoes wrapped in a square piece of brown cotton cloth. Every night my grandfather slept at a different house, until all the people he had met became in his mind like one big family.

Having heard the family lore throughout my childhood, I sometimes pictured my grandfather on his journey, as if I had been walking right beside him. As I did that, I could see him come through a town during a farmer's market, taking a seat on a makeshift bench to eat a bowl of noodles and to rest his weary feet. I would see him buying apples from a fruit stand, and eating two or three in a sitting, as all members of my family seem to do. I would imagine Grandfather having been bemused by the fact that apples were so expensive when they were plentiful in his home, where hundreds of apples from the family orchard were kept in storage. And, whenever I thought about Grandfather's journey on foot to Manchuria, I would imagine his various hosts talking about him long after his departure because they had never had such a distinctive man cross their threshold. His height and exceptional good looks must have been noted, too, for countryfolk in Korea even today have a naive way about them. "Why, that young man looks like a foreigner!" they must have said, for Myong-Hwan was tall and fair-skinned and had a nose with a prominent bridge, instead of a flat nose like most other Asians. To compare a Korean to a Caucasian was a compliment in those days, for Koreans felt such inferiority about their poverty and techno-logical underdevelopment. He had a fine physique, and the long topcoat he wore made him appear even taller than his five feet nine inches.

About a week after he left home, as he neared the Manchurian border, he began to hear news of the resistance in the homes where he took lodging. In border villages, even ordinary peasants and their families talked about what they had to do to regain their homeland. As freedom fighters went back and forth from Manchuria to wage guerilla warfare against the Japanese, these simple folks who eked out a living by farming and running small shops, gave what they could to help the resistance fighters. A small profit made from the sale of hens, a fattened pig, or a calf was put away for this purpose. Women hid money in the pockets of their pantaloon slips worn under their long Korean skirts, and sometimes gave it to the rebels without telling their husbands. People in whose homes he lodged treated Myong-Hwan like a long-lost kinsman when they learned that he was on his way to be with General Tong-Hwi Yi, Chang-Ho Ahn, and their compatriots. And when it was disclosed that General Yi was his wife's first cousin, people told him how honored they were to have him in their homes, and sometimes they refused to accept money for his food or lodging.

Some told Myong-Hwan that they had even seen Yi when he came through there with his soldiers from the Korean Royal Army, and they talked about his bravery as if they knew him intimately. Their tales about the number of Japanese he had ambushed and wild animals he had stalked while hiding with his soldiers in the mountains seemed exaggerated to my grandfather, but he was pleased to hear them at least for what they conveyed of General Yi's ability to inspire even these poor, uneducated villagers. By the time Korea was annexed by Japan in 1910, Yi had come to be a folk hero. He was held up as a model for Korean boys to emulate. On top of being an exemplary soldier with a strong physique and a big mustache that made him look like a European marshal, Yi was an educator who founded more schools than any Korean—141 in all—and an inspiring orator, whose message of salvation for his people in his booming voice moved his audiences to tears. Even while he was imprisoned by the Japanese soon after the Russo-Japanese War, General Yi did not flinch, and the story goes that Japanese guards treated him with great respect. My favorite was the story of the general's appearance before a gathering of students. Seated near the speaker's platform, he heard a young man tell his friend how he wished someday he could wear a suit like the general's. "You can have it now," General Yi said, removing his dark brown jacket and handing it over to the young man, who was too stunned to speak. If the general was known for his bravery and principles, he was equally well known for his warm heart and ample tears. Koreans love to cry; elderly people who heard him speak have told me the general cried a river over the fate of his country. Stories like these had made General Yi an endearing figure unique among Korean nationalist leaders.

In early November, my grandfather finally reached his destination. General Yi wept as he embraced my grandfather. It had been more than two years since they had last seen each other. My grandfather went with Yi to his home, where the general's wife and two daughters prepared foods that reminded him of home. Yi and my grandfather talked late into the night by the light of a kerosene lamp. He had arrived just in time. A harsh Manchurian winter was just beginning. A howling wind outside Yi's thatched mud house foretold of the bitter weather ahead. Grandfather learned that night how Yi desperately needed helpers to raise funds for the resistance. To raise money from Koreans in the United States, my grandfather's teacher from Taesong Academy, Chang-Ho Ahn, had gone to California, where his family lived.

Grandfather stayed with Yi's family until the blisters and swelling in his feet were sufficiently healed, before moving in with the family of a Korean exile who were already harboring several members of the Secret Association for Independence, a resistance group of educated young men. Many, like my grandfather, were from Taesong Academy. Members swore their loyalty in blood and promised never to reveal their assignments if they were captured by Japanese police.

Most of the younger resistance fighters lived with other families who treated them like their sons. Though the vast majority of the Korean exiles in Manchuria were poor, they were dedicated to the movement, and they gave what they could to support it. Manchuria's proximity to Korea made it easy for freedom fighters to go back and forth. The legacy of the Korean independence movement remains today: nearly two million ethnic Koreans live in China, half of them in the Yenpien Korean Autonomous District in southeast Manchuria.

My grandfather's main job was raising money and acting as a courier for General Yi. My grandfather visited Korean settlements throughout Manchuria, on foot and sometimes on the back of an oxcart, to solicit donations that were needed to smuggle in weapons from Siberia and to train soldiers in Manchuria. Everywhere he went, Koreans fed him and gave what they could. Old women, who sometimes reminded him of his mother, dug deep into their pantaloons and parted with pocket money that their sons had given them. That people who had so little were willing to give so much made a lasting impression on my grandfather and strengthened his resolve. If Myong-Hwan initially had been motivated to come because of loyalty to his mentors Yi and Ahn, now he was a convert.

Great-grandmother Bong-Keum waited anxiously for someone to bring news that her son was safe. About three months after his departure, Myong-Hwan's classmate from Taesong brought word that he was well and active in the resistance. She did not know much about the resistance, but she knew that it meant trouble if he were to get caught by the authorities, and she did not want her only son to become a victim of any cause, no matter how noble. She began to think that perhaps her son's marriage to a member of General Yi's family had been a mistake.

Ever since her son had left home, my great-grandmother had felt as if she were in mourning for someone who had died. She wanted to share her worries with her husband, but because he had become completely immersed in his work with the church and with handling business affairs for the family's orchard, my great-grandfather did not have time to fret over their son. If he did worry, he did not show it to his wife. In those days, churches in Korea did not have full-time ministers. Ministers rode the circuit, so the elder of the church did most of the work, including preaching. The burden of his work outside and at home looking after his extended family, besides worrying about the future of his son, must have been unbearable. But Great-grandfather Bong-Ho found solace in his new religion, as had so many new Korean converts. In the immediate aftermath of the Portsmouth Treaty of 1905, when Korea was forced into becoming a Japanese protectorate, the Protestant movement in Korea gained momentum from an evangelical fervor that swept Christian churches there. Korea had become a model for successful missionary work in Asia.

Korean churches became involved in the independence movement because Japanese officials banned Korean Christians from worshiping. Many leaders of the resistance, like Tong-Hwi Yi, were Christian converts. And, since his conversion three years earlier, Bong-Ho appeared to have become much more tolerant and accepting, and his old, quick-tempered personality had all but disappeared. So when he left for church after breakfast, Bong-Keum tried to sew or embroider to keep her mind off her son, but it always wandered back. She worried that he was not getting enough to eat, lacked comfortable lodging, and did not have anyone to cater to him. Tears fell on her sewing material; she would try to shake herself out of it but as soon as she calmed down, she would begin crying again. Since joining the Kang family as a fourteen-year-old bride, Bong-Keum had followed the Korean stricture that once you marry, you become a "ghost" in your in-laws' house. Girls of her day were taught to obey their in-laws and husbands. Her attitude was that if she made a sacrifice—quietly—there would be peace in the family. So, countless times she gave up her own food when an unexpected guest arrived at dinnertime. Nobody knew about it because she never told anyone. But servants eventually told other members of the family. Likewise, when she shed tears for her son, she did it when she was alone. She did not cry even in the presence of her daughter-in-law, my grandmother Myong-Hwa.

The two women were as different as night and day. Bong-Keum was quiet, but Myong-Hwa spoke her mind. True to the Korean superstition about women born in the Year of the Horse, Myong-Hwa preferred activity to being cooped up in the home, which was how Korean women of that era were supposed to spend their lives. Her father was the younger brother of General Yi's father. The Yi brothers, who were exceptionally close, each had only one offspring, and Myong-Hwa and Tong-Hwi were more like brother and sister than first cousins. She called Tong-Hwi "elder brother," and she lived vicariously through his success, as if his achievements were her own.

So my grandmother, unlike her mother-in-law, had quite the opposite reaction to Myong-Hwan's absence: she could not have been more proud of him. She had always viewed him as a spoiled and self-centered mama's boy who had temper tantrums when there were not enough side dishes on his dinner table, and so to see him place the interests of his country above his own comfort was immensely satisfying to her. And when she thought that her husband was working right alongside General Yi, the foremost nationalist leader in Manchuria and Siberia in the movement to free Korea, she even felt happy. She prayed that he would remain with General Yi, doing useful work. But Myong-Hwa did not reveal how she felt to her mother-in-law, though she assumed that Bong-Keum knew.

While her husband was away, she had enrolled at the Martha Wilson Women's Seminary in Wonsan, which was almost two hundred miles away from Tanchon, and moved there to live for six weeks. She had learned about the training program, which would qualify her as an evangelist, through missionaries who visited her father-in-law's church. My great-grandparents were aghast at the idea of a married woman, with a child, going off to school. This was unheard of in old Korea. My great-grandmother objected, but my great-grandfather neither supported nor opposed my grandmother's decision; he simply said nothing. With his sense of tradition, he must have felt he could not rightly object. Myong-Hwa went away to school, where she was a top student. But without the financial support from her in-laws it was difficult to continue, so she returned home without completing the program. Many years later we would hear her still complaining about this. She felt particularly hurt by her father-in-law, who, though a Westernized Christian, was still so tradition-bound when it came to his own daughter-in-law that he could not give her the backing she needed to finish school.

Myong-Hwan's Unfortunate Visit

After a year in Manchuria, my grandfather followed General Yi to Siberia to help set up new schools for the children of Korean exiles there. As early as the 1850s Koreans had lived in Siberia in the Russian Far East, just across the Tumen River at Korea's northern border with Russia. But the big Korean immigration to Russia had been precipitated by the great famines in the 1860s during which nearly five thousand Koreans from the northernmost province immigrated into Privorsk in the Russian Far East, in the Maritime Province. Lured by stories of the rich lands of Siberian valleys, and of how easy it was to make a living there, tens of thousands followed the homesteaders.

By 1910, the year Korea was annexed by Japan, an estimated two hundred thousand Korean exiles lived in Manchuria and in the Russian Far East. About forty thousand of them were in the Maritime Province, near Vladivostok, where their settlements were concentrated. While Russian policy toward Koreans varied from the administration of one provincial governor to the next, the indomitable Korean spirit, combined with Korean industriousness, made them successful immigrants, worthy of receiving official praise.

When my grandfather went to the Maritime Province in early 1912, he found a thriving Korean section called New Korean Village in the northwestern outskirts of the beautiful, hilly Vladivostok, surrounding the harbor that was the eastern terminus of the Trans-Siberian Railway. It amused him to see Koreans in native clothing on creaking oxcarts compete for space through the streets alongside Russians on their troikas, and galloping horses. He was heartened to see so many Korean settlers doing well as farmers and raising live-stock, and as contractors supplying meat and grain to the Russian forces. In the competition to win the military contracts, the Koreans had beaten out their Chinese neighbors by going into Manchuria, buying lean cattle, and fattening them up. Some Koreans had become quite prosperous. Eager to assimilate, many had converted to the Russian Orthodox Church. In some of the homes my grandfather visited, he saw pictures of the czar and czarina, as well as Jesus Christ and Greek saints, hanging on the walls. Some Koreans had even served in the Russian Army and fought in the Russo-Japanese War. Most were farmers who cultivated rice and vegetables, and raised livestock. Others worked as day laborers, hauling goods on their backs and on oxcarts in and around Vladivostok, and still others operated saloons, inns, and small shops.

Koreans had their own schools, and during his two stays in Siberia, my grandfather had taught at several of them. Since Russian-born Koreans had lived there for half a century, there were sufficient numbers of them to act as interpreters for independence leaders such as my grandmother's cousin, General Yi. The bulk of the urban Korean population consisted of newcomers and refugees who had actually experienced Japanese suppression and whose anti-Japanese sentiment was strong. The Maritime Province was both the tempo-rary home for working-class compatriots from the homeland and the base for patriots residing abroad. As in the Korean settlements in Manchuria, there was excitement in Siberia, too. Whether day labor-ers, prosperous farmers, or people like my grandfather, they were united in one goal: freeing their country from the yoke of the Japanese.

The Korean immigrant communities in Manchuria and Siberia were divided between peasants and resistance fighters. Farmers sup-ported the fighters who bought arms in Siberia and returned to Manchuria, risking their lives in the process. Siberia and Manchuria were twin bases for the independence movement, which later branched out to Shanghai as well.

Myong-Hwan was not a fighter like his grandfather Soo-Il or General Yi, but he was a good teacher. This suited him much more than raising money or doing other support activities. The children of Korean exiles became my grandfather's surrogate children and their education his mission.

In Siberia, for the first time in his life, Myong-Hwan shed his traditional Korean garb and learned to wear a Western suit much like the one General Yi wore. It took him a while to get used to wearing clothes that fit snugly, unlike the comfortable, loose jackets and the baggy Korean men's trousers that were tied at the ankle with ribbons. He soon found the Western clothing much more practical for getting around.

After almost three years of working with General Yi in Siberia and Manchuria, Myong-Hwan made a brief journey home to Tan-chon to raise money for his compatriots and to see his family. Resistance leaders like General Yi were idealistic: they thought if they could train a strong army, they could fight the Japanese. Yi, who admired Korean pioneers in Siberia and Manchuria, and had great faith in the people's volunteers and in any kind of armed struggle, said ten thousand Korean troops could cross the Yalu River in a month and annihilate all the Japanese in Korea. As unrealistic as that may sound in retrospect, at the time, it kept the movement going. But there was a limit to their fund-raising efforts in Manchuria and Russia.

Quietly, in the dark of the night, Myong-Hwan slipped into Boshigol. Apart from the familiar sounds of wolves in the distance, Boshigol was as quiet and peaceful as always, seemingly untouched by the events outside. As he neared his home on the road that he had walked countless times, he wanted to run those last few hundred yards to the house, but now that he was so close to his journey's end, he felt the fatigue of the past two weeks come over him. Myong-Hwan opened the small wooden door to the kitchen, bent his head to walk inside, and was immediately embraced by the familiar smells and warmth of his home. When she saw him, his mother broke into tears, clutched his hands, and embraced him. His visit home had been a complete surprise. Myong-Hwa stood silently, off to the side, glad to see her husband, but unable to say anything because of the unwritten Korean code requiring the daughter-in-law always to defer to her mother-in-law.

Afraid to call attention to Myong-Hwan's arrival even to the maid, who slept in the servants' quarters in a thatched-roof house next door, the two women rolled up their sleeves, added more firewood to the hearth, and cooked a meal in the middle of the night. My great-grandmother, so happy that she felt her heart would burst, sat next to her son, watching him while he ate. When Myong-Hwan finished his dinner, he went into his father's room and talked to him about the conditions in Manchuria and Siberia. That night, under a satin quilt Myong-Hwa had brought as a bride, my grandparents slept together, for the first time in nearly three years.

Myong-Hwan had been home less than ten days when Japanese police came to the house and took him off to jail. He was charged with violating national security laws because of his membership in the Secret Association for Independence. Occupying Japanese officials used national security laws to charge anyone they considered unfriendly to the state. Questioned about other members of the association from Tanchon, my grandfather refused to talk. He did not know that the leader of the association had been arrested earlier, and that he had broken down under police torture and revealed the names of the other members.

Punishment was swift. Myong-Hwan was hit in the cheek and then the head, kicked in the back and the legs, and then struck in the groin until he fainted and fell to the cement floor. During the many days before formal charges were filed against him, my grandfather was tortured daily. First, his arms were bound tightly together behind his back while he was seated upright on a chair, then two bamboo sticks were placed between his legs, which were bound together at the knees and ankles. Two policemen rotated the sticks, causing the ropes to cut into his flesh. Some days he was pulled out of his cell, made to lie flat on the floor, then beaten with bamboo rods until his flesh was raw. Some nights he was dragged into a dark underground dungeon, where he would spend the night on the cold dirt floor. After months of such daily torture, he was tried and convicted of violating national security laws and sentenced to eighteen months in prison. In 1914, while he was serving his sentence, my grandfather's first son, Joo-Han Kang, my father, was born.

Visiting the prison was difficult for my great-grandmother. It took a full week's journey on foot, by boat, and by train to see her son in the Hamhung Prison, where all the political prisoners from the northeastern part of the country were held. She visited him once, carrying a bundle containing his favorite foods. When she saw the bruises on her son's face, hands, and feet, she fainted. After that my great-grandfather discouraged her from going, and she obeyed him. My grandmother also visited her husband in the prison on her way home from Wonsan.

After he had served his sentence and was released, Myong-Hwan slipped out of the country again and went to Siberia, where he rejoined General Yi. He continued teaching the children of exiles in one of the many schools Yi had established. When the schools were closed for holidays or for summer and winter vacations, my grandfather traveled with association members to raise money for the movement. When he left Korea for the second time, Myong-Hwan vowed to return only after Korean independence had been restored. But after another three years away from home, he was tormented by thoughts of his family, especially his mother.

On a frigid night in Siberia, Myong-Hwan missed his mother more than he could bear. On the previous night, she had appeared in his dream, looking wan and frail in white clothing and with a scarf around her head. He could not bear the thought of his beloved mother dying without him seeing her. Donning the gray robe of a mendicant Buddhist monk, with straw shoes and a three-foot-wide bamboo hat the shape of a broad lampshade, he set off for the three-week journey home.

His son, who was a baby when he had left the second time for Siberia, was now almost five years old. His parents proudly told Myong-Hwan that their Joo-Han could already recite more than a thousand Chinese characters and other elementary Chinese classics. When Myong-Hwan called for his son to come to him, the boy looked at him as if he were just a visitor, and would not go to him. "Are you really my father?" the boy asked, merely looking at him, and holding his grandfather's hand. "Of course, he is your father. Go sit on your daddy's lap," his grandmother said. But the boy held back. The next morning after Myong-Hwan's arrival, just as he was having breakfast, the police came to the door. Someone had spotted Myong-Hwan during his journey and had told the police.

My father remembered his father's arrest. "Mother protested vigorously and pleaded with the policemen, but they pushed her aside and took him away," my father recalled years later. "In the middle of his breakfast, Father was taken to jail. I was just starting to accept the fact that he really was my father—and then he was gone."

Since he last was in prison, the Japanese police had added another device to their torture routine: they put a leather vest soaked in water on my grandfather's naked chest before the interrogation. As the questioning went on, the wet vest would start to dry and close in on him. It was slow, unbearable torture that would drive any man insane. He would faint and lose consciousness.

This time they never bothered to file charges against him. He was tortured and imprisoned for another eighteen months.

☯

On March 1, 1919, while my grandfather was in prison for the second time, there were nationwide demonstrations against the Japanese colonial rule. Organizers had taken to heart President Woodrow Wilson's doctrine of the self-determination of nations, enunciated in 1918, and they had risked their lives by rising up in an attempt to bring the world's attention to the Korean struggle for independence.

Wilson had announced it as an essential component of the post–World War I settlement to acknowledge and to respond to the rising independence aspirations among Europe's national minorities. The doctrine created independent Czechoslovakia, Yugoslavia, Poland, and Finland, among others. So Koreans greeted the American president's principle like a promise from heaven; at last the world was ready to usher in an age of justice and self-determination—even for small, powerless countries. The doctrine provided the inspiration to transform the Korean independence movement—which had been limited mostly to the activities of exiles and clandestine organizations, schools, churches—into a nationwide endeavor by Koreans to regain their country. Korean patriots meeting in Shanghai in January 1919 formed the New Korea Youth Association and sent Kiu-Shik Kim as its spokesman to the peace conference in Paris. The new group also dispatched representatives to Korea, Japan, Manchuria, Siberia, and elsewhere to develop a worldwide agenda for the movement.

Two events preceded and fed the protests. In December 1918, Japanese officials, anticipating problems over Korea at the forthcoming Paris Peace Conference concluding World War I, began to circulate a petition asking Koreans to renounce any desire for independence. This document was signed by several former high Korean officials, including Wan-Yong Yi, a former cabinet member. When Japanese officials presented the petition for Kojong's seal, the deposed king turned livid and refused to approve it. The tormented monarch had not resigned himself to accepting his country's fate. Kojong and his supporters continued clandestine struggles to regain Korea even after his efforts to persuade Theodore Roosevelt and the Second Hague Conference had failed. Ultimately, these efforts cost him his life. With spies everywhere, the occupying Japanese resident-general's office kept abreast of Kojong's every move.

The last straw came with Kojong's plot to send an emissary to the Paris Peace Conference to plead Korea's case, an endeavor that Japanese officials foiled. They decided the only way to stop Kojong was to deal him the fate of his late queen. Twenty-five years earlier, the Japanese minister to Korea, Goro Miura, had directed the murder

of Queen Min by using more than two dozen Japanese swordsmen
and Korean hirelings, because she was forming an alliance with Russia, Japan's main rival for superiority in Korea. Now, Japanese officials
plotted to eliminate Kojong. On January 21, 1919, a court herb
doctor, who was threatened and then bribed by the Japanese resident-
general's officials, had the emperor's favorite tea laced with poison.
Japanese officials delayed announcing Kojong's death for two days,
then said the king had died of apoplexy. No one believed this. Years
later, in her autobiography, Princess Bang-Ja, the Japanese princess
who was coerced into marrying the Korean Crown Prince Un Yi
in Japan's scheme to unite the two countries, said her father-in-law
was physically well on the eve of his death. He was in Toksu Palace,
where he had enjoyed the evening, reminiscing with attendants about
the old days. Late that night, as was his habit, he was served his
favorite tea. Then he retired to his chamber, but soon violent pains
attacked him and he died.

The word of foul play spread all over Korea and to Korean
communities overseas. The clandestine activities of Korean patriots
reached a feverish pitch. They chose the occasion of Kojong's funeral
procession on March 3, 1919, to attract the world's attention to
Korea's plight. Opinions ranged from capitalizing on the event to
initiate peaceful marches to using the occasion to mount an assault
on Japanese officials in Korea. Ultimately, planners adopted a policy
of non-violence. Anticipating extensive police deployments on the
day of the funeral, organizers moved up the date to March 1. The
protests, though months in the planning, took Japanese officials completely by surprise.

The organizers were thirty-three young men, many of them
Christians, but also Buddhists and members of the indigenous
Chondo-kyo Church, which preaches the equality of all people and
the virtue of meekness. Shortly before two o'clock in the afternoon,
they met at a restaurant in the heart of Seoul and signed a declaration
of Korean independence. The declaration was then read to crowds
at Pagoda Park across the street:

We herewith proclaim the independence of Korea and the liberty of the Korean people. We tell it to the world in witness of the equality of all nations and we pass it on to our posterity as their inherent right. We make this proclamation, having back of us five thousand years of history and twenty millions of united loyal people. We take this step to insure to our children, for all time to come, personal liberty in accord with the awakening consciousness of this new era. This is the clear leading of God, the moving principle of the present age, the whole human race's just claim. It is something that cannot be stamped out, or stifled, or gagged, or suppressed by any means. . .''

In the ensuing days and weeks spontaneous demonstrations spread across the country, with marching crowds waving Korean flags and chanting, *"Manse!"* (May Korea live ten thousand years!). The Japanese were ruthless in suppressing the peaceful protests. The demonstrations, which came to be known as the March First Independence Movement, hastened Japanese resolve to eradicate all vestiges of Korean nationalism. Thousands of Koreans were killed, arrested, imprisoned, and tortured. The March First Movement cost the lives of 7,645 Koreans and injured 45,562 more. The Japanese burned about a thousand churches, schools, and homes. In a village near Suwon, about twenty miles south of Seoul, the Japanese ordered all the villagers to gather inside their church for an important announcement. Then they set the church on fire and gunned down those who tried to escape.

In Tanchon, my father, who was almost five, witnessed Japanese gendarmes in their tan-colored uniforms, caps with red bands, and tall black boots, pursuing unarmed demonstrators. "Even old people in white topcoats and horsehair hats were running away from soldiers and gendarmes, who were going after them with bayonets and rifles," he said.

Dong-Yol Yu, a kindergarten teacher from our hometown, was

arrested for participating in the demonstrations. To punish her, Japanese policemen hung her upside down and pulled her pubic hair. The police had been keeping an eye on her for some time because she had taught her kindergarten pupils an anti-Japanese song that contained a derogatory word for Japanese—*woenom,* "little bastards"—because that mocked the short stature of most Japanese.

The brutal crackdown of the March First Movement stirred Koreans everywhere, including in America, and led to the creation of the Korean Provisional Government in Shanghai. In the United States, leaders convened a meeting of Koreans from twenty-seven organizations and from Mexico. During the three-day session, which began on April 14, 1919, in Philadelphia, the delegates issued a ten-point position paper encompassing the aims and aspirations of the Korean people, including the guarantee of basic human freedom and civil rights. They urged the League of Nations to recognize the Korean Provisional Government in Shanghai.

Just before they broke up, the delegates visited the Declaration Room in Independence Hall. Here, after reading the Korean Proclamation of Independence, they approached the old, cracked Liberty Bell. Placing their hands on the bell, and closing their eyes, they prayed for the freedom of Korea and the success of the new movement. Between 1919 and December 1920, an estimated seven thousand Koreans in the United States and Mexico donated $200,000— an enormous sum, considering that the average monthly income of a Korean immigrant laborer was $30.

☯

My father was too young to know it then, but the March First Movement was not only connected to the absence of his father and his uncle from his life, but was the most significant mass protest Koreans had ever engaged in. Although it crushed under the weight of Japan's occupation forces, it fed the struggle for Korean independence throughout the world. But the international community was apathetic to the bloodbath in Korea. The efforts of Western missionaries to publicize the Korean struggle for freedom failed to elicit much attention in the West. Korea was too far away and too small a country to arouse sustained interest. Tens of thousands of Koreans fled to China, Siberia, and America to foster the movement for Korean independence in exile. The Japanese responded with increased oppression.

After the March First Movement, the Japanese targeted Christians and put them under constant surveillance. They arrested pastors, elders, and church members at will and put them in prison, where they were interrogated and tortured. Often the mere suspicion of being anti-Japanese was sufficient cause for arrest and torture. With spies planted everywhere—even inside the churches—the Japanese did not run out of Koreans to mistreat.

My father, who had seen his father for less than a day before he was taken to prison the second time, grew up feeling as though he had no father. Consequently, he learned to be self-sufficient at a young age. When my grandfather was released from prison after his second eighteen-month term in 1921, he was a broken man, physically and mentally. "I could not recognize him," my father said. Once a fine orator, he hardly spoke now. He stopped all political and social activities. He saw only a handful of people who visited him at home. On occasion he would pen a piece and send it to the prestigious *Chosun Ilbo* newspaper, where he had been a regional correspondent. Otherwise, he rarely ventured outside the house—not even to church. He spent the rest of his life collecting antiques and artwork and writing calligraphy in his smoke-filled room. Many nights, members of my family would be startled awake in the middle of the night by the voice of my grandfather, singing *Aeguk-ka* (the Korean national anthem) in his sleep, his voice, like a knife, piercing the stillness of night.

3. JAPANESE COLONIAL RULE

(1910–1945)

We have nothing,

Neither sword nor pistol,

But we do not fear.

Even the might of the iron rule

Cannot move us.

We shoulder righteousness

And walk the path.

—Nam-Son Choe★ (1890–1957), *The Land and People of Korea*

MAIN CHARACTERS:
Joo-Han Kang, my father
Sok-Won Choe, my mother
Myong-Hwan Kang, my paternal grandfather
Ke-Son Han, my maternal grandmother

★Translated by S. E. Solberg

Erasing Korean Identity

Not long after Grandfather Myong-Hwan was released from prison for the second time, my father entered primary school. It was 1922. Japan had ruled Korea for almost twelve years, and its pervasive influence was stamped into every corner of Korean existence. Japanese had been made the official language, for instance. From the first grade, pupils were required to speak it. The Japanese language was taught two hours every day, while Korean was relegated to just one hour three times a week. Students were taught Japanese history, but not their own. And, with lightning speed, Japanese officials erected Shinto shrines with red torii gates everywhere.

My father had wanted to start school since he was four, having learned the essential one thousand Chinese characters under his grandfather's tutelage, but he had to wait for almost four more years because Tanchon Public School admitted older students first. There were youngsters in their teens who were trying to enroll in the first grade because of the scarcity of public institutions at the time. While waiting his turn, Joo-Han attended a church school, where he studied the Bible, arithmetic, music, and Korean.

Finally, on a crisp April morning, wearing new Korean cotton trousers, new straw shoes, and a jacket his grandmother had sewn, eight-year-old Joo-Han went off to school, accompanied by his grandfather. He was thrilled. There were 180 first-graders in three classes: A and B, and a separate class for a dozen girls. The boys were ordered to line up according to their height. Teachers marked off the first student to A class, the next one to B class, and so on until all the students were assigned an A or B designation. The classroom routine began with the youngsters arriving before their teacher and waiting for him. When the teacher entered the room, the "top boy," or the class president, ordered his classmates: "All rise. Attention. Bow. You may be seated." Like little soldiers, they did this at the beginning and end of each class, in a ritualized display of respect for the teacher, whose importance in Korean culture is still second only to that of the parent.

Some of the students in the elementary school were already married, since child marriages were prevalent because of the inordinate emphasis on family lineage. My father's seatmate was only ten, but he was a bridegroom, and he acted mature. He wore the silk trousers, the jacket, and the leather shoes of an adult, and lived in a rooming house in Tanchon City during the week. He went home to his village to his parents and bride after school on Saturday afternoon. What distinguished the married students from the unmarried ones was their clothing: only married students wore silk attire and leather shoes.

Soccer was the boys' favorite game, but there was only one ball at the school, which they were allowed to use just during the gym hour. So when they played after school, they improvised by kicking a tennis ball. And when a tennis ball was not available, they played with a ball made with old scraps of cloth, tightly bound with twine. I try to picture village boys playing soccer in loose-fitting traditional Korean clothing and recollect what my great-grandmother told my mother not long after her marriage to my father on May Day 1939. With more affection than complaint, my great-grand-mother told her granddaughter-in-law that when her grandson was a boy, he always came home after school with his clothes all torn. When he ran toward home, he looked like a bird in flight because his full *chogori* (jacket) sleeves were in shreds and billowing like wings. Every night my great-grandmother stayed up, getting his clothes ready for the next day.

In 1924, when my father was in the third grade, an edict from the Japanese education ministry required that Korean students shed their traditional clothing and wear the gray Japanese uniform that was called *kokura*. Though students had been taught Japanese from the first grade, until then they had not had to look Japanese. Now they did. Along with the uniform and a military-style cap with the insignia of a cherry blossom, Japan's national flower, at the crown, came a new hairstyle. All young Korean males were ordered to clip their hair to the scalp like Buddhist monks. My father did not like it, but he had no choice in the matter.

Japan's policy of remaking Koreans into second-class Japanese became more explicit and firm as Japan continued its first experiment in expansionism. Only the elderly, considered hopelessly old to learn Japanese, were left alone. For everybody else, assimilation was the order: Japanese became the official language. In the home, Koreans spoke Korean and sang their songs, but very quietly. With their tactics of fear, the Japanese police exercised social control down to even the smallest village. No one dared to go against the rules; to do so would mean punishment for everyone in the village.

Even Korean flowers were not immune. Japanese officials made Koreans dig up their national flower, the rose of Sharon, and plant cherry trees. Some families took great risks to keep rose of Sharon bushes in their garden. As a college student, Ok-Gil Kim, who later became the president of South Korea's most prestigious women's university, secretly rescued a rose of Sharon that had been uprooted from her university campus and planted it in the courtyard of her home, at great risk. When Korea was liberated many years later, she transplanted it to the garden of her alma mater. Harboring a bush may seem like a small thing, but in those times it was an act of courage and patriotism, and Koreans remember her for it.

Besides imposing a militaristic Japanese appearance on the Korean students and ordering that only Japanese be spoken, the Japanese also insisted that Koreans bow to Japanese gods at Shinto shrines and before the Japanese emperor's portrait. They were even told to make a deep bow once a day in the direction of the Japanese Imperial Palace hundreds of miles away. The imperial mythology was that the emperor was a descendant of the sun goddess, and therefore a divine being. Japan brought emperor worship to its colony, and enforced it with the power of the state. In a further attempt to remove all traces of Korean identity, Koreans were ordered to adopt a Japanese name or risk losing their livelihood. One of my father's teachers, Myun-O Kim, left for Manchuria rather than remain in Korea and adopt a Japanese name. Young Koreans such as my father wondered what it would be like to live in a free country ruled by their own people, without having to fear foreign colonizers and their collaborators. He would study maps and imagine many places around the world that he presumed were not occupied by the Japanese. He especially wanted to visit the United States and Canada because of his encounters with the missionaries whom his grandfather had invited to his church and into their home.

When he was in the sixth grade, Joo-Han decided to learn English, the language of the missionaries, who always seemed so well mannered, helpful, and generous. Like all other Korean children, my father thought the missionaries he saw were elderly because so many of them had light-colored hair. He also thought that Americans and Canadians, whom he could not distinguish by their appearance, looked rather odd with their narrow faces and small heads on their tall torsos. Their blue eyes seemed so un-human, and he wondered how they could see out of them. His desire to learn English, however, was not easily fulfilled, because so few Koreans spoke English. Missionaries visited his grandfather's church from time to time, but knowing how busy they were, Joo-Han did not feel he could impose on them. Eventually he heard about a man living in Tanchon City who spoke English. His name was Suh and he had just returned from San Francisco, where he had been a ginseng merchant in Chinatown. An adventurer, Suh had gone to San Francisco from Shanghai as a stowaway at the turn of the century and had lived there for some time, but he had returned to claim his inheritance upon learning that his well-to-do father had died.

My father, now in the seventh grade, went to see Suh. Suh's appearance took him aback. He looked like a dignified old man and acted very much like a foreigner—almost like an American, to my father. Suh had never married. Now an old bachelor, he had pictures of nude Western women hanging on the wall in his room. My father had never seen photographs of naked people, much less nude photos displayed like that, and he thought it strange. What manner of old man is this? he wondered, even as he told Suh why he had come.

"I don't have time to teach you English," Suh said, his blunt response very un-Korean.

Joo-Han did not know quite what to do next, whether to plead with him or just leave. He lingered, trying to think of a way to make his visit worthwhile. Seeing a safe in his room, he asked Suh, "What do you call a safe in English?"

"Strongbox," Suh replied in English. Again the answer was short. So un-Korean, he thought again.

"Strongbox," Joo-Han repeated after him.

Then, Joo-Han pointed to a picture on the wall and asked what Suh called it in English.

"Trull girl," Suh said.

"Trull girl," Joo-Han repeated.

Having learned two English words during his visit, Joo-Han thanked the old man and left. He did not know that a trull was a prostitute. During his long walk home, he tried to figure out how to justify a return visit. He decided to inquire about special foods Suh might like. Asking around, he learned that the old man enjoyed drinking more than eating. So he made another trip to Suh's home, this time with a bottle of rice wine. Suh appeared very pleased to see him.

"Sit down, my studious young man," he said, calling for the servant to bring him a cup. While he drank, Suh taught my father basic phrases, including "good morning," "good-bye," and "how are you?" From time to time thereafter, my father went to Suh's home with a bottle of rice wine to exchange for an English lesson. After several months of tutoring from Suh, he began to suspect that the old man's English might not be as good as he had originally thought. He had heard about another Tanchon man who spoke English, named Nak-Ku Kim, who had just returned from Japan after finishing high school. Joo-Han hurried to Kim's home and asked if he could teach him English.

"Of course," Kim said, complimenting Joo-Han's initiative. But to make the undertaking worthwhile, Kim told Joo-Han to gather other students who wanted to study English. My father located half a dozen classmates.

Borrowing a room in a local church, Kim taught *King's Crown Reader Book One* every morning for three months. By the end of the summer of 1930, Joo-Han had memorized the entire book and could write a letter in English. He ordered English-language books and dictionaries from Japan and studied constantly. His quiet life made the police suspicious, especially since everyone knew about his father and General Yi. One day, a Japanese police detective and a Korean operative, a collaborator, came to the house and searched for evidence of his supposedly subversive activities. They found nothing. Then, the Korean collaborator picked up an English–Japanese vocabulary notebook on Joo-Han's desk and thumbed through it, coming upon the word *revolution*, written in Japanese and English.

"Look at this," the collaborator told the Japanese.

The detective took a look at it. "What is the meaning of this?" he asked, looking at Joo-Han through narrowed eyes.

"It's simply a word," Joo-Han replied. "See this," he said, flipping through the well-worn notebook marked with many English words he had written.

The detectives left without further incident, but Joo-Han could hardly believe what had happened. He never thought that simply jotting down new words from his dictionary would alarm the police. He was certain that if *revolution* had been the only word he had written in the notebook, he would have been hauled to the police station for interrogation. He felt even more discouraged about living under Japanese rule. Learning English might be the only way to escape this oppression.

My father's big opportunity to study English full-time came one day in 1930. My great-grandfather, Bong-Ho, had gone to Ham-hung on church business, and while there, he had visited the local high school. Called Young Saeng (Eternal Life), it had been founded by Canadian missionaries. The principal, Kwan-Shik Kim, a cousin of the independence fighter Kiu-Shik Kim, who worked with General Yi in Shanghai, had given Bong-Ho a comprehensive tour of the school. When Bong-Ho returned home, he was determined to send his grandson to this wonderful school, the likes of which he had never before seen. He had been very impressed with the well-maintained brick building, complete with physics and chemistry labs,

Western-style indoor plumbing, and steam heat. My father did not like the idea of living away from home, but if that was the only way to study English, he decided he had to do it. So he lived in a boardinghouse in Hamhung during the week and returned home on weekends. He studied English day and night. When he walked, he read aloud to practice pronunciation, and he dreamed of becoming an English teacher someday.

The Reverend Dr. William Scott, the missionary who founded the school and spoke Korean fluently, cut an odd figure. In his dark-brown suit, he looked tall and very thin, and he wore a brown toupee and small rimless glasses. Devoted to teaching English, he took delight in Joo-Han's studiousness. In 1934, Dr. Scott prepared my father for the all-Korean secondary school students' oratorical contest in English. The competition, which was in Seoul, involved champions from all over Korea. When my father won first prize, he was so excited he dropped his trophy during the awards ceremony. When my father completed his schooling, and obtained his teaching credentials in 1940, Dr. Scott hired him to teach English at the school. In his mid-twenties, my father had already achieved his dream of becoming an English teacher.

While preparing for his teaching credentials, my father taught at an elementary school in Tanchon. It was during this time that my father met Sok-Won Choe, a young teacher from Hamhung who also taught at the school. After their marriage in 1939, my mother quit teaching, as was customary, and remained home. As the wife of the only son in two generations of Kangs, she went into the marriage with the burden of producing a son.

Outside the home, there were constant reminders of Japan's colonial rule. At work, my father and other Korean teachers suffered harassment and discrimination. In addition to getting paid considerably less than their Japanese colleagues, they had to watch every move they made as there were always informants in the teachers' room who stayed until all the teachers left, and kept track of everyone's comings and goings.

One of my father's responsibilities at Young Saeng was overseeing the school library. One day the principal ordered my father to throw away all the Korean books. Secretly, my father took the books home. When Korea was liberated, he returned the books to the library.

As a Christian, he especially detested the requirement that everyone take part in Shinto rituals. The teachers were required to bow before a Shinto shrine in the teacher's room (similar to faculty lounge) first thing in the morning when they reported to school and, thereafter, stand up at their desks and bow in the direction of the shrine on the wall every time they came in the teacher's room, and then bow again at the end of the day before they left for home. Twice a month, on the first and fifteenth, the teachers were also required to line up the students and accompany them on a march to the big Shinto shrine in the park and pay respect to Japanese gods. Since he was teaching at a Canadian mission school, there was much discussion about the Shinto rituals. The missionaries and Korean teachers decided to follow the Japanese order perfunctorily to avoid angering the Japanese and seeing their school closed. My father despised having to take his students before the shrine, detested having to cut his hair short like a temple priest, and loathed the Japanese for trying to destroy Korean identity and dignity so systematically and permanently.

Creating Second-Class Citizens

The resident-general's office in Seoul was a small-scale Japanese government with the single purpose of maintaining complete control of its colonial subjects. The first resident-general, Hirobumi Ito, oversaw the office, which was the instrument for carrying out Japan's design in Korea—total control of the territory and transformation of the country's twenty million Koreans into second-class Japanese (see chapter 2).

As a country, Japan had existed only half as long as Korea, and it embraced as its own much of Korean culture and art. In fact, Japan owed a great deal of its cultural and artistic heritage to Korea, especially to the Paekche Kingdom (18 B.C. to A.D. 660) in the southwestern part of the Korean peninsula. The Paekche Kingdom was known for the refinement of its culture, and its artists and artisans excelled in architecture, ceramics, and pottery, which they passed on to Japan. The Paekche Kingdom and Japan had friendly relations, and there was a lot of movement of the two peoples. One of the finest specimens of Paekche work lives on in the famous Horyuji Temple at Nara, built by Paekche artisans. And, during the seven-year war that followed Toyotomi Hideyoshi's invasion of Korea in 1592, countless Korean art treasures were stolen by Japanese forces and taken back to Japan. Japan also took as captives artisans such as distinguished potters, whose contributions to Japanese ceramics has been immeasurable.

Yet, as the Japanese Empire set upon a course of expansion, first in Korea and then throughout Asia, the Japanese mythology of the superior Yamato race was conjured up to rally its citizenry to compete with the West. This mythology of superiority was played out on the Korean peninsula with painstaking thoroughness, with the primary goal of destroying Korean identity and turning Koreans into second-class citizens. Through its propaganda, Japan skillfully convinced the outside world that everything it did in Korea actually represented progress for Koreans, even when the results were conspicuously the opposite. For instance, when the Japanese Ministry of Education established Seoul Imperial University in the late 1920s officials claimed that the school would go a long way toward improving education in Korea. But so few Koreans were admitted that its existence hardly mattered. A double standard practiced by school administrators resulted in only a handful of the best and brightest Korean students being admitted, while less qualified Japanese students were enrolled in large numbers. Japanese students who failed to get into an imperial university in Japan went to Korea and were routinely admitted to Seoul Imperial University.

With meticulous detail the resident-general's office established an administrative structure with a Japanese as the top official, thus ensuring that its edicts were enforced all the way from the central government in Seoul down to the smallest hamlet in the countryside.

In this way Japan, during its nearly four decades of colonial rule, was able to confiscate for its own use half of Korea's annual rice crop. Japan's design for global power, driven by expedited industrialization,. required vast material resources and a captive workforce to stoke its engine.

As colonizers, the Japanese were ingenious, petty, determined, and greedy in pursuing their goals. In the schools, a Korean could rarely become a principal, no matter how qualified he was or how long he had been there. When a Korean teacher approached the top rank, he would be assigned to a school in a bigger city where there would be a Japanese teacher higher in status than at the first school.

And Japanese administrators stifled Koreans in other ways, too. They made sure that only the Japanese got the lucrative concessions at train stations. Even in the most remote train stations in the country, the concessions were run by Japanese.

The agrarian Korean economy was restructured to suit the needs of the Japanese. Farmers were forced to sell the best crops— fruits, vegetables, and especially Korean rice, which Japanese preferred over their own—at artificially low prices to Japan, and they could keep only what was left over. With half of the crop going to Japan, rice became a scarce commodity in Korea. Koreans were ordered to make their rice go far by mixing it with a substance called *daedubak*, the residue left over after the oil is squeezed out of soybeans, which tasted like sawdust. The Japanese brought dried *daedubak* from Manchuria and sold it to Koreans to eat, though normally it was used as fertilizer. Only on special occasions, such as holidays, did most people get a chance to eat unadulterated rice.

But what most angered my parents was the constant reminder of where Korean rice and other crops were going. Every day they would see a mountain of rice, soybeans, and millet headed for Japan at the train stations. By midday the crops would disappear, only to be replaced next morning by another mountain of crops. Identical scenes were played at all major train stations throughout Korea for nearly thirty-five years.

The Japanese not only took food products but also snatched

people. Young Korean men were conscripted to work in mines and munitions factories in Japan, the Sakhalin Islands, and Manchuria to build the Japanese Empire's war machine. Young Korean women were abducted to work as sex slaves for Japanese soldiers. Venereal disease was rampant among Japanese soldiers, so a decision was made to provide them with virgins. The Japanese government took girls from their Korean colony for this purpose, and later on, as the Japanese Imperial Army's conquest of Asia expanded, Chinese, Filipina, Singaporan, Indonesian, and even Dutch women from Indonesia were also abducted, though in smaller numbers than Koreans.

Teishintai—the "comfort-women brigade"—was a dreaded word, known to every Korean. To avoid being abducted by Japanese agents, some girls dressed like boys and wore farmer's straw hats when they went outdoors. Poor peasant girls from the countryside were favorite targets, but everyone else worried, too. "We were warned about the *Teishintai* all the time," said my mother. Her parents kept a close watch over her and her two younger sisters, because every girl was a potential sex slave for the Japanese military. Innocent girls were kidnapped from their homes while picking wild vegetables for dinner or washing clothes by the stream. Poor country girls running errands in the marketplace were lured by tales of desirable factory jobs. All together, the Japanese recruited or abducted more than one hundred thousand Korean girls and young women, who were forced to follow Japanese soldiers to Manchuria and China, and later, throughout Southeast Asia. They moved with the Japanese troops and lived in barracks at the front. It was not until half a century later in the 1990s that these atrocities came to light and created an international scandal.

A horrendous example of Japan's disdain for Koreans' humanity occurred in 1923, following the Kanto earthquake, which leveled the Tokyo and Yokohama areas. Japanese police and soldiers, taking advantage of the postquake chaos and unfounded rumors that Korean residents of Japan were poisoning wells and setting fires, massacred six thousand Koreans. Recalling the horror stories he had heard from Korean survivors of the massacre, the Reverend Yun-Tae O, our family friend who was in charge of the Tokyo Korean Church we attended when we lived in Japan, told how even Japanese Christians showed no mercy. They, too, he said, were determined to kill all Koreans.

In one section of Tokyo, Koreans were taken to the banks of the Arakawa Canal, ten people at a time, their hands tied behind their backs, and mowed down with machine guns. Sixty years later, in 1982, a private group in Japan led by Yukie Kinuta, a primary school teacher, exhumed the remains of some of those Koreans who were killed. She organized the project, she said, to satisfy the souls of the slaughtered Koreans.

☯

And, in an irrational twist of fate, Koreans in Russia became victims because they were suspected of being potential spies for Japan. In the autumn of 1937, three months after Japan invaded Manchuria, nearly two hundred thousand Koreans were relocated by the Soviet leader Joseph Stalin from the Maritime Province in the Soviet Far East to Kazakhstan in Central Asia. With two days' notice and no explanation, they were put on trains like cattle for the long trip across Siberia, during which hundreds died. The relocation took from September to December of 1937. The descendants of these people still live throughout Russian Central Asia. The terrible irony was that Stalin suspected the Koreans of being potential or actual Japanese spies, but in fact, as was the case with some of my relatives, they had fled to the Soviet Union to escape Japanese oppression back home. Stalin's relocation would have gone unnoticed in history but for the Russian writer Alekxandr Solzhenitsyn. He was the first prominent non-Korean to disclose publicly the forced relocation in his book *Gulag Archipelago*. Listen to Solzhenitsyn's account of the relocation:

> In 1937 some tens of thousands of those suspicious Koreans—
> with Khalkhin-Gol in mind, face to face with Japanese imperialism,

who could trust those slant-eyed heathens?—from palsied old men to puling infants, with some portion of their beggarly belongings, were swiftly and quietly transferred from the Far East to Kazakstan. So swiftly that they spent the first winter in mud-brick houses without windows (where would all that glass have come from!). And so quietly that nobody except the neighboring Kazakhs learned of this resettlement, no one who counted let slip a word about it, no foreign correspondents uttered a squeak.

Elsewhere, Solzhenitsyn said the forced relocation of the Koreans was Stalin's "first experiment in mass arrest on the basis of race." After his disclosure, a handful of overseas Korean and Japanese scholars began investigating the circumstances surrounding the incident. But the isolation of the Koreans in the former Soviet republics and the scarcity of written records made it difficult for researchers to document the specifics. The Koreans who lived through the experience are the best witnesses, but they, for whatever reasons, have kept silent.

Larisa Kim, a fourth-generation Russian Korean, is a psychiatrist in Moscow. Her paternal grandfather was killed during Stalin's reign of terror, soon after relocating from the Soviet Far East to Central Asia, and her maternal grandfather escaped to Harbin to avoid the same fate. Kim grew up in Angren, a small town near Tashkent, the capital of Uzbekistan, and later in Moscow, where her parents are professors. Kim told me that her grandmother was so afraid of reprisal she kept the truth of her grandfather's murder a secret all her life. A number of Korean visitors to Soviet Central Asia have tried to find out about the 1937 evacuation, but elderly Russian Koreans remain reluctant to speak, preferring to take their tales of blood, sweat, and tears to the grave.

☯

The Japanese imperialism exacted a heavy toll on all Koreans. Then, as now, the voices of small countries fell on deaf international ears.

The differences of opinion among nationalist leaders added to the problem. The Korean Independence Movement was split into two factions—the American and the Siberia-Manchuria groups. Syngman Rhee, the leader of the American group operating out of Hawaii, believed in diplomacy and the help of the United States (despite his disappointing experience earlier with Theodore Roosevelt) as a way of obtaining Korean independence (see chapter 2). But Tong-Hwi Yi, who led the Siberia-Manchuria group, wanted to organize open warfare with the Japanese. General Yi had correctly surmised that the United States, which had helped Japan take over Korea, would not do anything to further Korean independence. He also predicted, correctly, that at some point in the future the United States and Japan would be at war. During a showdown between the two factions at a 1922 special meeting of the Korean Provisional Government in Shanghai, Yi lost to the pro-America faction's greater numbers. General Yi resigned the post of premier, and Chang-Ho Ahn quit as the director of the labor bureau. Returning to Siberia, Yi formed the Korea Socialist Party, because he believed that a strong revolutionary mass party was the only way to carry out his nationalist goals. The Soviet leader Vladimir Lenin was helpful toward that end and pledged monetary support. When Yi first went to Moscow from Siberia in 1918, he had no theory at all but only believed in a mass movement and in the Soviets. When Lenin asked him how many workers there were in Korea—in the factories, on the railways, on the farms—he could not answer. He had no idea. Lenin smiled and called in an aide, saying: "We must help Comrade Yi here. He has hot blood for Korean independence but no method. This is a natural Oriental condition. They have no revolutionary base but only a background of terrorism and military action."

Throughout this period, traitorous Korean collaborators aided Japan by inflicting pain on their own people. The Japanese sent its agents and Korean collaborators everywhere Koreans lived, at home and abroad. Even in Los Angeles, Susan Ahn, the eldest daughter of Chang-Ho Ahn, remembers as a child seeing Japanese agents spying on her family, watching those going in and out of their home. The collaborators enjoyed special privileges that enabled them to live comfortably and send their children to schools that the Japanese considered to be elite. The collaborators as a group exacted from the Korean soul a heavy price in the legacy that they left—eroding Koreans' core values and replacing them with a colonial mentality and sycophancy that would last long after Korea was liberated, extending into the behavior of decades of military regimes.

The Japanese takeover of Korea and the colonial rule affected five generation of Kangs, from my great-great-grandfather Soo-Il even down to me, as I have been deprived—it seems forever deprived—of access to my ancestral home in Tanchon. Like millions of other Koreans, our family's refusal to cooperate with the Japanese overlords cost us dearly. Soo-Il, whose powerful position was eliminated by the Japanese, lived through a quarter century of the colonial rule like an eagle with its wings cut off. Watching his only grandson, Myong-Hwan, become a broken man, must have pained him more than he could bear. But Soo-Il bore the tragedy with dignity, lavishing his attention on his only great-grandson, my father. His hobby in later years was growing tobacco for his pipe, taking care of his beloved light-gray donkeys (which he rode well into his late seventies) and doing a myriad of things for Joo-Han—building him a swing, walking him home from town, telling him stories. Soo-Il died in 1934 at the age of eighty-eight, when my father was twenty-one. He had lived up to his name, "Longevity Number One," for few people lived to be that old in Korea in those days. He was buried next to his first wife, whom he had married in 1859 when he was thirteen, just a hundred yards behind the Kang family house at our Boshigol estate.

My great-grandfather Bong-Ho also bore the burden that Japanese colonial rule imposed on his family with an uncommon strength drawn from his Christian faith. Sooner or later, he believed, Japan would fall. He preached to his flock to not let despair extinguish the flickering flame of hope, for righteousness would ultimately prevail, and to remember that people who do not believe in God cannot last long. Only through divine intervention would Koreans be freed from the yoke of Japan, he maintained, and he worked to convert as many nonbelievers to Christianity as he could. His movements were constantly watched by Japanese agents and Korean collaborators, but he was fearless. I suppose when you have God on your side, you feel strong despite the presence of oppressors like the Japanese. And, they mostly left him alone. Perhaps they reasoned that the Kangs had already paid a high price in the destruction of my grandfather Myong-Hwan.

Myong-Hwan's broken spirit after the years of imprisonment and torture cast a dark shadow over my entire family. As mentioned earlier, my grandfather kept to himself in his smoke-filled room, rarely venturing out. His unpredictable outbursts made family members feel uneasy. His condition would probably be what today is called post–traumatic stress syndrome. There were no such names for his condition then, but my great-grandmother Bong-Keum, intelligent as she was intuitive, made sure all the kitchen knives were hidden before she retired for the night. I try to imagine her anxiety and sadness, seeing how clouded her only son's mind had become, and I can feel her wrenching pain. What kind of fate was it that this daughter of wealth, whose nickname was the "Beautiful One," should end her days in such suffering? But for her grandson, my father, would she have had any sunlight in her life? I wish I had been old enough to have had a conversation with her.

My father coped by devoting himself to his studies. His love of the English language provided an escape from all this gloom, for it opened up for him an exciting world of English literature. My father devoured Tennyson, Shakespeare, Wordsworth, Robert and Elizabeth Barrett Browning, Keats, Yeats, and Hardy. He wanted to master English and studied all the time, assiduously avoiding political involvement. His proficiency in English was what gave him a modicum of independence under Japanese rule, for they recognized its importance as a tool for communication. I think English was his salvation. Just as my great-grandfather's conversion had changed the course of my family's life, so, too, my father's love of the English language irreversibly affected him and the next generation of the Kangs.

For thirty-five years, from August 22, 1910, until August 15, 1945, when Japan surrendered in World War II, there would be no escape from the tyranny of Japanese rulers. Without their country, and stripped of even their family names, language, national anthem, and flower, Koreans suffered under the Japanese as few peoples ever had under an invading country's rule. The only way that Korea might be free was a collision between the United States and Japan. General Yi had predicted there would be a war between those two powers, even as Japan had been scheming, with the help of the United States, to take over Korea. My family did not lose faith, and their faith was justified with the fall of Japan; but Korea, caught once again between whales, would find itself moving from one untenable situation to another.

4. LIBERATION IS A CRUEL HOAX

(1945–1950)

Come August 15 each passing year, we Koreans—at home and abroad—
are reminded of our age-old han called unquenched woes.
That day is supposed to be our Liberation Day from the brutal
Japanese rule which has left a deep scar in the soul of Koreans everywhere,
whether in Manchuria, China, Russia or America.
But this otherwise glorious and joyous date still mocks our dreams
and aspirations as one people.
We cry out for our unrequited liberation from our unacceptable fate.
It doesn't matter where we live. We are all exiles from our memory
of the Land of Morning Calm, once in one piece even under the
brute force of a savage neighbor.

—K.W. Lee, (1928–   )
Excerpts from interview with author in 1994.

MAIN CHARACTERS:
Joo-Han Kang, my father
Bong-Ho Kang, my paternal great-grandfather
Sok-Won Choe, my mother
Ke-Son Han, my maternal grandmother
The Reverend William Scott, my father's English teacher

World War II Brings Hope

My relatives, like other Koreans, were jubilant when the United States declared war against Japan on December 8, 1941, following the attack on Pearl Harbor. They saw it as a God-sent opportunity for Korea to free itself from Japan's rule. But life for Koreans became even more difficult now, as Japanese officials squeezed their colonial subjects even more to feed Japan's enormous war machine. Rationing of foods became stricter and police scrutiny tighter. With Western missionaries repatriated after the outbreak of the war, members of my family—already viewed as pro-American because they were Christians—came under greater police brutality. They were completely at the mercy of the Japanese and Korean collaborators.

Conspiracy against Japan was read into even the most benign actions. For instance, a milk cow that my great-grandfather Bong-Ho bought from a departing missionary family prompted a police investigation and punishment that led to his untimely death. Bong-Ho Kang, who by this time had established seventeen churches and was known throughout South Hamgyong Province, was summoned to the police station like a common criminal. Glaring at the seventy-four-year-old Presbyterian elder, his hair and mustache as white as snow, the police accused him of being an American spy. How else could he obtain the cow from a missionary, they said. My great-grandfather had paid the equivalent of $300 for the cow, a considerable sum in the Korea of 1941. Nevertheless, they insisted that it had been given to him. In deference to his age, however, they did not put him in lock-up. Instead, they ordered him to report to the police station at nine o'clock sharp every morning. For many months, Bong-Ho reported to the police station through blistering heat, rain, and snow, walking to and from his home. The toll on him was simply too much. He began to lose considerable weight, fell ill, and never recovered. He died on September 22, 1943, when I was ten months old. But I remember two things about him—his false teeth and shiny balding head. Years later, when I told my mother about putting my hands into my great-grandfather's mouth to try and grab his dentures she was astonished at my detailed recollection. Indeed, my mother said, whenever Great-grandfather held me, I would poke his balding head with my tiny hands. I have been grateful to my great-grandfather all my life. He was the only male member of my family to welcome my birth on November 11, 1942, in the midst of World War II.

I was delivered by a Korean Christian midwife named Martha on an exceptionally cold night, I was told, when winds from Siberia blew thick snow off the slate tiles of our home. I entered the world black and blue, from having the umbilical cord wrapped around my neck five times, but apparently I was determined to live. Three drops of herbal potion placed on my tongue by my maternal grandmother saved my life. When it was announced that a daughter was born, my father refused to acknowledge me. He had expected a son and had only one name ready—a boy's. For two weeks, he didn't look at me and refused to come into my mother's room, where women of the household gathered by her bedside to console her. It was like a wake, with all the women around my mother crying. But my great-grandfather chided his only grandson and comforted my mother: "I am a hungry man," he told the women by mother's bedside. "It makes no difference to me whether God gives me a boy or a girl child." Ten months later, as the old man lay dying in pain, he smiled. He was looking at a picture of me hanging on the wall taken on my 100th day. When my father finally accepted a girl for his first child, he went against the tradition of giving me a girl's flowery or simple name. Instead, he named me for his motto—Kyonshill, meaning "steady or constant" in Korean, as my name. It is unique; I've yet to meet or hear of another person by that name. (Connie, a diminutive of Constance, is the closest English equivalent of my Korean name.)

☯

When Okinawa fell in April 1945, my father, like many other Koreans, had anticipated that Japan's end was near. But when a Japanese colleague at the school where he taught solicited my father's opinion about who would win the war, my father was careful. "Most likely Japan," he said. With so many informants around, my father wasn't going to allow himself to fall into a trap as had others, who, having made minor anti-Japanese remarks, had been beaten and imprisoned, sometimes even without official charges against them. A childhood playmate of his in Tanchon, for instance, had been jailed after the war broke out for saying Japan's days were over.

Korean liberation came on VJ-Day—August 15, 1945. This was sooner than my father had expected. But he was still careful not to express joy, for Japanese soldiers and police were everywhere, and the fear was very real that they would kill as many Koreans as they could before surrendering. In Tokyo, the Japanese people heard for the first time the squeaky voice of Emperor Hirohito, broadcast over the radio, saying that Japan had lost the war. The emperor, who many believed to have divine origins, appeared to be merely human after all.

One of the first things my father did after liberation was to instruct a hesitant janitor to remove the Shinto shrine in the teachers' room. When the Japanese principal returned the following day, he immediately noticed the missing shrine and asked about it. There was silence. Finally, he called the janitor, who told the principal that my father had ordered him to get rid of the shrine. My father watched the principal, who, obviously aware of the difference between his position now and two days earlier, said nothing. My father, on the other hand, feeling all of his pent-up anger against the Japanese, could not contain himself. For months this principal had ordered teachers to take their students to nearby mountains to dig up pine roots. The oil from the roots was supposedly used for cleaning the parts of Japanese fighter planes. These excursions took as much as five and six hours a day, and my father resented the loss of study time for his students. Now, as he regarded the principal, stripped of his power, my father could not restrain himself any longer. How dare he still ask about the shrine? He struck the principal on the head and said, "How can you consider yourself an educator? You were more interested in having us bow before the shrine than teaching students. You were more interested in making the students go to the mountain to gather pine roots to please your superiors than educating them. How much oil do you think you got for your country out of the labor of the Korean students who could have better used their time studying?" He struck the principal again. The other teachers looked on in disbelief.

Japanese men and women who had sought refuge at the school, fearing retaliation from their Korean neighbors, were now gathering. My father glanced at their faces and thought they looked menacing, so he shifted his tactics. He proceeded to list, one by one, all of the Japanese principal's misdeeds during his tenure at the school.

When my father had finished, he told the principal: "Your country lost the war. What did you do for your country?"

The principal merely bowed his head in shame. The Japanese bystanders watched intently, without uttering a word.

Two days after VJ-Day, my father joined thousands of people who had gathered in Tanchon Park for a celebration. They waved Korean flags and sang the national anthem in public for the first time in many years. Years later he told me how full of hope he was then, that at long last Koreans would be able to live in freedom under their own flag. Little did he know how short-lived this new freedom would be.

A Brief Period of Hope and Excitement

In 1945, greater Tanchon was a midsized city with a population of forty thousand located in the mountainous and fertile area of what is now North Korea. Its rich soil produced the best soybeans in all Korea, and its proximity to the East Sea provided access to fresh seafood year-round. Its mountains contained gold, silver, copper, iron, and tungsten. On its fields grazed the Tanchon cow, famous for its beef (the Japanese even composed a song about the Tanchon cow entitled, "One of the Treasures of Tanchon"). Because of the city's resources, the Japanese built a big port in Tanchon to transport minerals, cattle, and soybeans back to Japan. Many Japanese lived in Tanchon because they had been brought over to supervise the factories, the mines, and the shipment of Japan-bound agricultural products. Some of the best homes were occupied by the Japanese, and only they were given leases to run lucrative concessions, such as shops in train stations. From 1910 until 1945, the Japanese in Tanchon lived well.

In the days immediately after the war, while awaiting instructions on repatriation, the Japanese gathered up their belongings and took refuge in the big high school in Tanchon, where they stayed, fully expecting revenge from Koreans. Under the Allied rules initiated by the United States in August 1945 and agreed to by the Soviet Union, the Russians were to receive the surrender of the Japanese troops north of the thirty-eighth parallel and the Americans south of the line. The choice of the thirty-eighth parallel, which roughly divided Korea in half, was a compromise between State Department officials who wanted to receive the surrender of Japanese troops as far north as possible and military men who held that it was logistically improbable to get U.S. troops to the northern part of Korea ahead of the Russians. The order was issued by General Douglas MacArthur, the supreme commander for the allied powers, on September 2, the day the Japanese signed the surrender aboard the USS *Missouri* in Tokyo Bay. It took the Russians about a week to move into North Korea. Not all Japanese waited for official repatriation, though. Their day of reckoning had come. Belatedly, confronted by the degree of their evil deeds, and the anger and resentment they had fomented, some quickly bought their way out on boats to the southeastern coast of Korea, and from there got to Japan on their own. But most waited for instructions. Their disciplined behavior under the circumstances impressed my father. He remembered, in particular, a large group of Japanese who had come to a Tanchon school to await their repatriation. Even in their desperate situation, they spent their time reading books or magazines, and remained orderly.

For the people of my ancestral county, those first few days after liberation were exhilarating. Intellectuals who had returned from their studies in Japan, Europe, and the United States during Japanese colonial rule, but who until now had been laying low or hiding, came out and moved into leadership positions. They confiscated weapons and promptly put many of the Japanese to work filling up the deep holes in the ground that Koreans had been forced to dig for air-raid shelters.

One memorable afternoon, the Japanese were lined up and marched with a Korean flag to the big Shinto shrine in Tanchon Park. Once there, they were ordered to raze the shrine. The Japanese worked very efficiently, saying not a word. They tied a rope around a torii and pulled it down. In the same fashion, they also brought down the Shinto shrine. But the Koreans' days of elite leadership were brief. Soon the Russian occupation forces appeared and took over Pyongyang, Hamhung, and other cities in the north, including Tanchon. The arrival of the Russians changed everything. Working with Korean Communists, the Russians formed in October 1945 the Provisional People's Committee, under the chairmanship of Il-Sung Kim, who had been trained in the Soviet Army. After purging many prominent nationalists who had returned from China, Manchuria, and Siberia, they enforced a policy of communization. People's Committees were formed throughout the north, with members re-cruited from the ranks of the unschooled peasantry. A power struggle ensued between the Communist peasantry and the Korean intelligentsia. With Russian backing, peasants fought the educated class and confiscated their weapons. Russians arrested many members of the intelligentsia, preventing what could have been an enlightened leadership from emerging. Almost every day Communists, waving red flags and singing pro-labor songs, held marches, to which only the poor and uneducated people came.

The People's Committees now dispatched their representatives to all the public institutions, including schools, where they required the teachers to bring their students with them to rallies and meetings. Almost every day a meeting was called, and records were kept of who came and who did not. While my father took his students to public rallies as required, he ignored invitations to other functions in the evenings and on Sundays. People's Committee members took notice of this and would use it as an excuse to detain him. Koreans had expected that the Allied victory would mean Korea's liberation from Japanese oppression, but now it appeared that one oppressor would be replaced by another. Instead of Japanese imperialism, it would be Communism, and its control would become, in some ways, even tighter than that of the Japanese.

My father spent his first Christmas after liberation in jail because the Communists had marked him as uncooperative. Three days before Christmas, he was getting ready to go to bed after returning from church, where he taught an English class, when two plain-clothes policemen showed up at the house. They told him to follow them to the police station. When he asked why, they would only say that it was an order from the "authorities." "Normally, we would use handcuffs, but out of respect for your profession we're not doing that," one of the policemen said.

When my father arrived at the police station, he saw an old primary school classmate with whom he had been friendly. "What have I done to be brought here like this?" my father demanded. The classmate's answer was the same—"an order from the authorities." He was led to a small cell with a tiny window very high up and a latrine hidden from direct view by a dirty blanket hanging from the ceiling like a curtain.

The stench from the latrine and people who had not bathed in a long time was unbearable. Lice and fleas were everywhere. There were seven or eight people sitting on the wooden floor in the room. My father recognized two of them. One was a friend of his father's from his Siberia days. The second man was a pro-Japanese collaborator who had caused misery for Koreans. A third man had committed murder. The fourth Korean said he had been captured trying to escape to Seoul. My father, recalling his father telling him years ago that there is always a plant in prison, thought that this man might be a spy. Another man was a tennis champion whose crime was listening to a Seoul radio program on his shortwave. All of the men had been in the cell for several days.

To pass the time, they took turns telling stories. My grandfather's friend from Siberia talked about seeing a tiger on one of his journeys. The man my father had decided was an informant kept criticizing Communists, which prompted some of the cellmates to join in the criticism. Outside the cell, a tall, grim-faced Russian soldier walked back and forth, patrolling with a machine gun. My father found the soldier's presence unnerving.

On the following day my father waited and waited to be called for questioning, but he was not summoned. Only the tennis champion was taken away. When he returned, he was limping from the beating he had received during the interrogation. Over the next two days, one by one everybody in the cell was called except my father. He spent the days reading his Bible and trying to ignore the anti-Communist tirades of the man he suspected of being a spy.

His third day in jail was Christmas Eve. From his cell he heard distant church bells ringing. How was it possible that he, whose only interest was in his studies and teaching, should be spending the first Christmas Eve after liberation from the Japanese in jail? How was it possible that he, who assiduously avoided politics because of what it had done to his father, could be held in prison not by the enemy but by his own people? He kept reading the Bible.

On Christmas Day, his fourth day in the cell, he was finally taken to see the police chief. My father knew the man because he came from the same village as my father's mother. The minute he saw him, my father complained about being put in jail when he had done nothing wrong. "What is the meaning of this? Explain to me, why was I put into a flea-infested cell for three days? What did I ever do to deserve this?"

The police chief let out a half-hearted laugh. "Teacher Kang, how naive can you get?" he said. "In this new liberated world of ours it is not enough to devote yourself to your scholarly pursuits. Let's have a little social commitment from you. Your father was a revolutionary. He is my esteemed senior for whom I have only the highest respect. How can the only son of a man who sacrificed himself for our country be so indifferent to what's happening to our motherland?"

My father told the police chief that he had no interest in politics, that he had seen what politics had done to his father, and that all his life he had sought to avoid any such involvements. His only preoccupation, he said, was studying languages, especially English and teaching.

With a sigh of disgust the police chief let him go, admonishing him once again. "Teacher Kang, from now on, don't devote yourself only to your studies and teaching. You have to demonstrate some commitment to society. As a member of the intelligentsia, you have a duty."

My father was joined by my mother, who had been waiting for him at the police station with me strapped on her back. She had been alerted about his release. They began the long trek toward our home. On the way, they passed by the Railroad Hospital and saw Mrs. Yoo, the wife of the hospital director, whose younger daughter had been one of my father's students. Mrs. Yoo invited them in for a much-needed bath and a rest, after which they were treated to a hearty meal before heading again for home.

Later my father learned why the police chief had released him. My grandfather had gone to plead with the chief, insisting that his son neither understood nor had any interest in politics, and that ever since his son had seen what his own involvement in politics had done to him, his only obsession had been his studies. My father, he insisted, posed absolutely no threat and it served no purpose whatsoever to detain him. Yet the experience convinced my father that he could no longer live in the North, that he had no choice but to leave home. He continued to teach until the end of the semester, then left for Seoul, accompanied by my maternal grandmother, who knew her way around the border, eleven days later on March 31, 1946.

For now, my mother and I stayed behind. My maternal grandmother, Ke-Son Han, was the master planner in the family's move to the South. She had crossed the border soon after liberation by herself to check out the situation. A widow who ran her own business after her husband's death, Ke-Son was an extraordinary and courageous woman. She knew her way across the thirty-eighth parallel better than any guide. Upon her return, she planned it so that she would accompany my father alone, then return and guide us next to Seoul. She knew that it would raise too much suspicion for the whole family to leave at once. I was two and a half years old when my father left for Seoul. I do not remember his departure, but I do remember playing on our country estate, hearing cuckoo birds, looking at my father's glass-enclosed bookcase and a statue of a horse, and riding on a swing inside our family rooms.

Crossing the Thirty-eighth Parallel

It was late March 1946, and cold wind from Manchuria sent a chill through the bones even though spring had officially arrived. In these parts of northern Korea, spring was short. If my father could stay another month, he would see his two hundred apple trees turn Boshigol into a flowering forest of perfume. But there was no time for this. He knew he had to hurry.

A month earlier, in February, there had been a mass meeting in Pyongyang welcoming the establishment of the North Korean Provisional People's Committee by the guerrilla leader Il-Sung Kim, who had returned from the Soviet Union five months earlier. There was talk of land reform and demonstrations by peasants. Since his Christmas detention, my father had been preoccupied with leaving the North. Some of his colleagues at the school had already left or were planning to depart. The talk around the school had been that before the end of the year, the thirty-eighth parallel line would be shut tight, and Il-Sung Kim would be firmly in control. Every day, more and more people, anticipating the worst, made their way to the South.

What kind of liberation was this? my father asked himself bitterly, cursing the fate that was forcing him to choose between staying and leaving. A country divided: Joseph Stalin, Winston Churchill, and Franklin Roosevelt, without consulting even one Korean, had chopped the country in half—Russians on one side and Americans on the other. Had Roosevelt or Churchill, for one moment, considered what their actions might do to Koreans? Did they, for a moment, ask themselves what it would be like if they could not visit their relatives in another part of their country? Was the Korean peninsula a remote place they neither knew about nor cared about? In terms of Korea, Stalin had gotten his way at the 1945 Yalta Conference. Now two Roosevelts had betrayed Koreans. The United States, the supposed protector of democracy, had once again turned its back on Korea just as it was finally on the verge of freedom and human dignity. My father cursed the two Roosevelts: cowboy Teddy, for conniving with Japan in her takeover of Korea, then refusing to acknowledge the Korean government in exile; and FDR for selling out to Stalin in Yalta and at the 1945 Potsdam Conference. It angered him to even think about it. Adding to my father's grief was the death in October of 1945, of his paternal grandmother, the oasis of his lonely childhood. Thankfully, she had lived long enough to see Korean independence, but died two months later. She had been ailing since her husband's death two years earlier. He had been mostly reared by his grandparents.

Tens of thousands of Koreans, who, like my father, could not endure life under the emerging Communist rule, left behind everything they had for freedom in the South across the thirty-eighth parallel. In the first two years after the liberation, eight hundred thousand northerners moved south. In my immediate family, only my paternal grandparents stayed behind. My grandfather had insisted that the Communists could not inflict greater suffering than that heaped on him by the Japanese. Even had my grandparents wanted to, they could not have traveled because of their frail health. But they urged my parents to head south. "Young people have no future here," they said. "You must leave as soon as is feasible."

U.S. Military Government and Occupation Forces

In the South following Japan's surrender, U.S. forces established a temporary military government headed by Lt. Gen. John R. Hodge, the commander of U.S. forces on Okinawa. He was a tough soldier who had led the successful capture of Okinawa, one of the bloodiest and prolonged battles in the Pacific. But the main consideration in assigning Hodge to Korea was that he was stationed nearby, not because of any expertise on Korea—he had none. In fact, Hodge and his men knew practically nothing about conditions within Korea, and this ignorance led to many decisions that disappointed Koreans. One blunder was his refusal to recognize the legitimacy of the Korean government in exile in Shanghai or the new People's Republic in Seoul and his choice, instead, to retain Japanese officials until the transfer could be completed. The Shanghai government, established in April 1919, had been the symbol of the Korean independence movement. It was the product of a merger of an earlier exile government in Vladivostok and a later one established in Shanghai. The Vladivostok government, which represented Koreans in Russia and Manchuria, had a bigger constituency because of the greater number of Koreans there than in Shanghai, but the location in the relatively free French Concession of Shanghai was an important consideration. The uniting of the two exile governments had been the handiwork of Chang-Ho Ahn, who believed that the success of the independence movement depended on Korean leaders speaking in one voice. To the outside world, there appeared to be division. Thus, in absentia, Syngman Rhee, whose base was Washington, was chosen as the president, and General Tong-Hwi Yi was elected the premier. Ahn, a conciliator whose skills were as a tactician, ran the organization until General Yi could relocate to Shanghai in September 1919 to take over the reins of the infant government. Ahn served as the director of labor.

But sadly for Korea, by the time Koreans had regained their country, two of the three most forceful leaders of the Shanghai government were dead. Ahn, captured by Japanese police in China and taken to Seoul, died in prison there, and Yi met his death at the hands of a Communist assassin in Vladivostok. The lone survivor was Rhee, better known than the other two by American officials because he had lived in the United States for some four decades. But Rhee, self-righteous and unaccommodating of divergent viewpoints, had the biggest ego of them all.

Three other notable survivors of exile in Shanghai—Ku Kim, Kiu-Shik Kim, and Wun-Hyung Lyuh—were available, but Hodge and MacArthur preferred Rhee, the only one who spoke fluent English among Korean leaders at the time. Ku Kim was a conservative, an indigenous patriot who always wore traditional Korean *hanbok* (attire) and was the head of the police in the Shanghai government. Kiu-Shik Kim, who had gone to the Paris Peace Conference as the representative of the Provisional Government after World War I to seek recognition of Korea, was a moderate. Lyuh, a moderate leftist who espoused agrarian reforms, had held no official post in Shanghai, but he had a sizeable following among the masses who longed to possess their own land.

In the summer of 1945, when Japan's surrender was imminent, the top Japanese administrator in Korea, Nobuyuki Abe, had approached several Korean nationalist leaders, including Lyuh, about the possibility of forming an interim Korean government prior to the Japanese surrender. Abe's motive was more to benefit his people—he believed a transition administration composed of Korean leaders was needed to maintain order and avert reprisals against the Japanese— but nonetheless, the proposal made sense. At Abe's behest, Lyuh agreed to accept the position as the head of the transition team until the Americans arrived.

Lyuh's interim administration was largely successful in preventing violence, and Lyuh developed considerable grassroots support by forming People's Committees throughout the countryside. Lyuh also advocated several other popular reforms, such as allowing tenant farmers to acquire their own land on easy terms, ousting Japanese nationals and Korean collaborators from positions of power, and strictly regulating government monopolies. These measures quickly gained popular support, but by September 8, 1945, U.S. forces arrived and the Americans effectively ended progress on any of his programs.

When Hodge arrived in Inchon as the commander of the U.S. military occupation, he was met by officials of the transition government. But the general snubbed the eager Koreans who had come to welcome him by saying that he knew nothing of Lyuh or his administration. This was an insult and a humiliating lesson for Lyuh and other Korean leaders. They had mistakenly assumed that they would be received with open arms into the U.S. military government, even though the matter had not been discussed. Had they been exposed to Western culture, they would have known that Americans would not assume something as important as who would run the interim government without discussing it first. In the Korean culture, much is left unsaid because spelling out would take away room for nonverbal negotiating and face-saving later. This misunderstanding would be one of countless cultural clashes that would strain Korean relationship with occupying American forces. The general's position was backed up by his superior, MacArthur, who said that Korea would be ruled under his, MacArthur's, authority. Lyuh and his People's Republic found themselves out in the cold. Ignoring Lyuh, Hodge retained Abe and other Japanese officials to help inaugurate a military government—an action that infuriated Koreans and set the tone for the discontent and frictions that would follow.

There seemingly was no end to Hodge's arsenal of decisions that angered and insulted Koreans. For instance, U.S. military personnel were ordered not to accept any food from Koreans. Although the order had been issued because Koreans were poor and had little food for themselves, it was nevertheless taken as a slap in the face of Koreans, who very much mind form. My father, who was working for the U.S. military government, remembers the awkwardness created on both sides when Americans who were invited to Korean gatherings declined offerings of food. Koreans, already suffering from an inferiority complex about their poverty and primitive living conditions, believed that the general had directed his men not to partake of Korean food because he looked down on them and considered their living conditions too unsanitary. The directive was so contrary to the Korean concept of hospitality that no amount of explanation from the American side could assuage Koreans' wounded pride.

Still, there was one thing that the U.S. military government provided: political freedom. This led to the rise of more than four dozen political parties—and chaos. The return of the now septuagenarian Rhee from the United States and Ku Kim and other lesser figures in the Provisional Government from China exacerbated the confusion and political unrest. Both Lyuh and Kim were killed by assassins; it has long been suspected that killers were agents of Rhee's supporters.

Beyond the political confusion, there were other factors that wrought economic turmoil in the wake of partitioning the country. For example, the predominantly agricultural South was now entirely separated from the heavy industry of the North. The U.S. decision to split Korea along the thirty-eighth parallel because it was roughly at the middle point of the country reflected a profound ignorance of the fact that neither side could survive independently. Furthermore, Japanese authorities triggered severe inflation by intentionally circulating a huge sum of the Japanese currency (3.5 billion Japanese yen, compared to about 5 billion yen total in banknotes outstanding) in the first weeks following Japan's surrender. Every week the price of rice, along with everything else, doubled. With more than two million Koreans crossing into the southern zone from the North or returning home from China and Japan, economic havoc reigned during the first two years after liberation.

In our family, my father was the first to leave, since he was the most likely target of the Communists. Dressed like a woodcutter, he departed with a knapsack containing only his pocket-size English and German dictionaries, a Bible, a change of clothing, a pair of shoes, and fifteen hundred won (enough money to buy a two month's supply of rice for two adults) rolled around his waistband. My maternal grandmother, Ke-Son, was the only other person who went with him, as had been planned. She would return to take Mother and me when my father got established in Seoul.

The sky was deep blue-gray when he left Boshigol at dawn, heading first to Orori to my grandmother's home, then by train to Chongok, a border town where travelers to and from the South were cleared. They spent the night at an inn where they shared a room with a dozen others. Early the next morning they crossed a railway bridge over the Hantan River. The southern side of the river was patrolled by American soldiers, the north by Russians. A long line of people, perhaps a hundred or more, were queued up on the northern side when my father and grandmother arrived. A Soviet soldier with a submachine gun checked each person and his or her baggage.

On the other side of the bridge, people underwent a similar inspection by a U.S. military policeman. I do not think my father was ever more happy to use his English than when he greeted the young American military man.

As soon as the travelers were cleared, U.S. military personnel sprayed all of them with hefty doses of DDT from army-green cans to delouse them. The powder turned everybody's hair and clothing white, but the travelers merely brushed it off with their bare hands and walked toward Tongdu-chon, the closest town south of the thirty-eighth parallel, where with many other refugees from the North, my father and grandmother boarded a train bound for Seoul.

My grandmother and my father sat next to each other on the train without saying much. Both were submerged in their own thoughts. Nearby, several passengers were engaged in a heated criticism of Russians and the North Korean Communists, but my father was too preoccupied to pay attention to them—except when their voices rose and interrupted his thoughts. He wondered how long it would be before he could return home. A year, perhaps? How could he live even a year away from home? Even the thought of being away for a year pricked his heart. What good was freedom if he must give up his home to win it? At least under the Japanese he could live in his native place. It had not even been a full day since he had left home, and already he missed Boshigol as he pictured the orchard, the two little brooks that meandered along the house, and the mountain beyond. But then with a chill he remembered his brief imprisonment and the speed with which Russians and Korean Communists made life for the people, especially landowners, unbearable. He had been startled to see so many people come forward to cooperate with the Communists. They had helped Russians confiscate rice and other crops from the well-to-do and, in some instances, forced them out of their homes without so much as a day's notice. Thus, he comforted himself by thinking that within a year or so the political situation would stabilize and that he would be able to return home, if not to live, at least to visit. He also looked forward to being reunited with my mother and me, as it was my maternal grandmother's plan to go back within a few weeks and bring us out of the North. Thinking about my mother and me, he gained strength and told himself that he must not lose faith and that he must start a new life in Seoul, however long that might last, until he could return to Boshigol. He had heard jobs were plentiful for people who spoke English.

My grandmother, having crossed the thirty-eighth parallel once before to buy medications and canvas shoes that were much in demand in the North, thought about the merchandise she would return with this time, and the preparations she would have to make to convey my mother and me to the South. She feared that soon the thirty-eighth parallel would be closed to all travel, as the Russians and their Korean sympathizers solidified their power in the North. Having operated a hardware store since her husband's death, she was an astute businesswoman. Each time she went back, she would take goods from the South and make a profit. She was fifty-one, my age as I write these words; I wonder if I would have had the courage, vision, and strength she possessed to see that her family members got safe passage.

Since liberation the word was out that Russians would be temporarily occupying the North, and thousands of people, especially Christians and the well-to-do, had begun to move to the South. The refugees went everywhere in the South, but rural areas were so unaccommodating to northerners that almost a third of them ended up in the capital. With half of the labor force in the South unemployed, even educated people from the North took to peddling goods in street market stalls. Many took advantage of the rice shortage in Seoul by going to the countryside and carrying the rice back for sale in the city. People who had no relatives or friends to stay with lived where they could, renting space even in entryways. When they could not get even that, they put up a few boards with a sheet over them for a roof and lived under them. But the makeshift supplies were hard to come by, and everything was hauled either on women's heads or on an A-frame on men's backs. Food was in short supply; women stood in line for hours for a bucket of drinking water.

☯

At Seoul Station my father and my grandmother parted. Their relationship had been polite but cool. My grandmother was proud of my father's professional achievements, his intellectual prowess, and his basic decency and honesty. But she considered him cold and arrogant. My father had a Confucian respect for scholarly pursuits and a disdain for businesspeople. My mother's people were mostly merchants. And, like so many other Korean men, my father could not bring himself to thank my grandmother for the many kind things she had done for her son-in-law, such as taking care of him when he was laid up with typhoid fever soon after his marriage. She attributed what she considered to be his shortcomings to the fact that he was an only child and had been spoiled by his grandparents because his father had not been around to raise him. In any case, he could not go with her, since my grandmother was in no position to provide lodging for him. She would be staying with a friend from her home-town, whose family had come to the South the year before and was living in one rented room. My father looked for an inn where he could spend the night, and there were a number near the station. They were traditional Korean houses with a small sign reading *yogwan* (inn) posted at the front gate. My father chose one that looked clean.

A pleasant-looking woman with a pleasing Seoul accent greeted my father as he entered the gate. When she told him the rate for a single room was a hundred won per day, with two meals included, my father could hardly believe it. At that price his money would run out in fifteen days, he thought. The inn was an L-shaped house with a courtyard in front, and there were potted plants, a clothesline with sheets pinned to it, a faucet, and a trough. His room, a typical Korean one with a low ceiling and no furniture, was barely six feet by six feet, and the yellowed wallpaper made it seem even smaller. There were three hooks on the wall by the sliding doors to hang clothes, and a face towel hung from one hook. In one corner were folded quilts. A lone electric lightbulb dangled from the ceiling in the middle of the room. Our servants in Boshigal lived in bigger rooms, he thought. The room seemed to sum up his life: his future seemed as bleak as this cubicle.

That very morning, my father went to the Capitol Building, about a twenty-five-minute walk from the inn, to check out his prospects for work. He was walking on the capitol grounds, headed toward the main building, where the U.S. military government was located, when he heard someone call out, "Teacher." It was Hogun Yun, a former student at Young Saeng High School. My father learned that Yun had arrived in Seoul several months earlier and was working for an American officer in the capital building. Yun introduced my father to his boss, who showed pleasure at my father's command of English. My father was immediately hired as his interpreter and translator. Afterward, though, my father wondered how he would manage on his salary of fifteen hundred won a month when his lodging alone cost one hundred won a day. Even so, as he walked back to the inn, he felt more optimistic than when he had arrived in the morning. He felt hopeful that other opportunities would come up, as Yun had suggested.

My father had been in Seoul almost two weeks, and the money he had brought with him was quickly running out, when he ran into the son of a family friend in a bookstore. He invited my father to stay with his family, saying that they could spare a room. For a time, at least, my father did not have to worry about where to sleep until his payday, which was not until the end of April. But he got soaked every day from the rain because he could not afford to buy an umbrella. By the time he got to work, his one suit was drenched. It dried on body heat during the day at the office. In the evenings, he came home wet again. The suit dried overnight, while he slept.

☽

In Tanchon, my mother waited eagerly for my grandmother's return. Rumors were rampant that any day, the border would be closed off. She could feel, too, the Communists tightening their control. Left and right, men were being conscripted for military training, leaving only the old men to work in the factories and farms. A gloomy atmosphere prevailed. Anticipating the shutdown of the border, it seemed that practically everyone my mother knew was leaving for the South. Mother organized her closets and removed what she thought she would need to take with her. When she came across new silk and satin Korean dresses and the china she had considered too good to use, she cried. In early May, Grandmother Ke-Son returned alone to the North, taking with her medication and other goods to sell. Within days after her return, the border was officially shut. From that point on, people would have to cross covertly, and possibly even risk being sent back to the North. Their right to cross the border would rest on the whim and generosity of authorities on both sides. The closure did not change my grandmother's plan to get Mother and me to Seoul. She wanted to evacuate all of her family from the North. On the day of our departure, my paternal grandmother held my hands, and with tears in her eyes, said: "When will I see you again, my little one?" That was the last time I saw her; I was three and a half years old.

My mother carried me on her back. I sat over a rice container, filled with rice with seaweed over it, with a false bottom in which my mother put her life's savings. So nothing was visible from the outside, she draped over me a quilted silk wrap of the type used to put over children who were carried on the back. It was mid-May of 1946. Our party included my grandmother, a family friend (also a middle-aged woman), and Mother and me. We traveled by train, three hundred miles to Chulwon. Mother and Grandmother also carried a small bundle containing mostly clothing. We were to switch trains in Chulwon, which was two train stations before the border town of Tongdu-chon. To economize, my grandmother and her friend headed for Yonchon on foot, but hired an oxcart for Mother and me. Before we got to Yonchon, we were stopped by police inspectors. They opened Mother's bundle and checked everything, but they did not ask her to undo the quilted wrap. The money under the rice was intact. Before we were ushered inside the police station where North Korean authorities interrogated people leaving for the South, my mother and I had agreed that I was to cry when she pinched my feet. My mother pinched me again and again and I cried and cried. To get rid of a bawling child, North Korean officials let Mother through the interrogation line quickly.

As we were resuming our journey to Yonchon, where we were to meet Grandmother and her friend, we saw them coming toward us, this time on a cart. When we had not arrived as anticipated, my grandmother had gotten worried and had headed back. There, we spent a night at a Yonchon inn and waited until dawn to make our getaway. With a young hired male guide, we crossed the Yonchon River. Lifting up their long Korean skirts, Grandmother, her friend, and Mother crossed the water, which in some places came up to their stomachs. What I remember vividly about the river crossing is how cold the water was. From my mother's back, my feet dangled just enough to touch the cold water. "My feet are cold. My feet are cold," I yelled, and my mother put a piece of candy in my mouth to hush me. The crossing felt like an eternity, but actually it took only twenty-five minutes, my mother told me years later. Once over the river, we walked to Tongdu-chon, the next train stop, from where we took the train to Seoul.

Unlike two months earlier when my father had crossed the thirty-eighth parallel, there were no U.S. military police standing with DDT cans to delouse us. The border was closed; we were crossing at our own risk.

"Now we're free; we can go to church without fear," were my grandmother's first words after crossing safely to the South.

It was evening when we reached the house where my father was staying.

"You're here, Kyonshill," my father exclaimed happily, lifting me from my mother's back and holding me in his arms. My refugee days had begun.

A month later, Grandmother returned to North Korea to bring her son, Suk-Hoon, and younger daughter, Suk-Bin, to Seoul. It was her fourth trip across the thirty-eighth parallel. A few months later, after renting a room for my uncle and aunt, Grandmother made her fifth trip, this time to get her sister and her family out of the North. By the autumn of 1946, Grandmother Ke-Son had gotten everybody who wanted to leave across the border. But she had to return once again to take care of her ailing mother, who was in her eighties. Great-grandmother Park, a tiny woman whom my mother once described to me as looking like a butterfly in her summer gossamer dress, wanted to die at home and then be buried by her daughter. So Ke-Son remained in North Korea and nursed her mother, who died in her sleep, holding her daughter's hands. The pressures Ke-Son endured during her numerous crossings over the thirty-eighth parallel no doubt led to her death during Easter week of 1952 of a stroke, at age fifty-six.

About a month after we arrived in Seoul, we had to move out to make room for the owners' relatives who had arrived from the

North. With the help of Elder Neung-Keun Kim, my father's colleague from Young Saeng High School, we found temporary lodging
in a dormitory room at a girls' high school. By then I was almost
four years old and felt keenly the refugee life through my stomach:
we never had enough to eat. How I wished I could eat as much
rice as I wanted! But rice was so expensive that we had it only once
a day. We mostly ate *sujaebi*—dumpling soup made of wheat flour
mixed in thin soy sauce broth. We did not even always have enough
sujaebi. Acquaintances from the North who were even worse off than
we were—my father's former students and distant relatives—found
their way to our small dormitory room. My mother gave up her
meager dumpling soup for an unexpected guest. I saw her often just
lying down in the afternoons because she felt faint from hunger.
After learning from a friend that one way to silence hunger pangs
was to boil chaff from barley and wheat and drink the broth, she
did that often. Birthdays and holidays came and went, hardly noticed.

One afternoon while my mother was at the East Gate Market
to buy cabbages to make pickles—our only side dish—she ran into
an old friend from high school. Through her, we rented a room in
an old Korean-style house in Chong-no, then the central district in
the capital, and moved out of the dormitory. The room was small,
only seven feet by seven feet, but it was still an improvement over
where we had been. Now mother could cook in the landlord's courtyard instead of on the one hotplate we had used in the dormitory.
Our kitchenware consisted of two pots, one for cooking rice and
the other for soup or stew.

Adjusting to a life of a refugee was humiliating for my mother.
She was so embarrassed to have to carry small bundles of firewood
for cooking that she carried them home from the market wrapped
in silk scarves. Back home, there was no shortage of male and female
servants living on our property. Here, as she carried firewood from
the market, she stood out, too, because she wore an elegant black
velvet Korean skirt and a pale gold satin jacket, as she had done in
the North. She did not have clothes to suit her new, lowly economic
status. My mother cried often. Sometimes, I would see tears stream

down her cheeks as she lit the fire outside in the landlord's courtyard to prepare our meals, since we had no kitchen. When it rained, she took the brazier under the eaves, but the fire would go out and she would try again, rolling up newspapers and fanning the flames furiously to keep the fire from going out. I wanted to console my mother, but I did not know how. Our predicament humiliated her much more than my father because he was out working, but she had to contend with trying to put food on the table with so little money. The inflation got worse by day. One had to take a fistful of money to buy a few things at the market.

For me, the hardest thing about this period of our life was trying to cope with the tantalizing smell of food cooking in the kitchen of the landlord's house. As in all traditional Korean homes, their kitchen faced an open courtyard, and the door was left ajar because the water faucet and trough were in the courtyard. I would smell the aroma of different foods and imagine how they might taste. How much I wanted to be invited over to eat! But I never was. Ever quick to notice my longing, my mother always called me to our room whenever the landlady prepared the dinner table for her husband. My mother was too proud to have her daughter look like she was hungry. Once I badly wanted to eat a melon, so I picked the freshly discarded innards from a rusty garbage can outside the house and tasted it. Forty-five years later, when I see homeless people in American cities go through a garbage can, the picture of me picking out a discarded slice of melon comes back to remind me of my own hunger and homelessness. It must have been gnawing for my parents to see their only child going hungry.

The demand for my father's services grew as people learned about his proficiency in English, since there was a dearth of people with a good command of the language then. With the U.S. military government in control, interpreters and translators were sought after. My father continued to work as an interpreter and translator at the occupation government. To augment his meager government monthly salary of fifteen hundred won, which was officially about $35 but in actuality only $15—just enough to buy rice to feed a family of three for a month—my father did outside translation work.

About six months after my mother and I had arrived in Seoul, my father was offered a full-time teaching job at Bosung High School, a reputable private school. Soon thereafter, he was invited to teach English at Seoul National University, his alma mater, which was and still is the most prestigious university in Korea. His dream had come true—much quicker than he had anticipated. He was pleased, even though we were still living in the tiny seven-by-seven-foot room in Chong-no. With more income, we ate better—rice, vegetable side dishes, and sometimes even a piece of broiled fish. But it was still a drastic change from life in the North. One evening, Elder Kim visited us and told my father about a teaching position at the school where he was the head teacher, and he said that housing would be provided. It was an offer my father could not refuse. So, the following summer, after the teachers' residences were completed, we moved to Wangshim-ni, a district at the western edge of Seoul. Along the main unpaved dirt road were fields of corn, cabbage, and other vegetables as far as my eyes could see. The smell of manure was ever-present, following us everywhere and giving us the feeling of uncleanliness. Vendors spread out their wares along the dusty road, and this is where residents went to do marketing, unless they took the streetcar to the East Gate Market.

Our new three-room home seemed like a palace to me. In the garden we shared with two other families of Muhak teachers who also lived on the compound, we planted balsam, dahlias, and myrtle. My playmates were their children. At night after dinner, we sat on the veranda and sang songs. Our favorite was an ode to the moon: "Oh Moon, you bright moon, where Li Po played . . ." Li Po was the eighth-century wine-loving Chinese poet who drowned when he tried to fetch the moon he saw reflected in a lake one night. I quickly forgot what hunger was. I was happy.

In my father's second year at the new school, five of his students were accepted into Seoul National University—a first for the school. My father continued to teach at the university, too, a forty-five-minute walk from the high school, which meant he was drawing a salary and getting rations from two places. I remember, as a five-year-old, being very proud to be his daughter. Sometimes I walked over to the campus, which was surrounded by forsythias, and played there with my friends. If a guard questioned us, I would say simply, "I'm Teacher Kang's daughter," nothing more, and that would be enough.

For the first time since my family's arrival in Seoul, we had a semblance of stability. After moving from one room to another for more than a year, I had finally found a cozy nest. After a while I even got used to the smell of Wangshim-ni. The two-and-a-half-year period from September 1947 until March 1950 before my father went to the United States stands out in my mind as the longest period of calm in my childhood. As I was still too young to go to school, my days were occupied with playing doll house and *gomujul* (jumping over a rubber string held by two playmates) and waiting for the taffy man's cart in the afternoons. Because of frequent power outages, we kept kerosene lamps. And I looked forward to my routine as I do now to reading or walking by the sea.

We had lived in Wangshim-ni less than a year when my father's school provided us with even better housing—this time in Shindang-dong, a fine residential neighborhood. There were five Japanese-style homes for teachers in a cul-de-sac. Compared to Wangshim-ni, Shindang-dong was high class. One look at our future home, and my mother and I were ecstatic. It even had a large cast-iron tub in the bathroom and a roomy kitchen. My mother was so pleased with her new home, she plunged into housekeeping with fervor—she even learned to make doughnuts and rolls stuffed with sweet red beans.

It was 1948 and an election year. My grandmother, who followed politics, left her stall at the East Gate Market to my aunt's care and took me to listen to Syngman Rhee speak at the nearby

Seoul Stadium. Rhee, who had the distinction of being the first Korean to earn a Ph.D. in the United States, was referred to as "doctor"—a title he preferred to "president" later in his life. In the stadium, which was so packed that I was almost swept away in the crowd, I listened to the man about whom I had heard so much deliver a long-winded speech in the oddest-sounding Korean—he spoke like a foreigner. When I mentioned this, my grandmother attributed that to his long life in America. "He spoke English for so long that his tongue had curled up, pronouncing difficult foreign words," she said. The peculiar way Rhee spoke Korean is all I re-member about that event. But my first attendance at a political rally changed my childhood habits right away, at least briefly. I no longer had time for a doll house or *gomujul*. I wanted to run for office. Mimicking candidates who campaigned with loudspeakers, I went outside every day and gathered neighborhood children and made speeches. Standing atop an apple box, I urged them in my best politician's voice: "Let's send Kyonshill to the National Assembly." The children applauded. I was a precocious five-year-old.

The election that year, supervised by the United Nations, took place, but the Russians in the North denied access to UN officials, so the voting was conducted only in the South. I did not know it then, but pivotal events had occurred before the election. By Sep-tember 1947, two years into the administration of the U.S. military government, Washington had concluded, based on the recommenda-tion of the Joint Chiefs of Staff, whose chairman was General Dwight D. Eisenhower, that forty-five thousand American occupying forces in Korea "could well be used elsewhere," and their withdrawal "would not impair the military position of the Far East Command." Under the plan, American troops would withdraw in several stages, with all gone from the peninsula by June 1950. Even as it approved the phase-out plan, the United States also proposed that the United Nations name a panel to conduct free elections in Korea under its auspices before the end of March 1948. It was the U.S. premise that the government thus elected would control the entire peninsula, and the United States and the Soviet Union would withdraw their troops.

The Soviets balked, arguing that the UN lacked authority to do any such thing, since Korea was not a member state. The UN General Assembly went ahead and approved the U.S. proposal, but the Soviets said they would not take part in any elections. The question of how the new-born Republic of Korea could survive in the face of a constant military buildup in the North was never seriously discussed.

In the South, the right-wing Rhee supporters clearly had the upper hand. With smear tactics that presaged McCarthyism in the United States, Rhee's supporters waged propaganda campaigns to discredit anyone who spoke with a moderate voice or advocated negotiations with Communists in the North. Anyone who urged uniting the country was branded as a Communist, including such dedicated resistance leaders as Ku Kim and Kiu-Shik Kim, who went to Pyongyang to participate in unification talks. But conscience was an elusive commodity in the Korea of postliberation era, when expedience and hunger for power blinded so many people. Too many leaders, motivated by self-interest, had failed to rise to the occasion. In an irony of ironies, Rhee supporters, many of whom had been collaborators under the Japanese colonial rule, were able to use the organizational skills they had learned under the enemy and push out of contention patriots like the two Kims or Lyuh—men who had put their lives on the line in the resistance movement in China and Manchuria—while Rhee, living in the United States, at least did not have to worry about risking his life.

The Communists tried to boycott the election in the South, too, but the effort failed. They then resorted to terrorism on election day, May 11, killing scores of people in and around polling places. Nonetheless, the turnout exceeded 90 percent of the registered voters, and the UN commission later called the election "a valid expression of the free will of the electorate." Koreans elected their representatives to the National Assembly, which in turn, on May 31, chose Rhee as the chairman and proceeded to write a constitution. The constitution was proclaimed on July 17, 1948, and three days later Rhee was elected the first president of the Republic of Korea. The election of Rhee meant that the formal end of the

U.S. occupation of South Korea came in August 1948. The question of how the new Republic of Korea could survive in the face of the Communist stronghold in the North never received thoughtful consideration in Washington.

In September, just two months after Rhee's inaugural, the Soviets announced the establishment of the Democratic People's Republic of Korea in the North under Premier Il-Sung Kim. The Russians also said they would remove their troops out of the North by the end of the year, and they contended that American soldiers should pull out of the South at the same time. Thus, two Koreas were born. The thirty-eighth parallel, which was to have been just a temporary demarcation to receive the surrender of Japanese soldiers, became permanent. The Russians and Americans then left the peninsula.

☯

My parents and my grandmother had anticipated this scenario, which is why they left home in the North in the first place. But to see it actually happen and so quickly was another story, and we were completely cut off from our beloved Boshigol. It was around this time that a song called "The Thirty-eighth Parallel" became popular. It was a ballad lamenting the fate of our people and the cursed line imposed by two colonels, one of whom was Dean Rusk (later to become the secretary of state under John F. Kennedy) during an emergency meeting of the state and armed forces officials. Still, people in the North risked their lives to cross the border. From these people we heard about the dire conditions in the North—the purges and bloodbaths of indescribable proportions. Premier Kim was getting rid of anybody who posed even the least bit of threat, including nationalists who had struggled for Korean independence. If life in the South was corrupt and callous, in the North it was a living hell. My father, who never had a chance to grow close to his parents, seldom talked about them. But we heard through hometown people who had escaped later that my paternal grandmother, Myong-Hwa, had died in 1947, and that my grandfather was living with the servants in Boshigol and was experiencing great economic hardships. He was in such a bad condition that he had gone to Hamhung, my mother's relative's place, to claim a sewing machine that had been left there to sell. The Singer machine, which was priceless in those days, had been my great-grandfather's gift to my mother after I was born. My grandfather had never worked a day in his life and had no clue as to how to take care of the orchard and the property.

☯

Now, in early February 1950, the Reverend William Scott, the Canadian missionary who was my father's mentor from Young Saeng High School, came to our home and asked his former student if he wanted to go to the United States to study. When my father was young and studying English day and night, he had very much wanted to go to America, but now that he had achieved his goal of teaching at a university, he no longer wanted to leave Korea. Besides, after four years of struggling to survive and of working three jobs, he was finally settling down. He wanted to enjoy this lull and the reasonable material comfort. He could not go home to the North, but at least the situation had been resolved, and bad or good, he knew what to expect. Having lost my younger sister, Eunshill, only two weeks after her birth in December 1949, to pneumonia, my parents wanted to have more children, too. But again, something beyond my father's control intervened to change the direction of his life. His teacher, who had founded the missionary school, had high hopes for his star student. Dr. Scott was insistent, as my father hesitated and tried to think of excuses for why he did not want to leave Korea.

"This is only for four months," Dr. Scott said, urging him to go. "Four months will be gone in a flash."

My father yielded. Dr. Scott said he would do all the paperwork. The only thing my father had to do was to pass the tests at the American embassy and the Ministry of Education.

In March 1950, my father, along with eight other English teachers, left Korea for the University of Michigan as Fulbright fellows for a special training program at the renowned English Language Institute. They were the first group of Korean educators in the program. Their trip was widely publicized in the press and everybody in the country seemed to know about it. I was so proud of my father and excited about his trip that I did not even think about what it would be like to live without him for four months.

To Koreans of the time, America seemed as close to paradise on earth as possible. People said going to America was as difficult as "catching a star in the sky." On the day of his departure, we went to Kimpo International Airport, and I learned for the first time words like "Northwest Airlines." Amid the activities of people taking pictures, I also saw for the first time a woman wearing nylon stockings. It was still cold in March, but an American who presented flowers to my father's delegation wore hose that you could see through. "Glass stockings," I called them. Her stockings became embedded in the memory of a seven-year-old on that cold day at Kimpo amid picture taking, flower bouquets, and the press of well-wishers. On that auspicious day I could not have imagined that in three months the Korean peninsula would be embroiled in a war and that my father would not set forth on Korean soil again for seventeen years. Aside from my great-grandfather Bong-Ho's conversion to Christianity, my father's journey to America was a signal event that irrevocably changed the direction of our family's collective destiny. While my great-grandfather's conversion had brought a Western religion into our lives, my father's decision physically moved us out of Korea into other worlds. Who could have imagined that my parents would grow old in America and that their offspring would become Americans?

5. THE KOREAN WAR

(1950–1953)

Our wish is unification,

Awake or asleep, our wish is unification.

—Refrain from a Korean children's song

MAIN CHARACTERS:
Sok-Won Choe, my mother
Ke-Son Han, my maternal grandmother
Teacher Song, our next-door neighbor
Suk-Bin Choi, my maternal aunt
William Scott, my father's English teacher

A Surprise Attack

It was late June 1950, and already at half past seven, when we had breakfast, cicadas in the nearby acacia trees greeted the day with their boisterous chorus. Their incessant music made it seem even hotter. Not knowing, of course, of the events that would intervene, I began to count the days until my father was to return from the United States in the second week of July.

On our quiet cul-de-sac in Shindang-dong, my friends and I played a game of *gomujul* religiously, wearing loose white cotton short pants and shirts. "One, two, three, four, five," two girls counted as they jumped in opposite directions over a scarlet-colored rubber string four feet long, a foot above the ground, held by two smaller children. One stood by to keep the score. The goal was to jump over the rubber string one hundred times without touching it. Korean children of my generation did not have ready-made toys to play with, so we improvised with what was around—rubber strings, scraps of leftover cloth, pins, straws, tin cans, broken dishes, and stones. A favorite game for little girls was *gong-gi*, the trick of turning five smooth stones that were on the back of your hand and catching them when you turned your palms up. When we could not find smooth stones, we made *gong-gi* out of broken pieces of roof tiles and spent many hours polishing them.

Anticipating my father's homecoming, I would mark off the days on the calendar on the wall. I would imagine him getting off the plane with suitcases filled with Hershey chocolates and Nabisco wafers and perhaps even a few American dolls. Since his departure in March, we had received letters from America in airmail envelopes with blue and red stripes on the edges. In photographs my father sent, I thought that he looked like an American already in his new "Made in the U.S.A." attire and rimless glasses. Gift packages also arrived. One contained a gorgeous silky fabric in smoky cherry pink with thin gray stripes and a satiny backing. I was thrilled; I felt the material again and again, wondering if in the United States everybody wore clothes made of such beautiful cloth.

One afternoon in June, after church, my mother and I went to a neighborhood seamstress and ordered new matching dresses. The dressmaker admired the American fabric and said that she was honored to have a chance to work with it. My father would be returning on July 10, and we wanted to look our best at the airport. The day was June 25, 1950. And as we talked with the seamstress, we did not know that in the wee hours of that very morning while we had been asleep, North Korea had made a surprise attack on the South and that columns of North Korean soldiers were moving toward Seoul in their Soviet tanks.

We did not learn about the war until the following day when my mother heard the news on the radio. Mother said she had to go to the East Gate Market, where my grandmother had a stall, to break the news. My grandmother sold what Koreans then called "Yankee *mulgon,*" American products. Quality clothing was so scarce that even used American uniforms, sweaters, and jackets were in great demand. Walking alongside my mother, I wondered if I would ever see my father again. I was afraid he would not be able to return from the United States.

My grandmother's face turned ashen when my mother told her about the Communist attack. She looked so old and frail, and I was afraid she might faint. After a long silence, Grandmother said: "What shall we do? What shall we do?" She was just barely getting settled in Seoul and was putting my uncle through medical school. The prospect of the Communists overtaking Seoul must have been a nightmare come true for my grandmother, who had left her home, her business, and her friends just to get away from them. When she had regained her composure, Grandmother walked over to whisper the news to nearby vendors, who reacted to the news as if the sky had fallen on them. Grandmother closed her business for the day.

My maternal grandmother was a strong-willed woman. In her early thirties, she had risked alienating her mother by converting to Christianity. Her mother, like most other Koreans, believed in shamanism and spent a small fortune engaging the services of a *mudang,* a medicine woman, to appease the spirits that cause illnesses and other of life's unpleasant turns. In 1931 my grandmother, who had been surreptitiously attending a neighborhood Christian church, told her minister she wanted to be baptized. She had already received her husband's permission. But there was one remaining unfinished item of business: What was she to do with her mother's altar for the spirits she worshiped? When there was a problem in the household, her mother would light a strip of white paper at the altar and pray to the spirits. Whenever a member of her household became ill, she called a medicine woman to perform a magical rite. A pig would be slaughtered for the occasion, rice cakes prepared, and a table set by the sick person's room. On it were placed boiled rice, grilled fish, apples, pears, chestnuts, jujubes, boiled cow hooves, dried pollack, and a pig head, and then candles were lit. Afterward, the entire neighborhood would be invited to partake of the food.

Like other Korean Christians of her day, my grandmother's faith was rather conservative, similar to evangelical fundamentalism today, and she found it extremely difficult to live with her mother's many gods. As long as the altar and the rituals persisted, her conscience was not clear. So she got rid of the altar while her mother was not around. Her action infuriated her mother, who did not speak to her for several years. Try as she did, the old woman could not understand her daughter's intolerance for her spirits. My grandmother's action also antagonized the richest woman in her neighborhood, who claimed that the evicted spirits had now settled in her home, which meant that she had that many more ghosts to appease. But my grandmother did not flinch in her conviction. So it was throughout her life; her faith was central. It was the driving motivation behind her leaving North Korea and the Communists. The news of the Communist attack suddenly brought all of this back for my grandmother—her sole reason for leaving her comfortable life behind in the North to become a refugee in Seoul. Was that freedom—her freedom to worship—about to be taken away from her?

Mother and Grandmother trudged home, after stopping at stalls at the market to pick up some fruits and vegetables. We ate dinner in silence, as if there had been a death in the family. Later in the evening, Teacher Song and his wife, who lived next door, came over with their infant son. The Songs, too, were refugees from the North and were also Christians. I never saw a bunch of adults look so forlorn and dejected as then. As for me, I mostly thought about my father and what would happen to him. I had missed him so much. The more I thought, the more likely it seemed to me that he would not be able to come home.

On Monday night, the day after the Communist invasion, we heard President Syngman Rhee on the radio, telling his people to remain in Seoul, just as he was doing. We would not learn until several days later that his message had been prerecorded, and that he, along with his entourage, had already fled from Seoul. What my grandmother and mother had heard was that the president, his wife, and a host of hangers-on and their families had headed south on two special trains—first to Suwon, twenty miles south of the capital, then to Taejon, seventy miles further south from there. We later heard that the government officials managed to take much with them— "even pianos and pillows," people said with disgust. Rhee was among the first to leave Seoul—well ahead of foreign diplomats, including the American ambassador to Korea, and the British minister and the French chargé d'affaires.

The news of Rhee's cowardly departure raised the tension level. Panicky civilians raced to the railway station to catch any train heading south. People who could not find room on a train, many with small children in tow, put their belongings on their backs and heads and walked south. Late Tuesday night, one of my father's closest friends, Elder Kim, came to our home and said his family was leaving and suggested that we come along. But my grandmother and mother, looking despondent, said they could not muster the strength to leave, nor could our neighbor, Teacher Song, and his family. The Songs had a relative living with them who was suffering from encephalitis and a baby only a few months old. Looking back to those shocking, then numbing days immediately after the outbreak of the Korean War, I think my grandmother made the decision for the family to remain in Seoul because she had not recovered from her previous trips across the thirty-eighth parallel. Suffering from a heart condition, which she attributed to her harrowing trips, even a woman as strong as my grandmother had her limits. She was simply too exhausted to go through the ordeal of moving the family again.

Bridge Over the River Han

The Han River, which bisects modern Seoul, is to the South Korean capital what the Seine is to Paris. But instead of East and West Bank, the demarcations are South of the River (Kangnam), and North of the River (Kangbuk). Kangbuk is the old Seoul of palaces and traditional-style Korean homes. Kangnam is the new capital of concrete and glass, trendy shops and luxury condos—so much so that Seoulites refer to it as "Manhattan." Back in the Seoul of 1950, however, Kangnam was practically country. In the summer, children swam, took boat rides, and sometimes even looked for fish in the river. In the winter, people came to skate when the river froze. Poets immortalized it. When I was a child, the Han held an alluring mystery for me. Trains traveling across the river over the big bridge fascinated me, and I would imagine all the places I would go by if I hopped on one.

The Han and the bridge were among the first casualties of the war. The Han separates Seoul from the rest of the southern part of the peninsula. As North Korean soldiers marched south toward Seoul, South Korean defense officials ordered roadblocks and explosives set up at the bridge complex and on roads north of Seoul. By blowing up the bridge, they had hoped to prevent North Koreans from rolling tanks across the Han and advancing further south, although soldiers could still cross the river on ferries. But nervous officials directed the bombing of the bridge shortly after 2:00 A.M., Wednesday, June 28, while some ten thousand South Korean soldiers and their equipment were still on the northern side. When the bridge plummeted into the river, it took with it some one thousand people who had been walking across. The hasty decision would be just one of countless snafus that inept South Korean officials would commit during the war.

I felt sick to my stomach when my grandmother and mother told me what had happened. I was glad we had decided to remain in Seoul, but I worried about Elder Kim's family and wondered whether they had made it across to the south of the river before the bombing. For days after that I could not put out of mind the image of hundreds of people falling to their death in the dark of the night. I sometimes dreamed of children who looked like water ghosts, with skimpy wet clothing hanging like rags over their skeletal bodies and their eyes half closed, reaching out to me and crying out, "Help me, help me!" I would try to run away from them, but my feet would not move.

By Wednesday night, we could hear the sounds of cannons from afar. Within days thereafter, Russian tanks had arrived at Kwang-Wha-Mun, the heart of Seoul and the entrance to the old palaces. After Seoul was occupied, we saw North Korean People's Army soldiers even in our relatively quiet residential neighborhood. Their faces appeared intense, their eyes moving constantly as if to size up their surroundings. They looked every bit as scary to me as I had heard that they were from adults and other children.

In the ensuing weeks, life began to change. What surprised us were the number of Communist sympathizers in the neighborhood. People we never suspected suddenly were Communists or sympathizers, and they began to form block committees, whose job it was to keep track of people in the neighborhood, their movements and activities. They went from house to house and signed up all able-bodied adults for work assignments. Every house was issued poster pictures of Joseph Stalin and Il-Sung Kim, with orders to display them prominently.

Men were conscripted as porters to haul ammunition for the North Korean Army. My aunt's husband, Chang-Kyu, and Teacher Song, the next-door neighbor, both being in their mid-thirties, were ideal targets to be drafted into the North Korean Army. Grandmother and Mother suggested that we hide the two men in our home. Since everyone in the neighborhood knew my father was away in America, they would not suspect. There were two places to hide them: the storage space underneath the den, and the crawl space above the ceiling joists. Access to the crawl space was through a closet in my father's study, and one had to be intimately familiar with the layout of the house to know this. The ceiling had a double layer of plywood, which would provide strong support. Teacher Song, a slender man, fit easily into the crawl space. Chang-Kyu would hide in the crawl space under the floor. Since the flues were not used to heat the rooms in the summer, he could be made reasonably comfortable. We had a flower-patterned straw mat covering the floor, as was the custom in Seoul, and a table in the middle of the room, and no one would suspect there was a storage room beneath it.

That very evening, the two men tried out their respective hideaways. They could manage. I was drafted to play a key role in all this: I was to keep the household posted on any suspicious people in the neighborhood, and then to signal the men ahead of time to make them keep still. Though I was just seven, I did not feel left out in the discussions grownups had. Being the only child, I was always among adults. Unlike my friends, whose family members talked down to them or shunned them when they discussed adult business, I was allowed to listen in. I instinctively felt that this was a privilege I should not abuse. Watching Teacher Song and Uncle Chang-Kyu do a dress rehearsal of what would be their summer-long drama, and being told their lives depended on my ability to keep this secret, I felt important. It was exciting and scary at the same time. When I could put out of my mind the thought of my father in America, I could almost feel like this was fun.

Life began to change immediately after the Communist occupation of Seoul. Schools closed throughout the city. A constant stream of strangers roamed the neighborhoods. I became eyes and ears for my family and Teacher Song's household, and I spent most of my time outside, playing with other children but always keeping a keen eye on the comings and goings of strangers, and reporting any unusual happenings to my mother and grandmother so they could in turn warn Teacher Song and Uncle Chang-Kyu. Mother would tap the floor and ceiling three times rapidly with a stick used for beating laundry clean. When the danger was over, she tapped the ceiling and the floor twice very slowly. The men had other signals for going to the bathroom and so on.

As days stretched into weeks, it became clear to me that it would be a long time before I would see my father again. As a seven-year-old, I could not comprehend the meaning of the words *communism* and *democracy*, even though I repeated those words myself, mimicking adults. But I understood one immediate effect of the war on my life: the letters from my father in America stopped coming. I had so much looked forward to receiving those letters, filled with descriptions of a world so different from my own. He had written me about his visit to Niagara Falls, Philadelphia, Washington, D.C., and New York. My father's depictions of buildings of steel and glass in New York really impressed me. Try as I might, I could not visualize tall buildings of glass, but they sounded fantastic to me. I decided that America was the most beautiful place in the world, so I tried to imagine what it was like. Would I be able to go there someday and see for myself those glass buildings he described in his letters?

As days went on, Teacher Song and Uncle Chang-Kyu turned more pale and sallow. Sometimes Teacher Song's steps were unsteady when he tried to walk after a whole day spent lying or sitting in the dark crawl space. Uncle Chang-Kyu's bedding was always damp and had to be aired out. Both men complained of constipation.

☯

American airplanes became a regular presence in the skies over Seoul. During air raids, we ran to a small room in the basement where we kept old blankets, quilts, and pillows. Some nights, we slept there. B-29 bombers began to arrive in Munsan near the thirty-eighth parallel in July, and their bombs heavily damaged railroad lines. When the shiny silver B-29s were in the sky, we children ran inside our homes immediately. Most of the targets were factories and other places where the North Koreans kept their supplies. But one time, American pilots made a mistake and bombed a neighborhood school where people had gone to seek refuge; many civilians died. Bombings sometimes lasted an hour or more.

In the third week of July, three high school girls who were Communist sympathizers came to our home and asked that they be given a room to stay. We were in no position to refuse them, so they moved into the room by the kitchen, which had been our maid's room. My mother had sent the maid home to her family in the countryside a few days after the outbreak of the war, so her room was available. One of the students, much to our surprise, was a former student of my father's at Muhak. With Communists living under the same roof, we had to do everything possible to keep them from finding out about the two men. My mother instructed me to say "I don't know" to all the questions the students might ask me.

"Our lives depend on you," Teacher Song said, stroking my head when he had come down from the crawl space to take his meal. "If you open your mouth, we're going to be dead," Uncle Chang-Kyu said. This was an awesome charge for a seven-year-old, and I felt very grown up doing this important work, so I vowed to pretend to appear to know nothing and act stupid around the students. The girls liked me, and they told me about the virtues of Communism and instructed me to address people as "comrade." They constantly talked about the "evil Americans—imperialist Americans— who were killing innocent civilians" and predicted a "people's victory." "We will kill those American bastards like this," one said, demonstrating with a bamboo spear that was kept in the kitchen by order of the neighborhood women's committee, a Communist group.

One afternoon, after an air raid, one of the students asked me if I knew why the planes came. I shook my head. My father's former student proceeded to tell me how the "evil Americans" were "trying to kill us all."

"Really?" I responded. My mother in the next room winced that I might forget her admonition and say something incriminating.

Later, when the students were out again, my mother warned me never to say anything when they asked me about the planes, and never to let on that we were rooting for the Americans.

"I won't. But do you really want the American planes to come and bomb everything, Mommy?"

"There is no other way to end this war," she replied. "Americans have to win. They are on our side."

Fortunately, the students were out more than they were in. In the evenings, they joined different neighborhood committees to recruit women. Initially organizers had recruited men for the duties of carrying ammunition and supplies at night, but as the summer wore on, they began drafting able-bodied women as well, after most of the men were gone. Neighborhood organizers were always recruiting people for meetings. In every household, women were given a bamboo spear, which they were to use to kill American soldiers if they parachuted into the area, and drills were held in schools.

At night, all able-bodied neighborhood women had to attend the bayonet drills, during which they would march to a middle school in the neighborhood and practice motions of killing Americans with bamboo bayonets under the direction of Communist leaders. The women were to be citizen soldiers.

"I can't go to the drills because I'm alone with my girl, Kyonshill," my mother pleaded with the leader of the Women's League (the umbrella group for various neighborhood women's committees), who happened to be a friend from middle school in North Korea. Even though she was a Communist, which my mother discovered only after the outbreak of the war, her old friend excused her from the drills.

As the summer wore on, food supplies became scarce. Our supply of rice was dwindling because we were sharing it with the students and relatives who needed help. Initially, we started to mix the rice with barley to make it go farther. Side dishes were becoming scarcer, too. Grandmother began to hide rice in small earthen jars in different places throughout the house to discourage the Communist students from taking so much of it. She also put rice in small bags inside pillows, stuffed with rice chaff. She was uncertain that the supply of rice she had bought would last until fall, when a new crop of rice would be on the market. She wondered whether there would be money left for food then.

Knowing that Seoulites did not keep large stocks of food on hand, farmers came to Seoul to peddle rice and other crops in exchange for precious commodities such as sewing machines or lacquer chests inlaid with mother-of-pearl, fabric, and even gold and precious stones. In some homes, women were even exchanging their wedding jewelry for rice. I heard my mother talk about a farmer who had managed to exchange a bolt of precious lace from Switzerland from a rich man's home in the neighborhood for one eighty-pound sack of rice. The rich man needed rice more than the Swiss cloth.

And, of course, there was the constant fear that North Korean soldiers might barge in at night and find the two men in hiding. There was a close call one afternoon, when, making the rounds of the neighborhood, North Korean soldiers stopped and went through the entire house, without taking off their shoes. They even went down to the basement bomb shelter and shook pillows. Grandmother looked toward heaven when the soldiers did that. During another close call soldiers showed up before I had a chance to alert my mother. While the soldiers were looking for food in the house, my mother and I heard the ceiling creak once when Teacher Song shifted his position in the attic. I prayed that he would sit still. He did. Afterward, when he came down for his evening meal, we talked about the close call.

☯

By June 1950, North Korea was well poised to attack the South. In the previous four years since the liberation, it had built a well-trained army numbering almost two hundred thousand with each of its twelve divisions headed by soldiers trained and indoctrinated in the Soviet Union. A fifth of the North Korean army had been volunteers fighting on the side of Communists during the Chinese Civil War, from 1945 through 1949. Also, about ten thousand soldiers had been handpicked young men, trained in the Soviet Union while the North was within the Soviet zone after liberation. The North Korean army was well supplied with modern arms—Russian T-34 tanks, trucks, automatic weapons, and YAK fighter planes. By comparison, the Republic of Korea's Army could hardly be called that. Begun as a constabulary after liberation, Rhee's army was not even half the size of Kim's. It had no tanks, heavy artillery, or combat airplanes. Half of its vehicles were in disrepair without replacement parts. Most important, like its government, the army was corrupt and the morale of its men at rock bottom.

The United States did not help matters. Its Korean policy was to disengage from the peninsula as soon as possible. Thus, within two months after Rhee's government was installed in 1948, U.S. occupation forces began to pull out. By June 1949—a year before the Korean War—only about five hundred military advisors were left in Korea. And in a speech to the National Press Club in Washington just six months before the war, Secretary of State Dean Acheson had declared that Korea was outside the U.S. "defense perimeter."

But the Soviet Union had other designs on the country, whose strategic importance had prompted it to go to war with Japan. During its occupation of the North, the Soviet Union seized the chance to build a Soviet-style government under Stalin's protégé, Il-Sung Kim. North Koreans were easy converts to Communism, since they believed it offered the only way to break Koreans away from centuries of corrupt rule and class inequality. The Soviet Union spared no cost in promoting this dream among North Koreans.

The news of the North Korean attack came as a total surprise. It was late Saturday night (June 24) in Washington, and Acheson immediately called vacationing President Truman in Independence, Missouri. By Sunday evening when Truman returned to Washington, the UN Security Council, meeting in an emergency session at the behest of South Korean and U.S. officials, had passed a resolution condemning the North Korean attack and calling for the withdrawal of Kim's forces south of the thirty-eighth parallel. By late Monday (June 26), Truman committed U.S. air and naval forces to defend Korea—the first time the United States had come to Korea's aid since the signing of the Treaty of Amity in 1882. On Tuesday night, the UN Security Council passed a U.S.-sponsored resolution calling on member nations to "render such assistance" as may be necessary to repel the armed attack and "to restore international peace and security to the area"—a decision that would later involve sixteen member nations, including Great Britain, France, Germany, Australia, Canada, and Turkey, which sent forces under the blue flag of the United Nations.

By Wednesday in Tokyo, General MacArthur had dispatched an inspection team to Seoul, and he flew to Korea the following day to assess the situation. Upon his return, he persuaded Truman to grant him "full authority" to use the forces under his command. MacArthur dispatched the first contingent of American troops on Friday, June 30. Their mission was to stop the North Korean advances until the rest of the Twenty-fourth Division could arrive. American occupation soldiers, airlifted out of their easy life in postwar Japan, were no match for the North Korean soldiers, whose second nature was living with hardship. Their face-off on July 1 was a disastrous retreat. With the congressional cutbacks, befitting the mood of the country after World War II, the military was being downsized. The first battalion of soldiers deployed from Japan were poorly trained and equipped, a majority of them young men twenty or younger. They were injected into the blistering heat and monsoons of Korea and had to contend with not only its steep mountains, meandering valleys, and narrow dirt roads that were built for oxcarts, but also the nauseating stench of excrement in the rice paddies. Even after the arrival of the Twenty-fourth Division and additional troop reinforcements throughout July and August, the North Koreans advanced steadily south. South Korean and U.S. forces retreated until they barely held onto less than a tenth of the territory at the south-eastern tip of Korea, which became known as the Pusan Perimeter. North Korean troops, which hid by day and fought by night, concealed themselves among columns of refugees and then came out of nowhere to ambush American soldiers. They shed their uniforms and easily blended into villages, a classic guerilla technique. Throughout July until the First Marine Brigade reached Korea in early August, the news from the UN battlefront was bad. Then, in mid-August, U.S. troops for the first time made two attacks in a fierce battle over the Naktong River, which provided a natural moat for the Pusan Perimeter, since the river made a semicircle around it. By night, American bombers hammered North Korean crossings.

The news from the front, which came to us by word of mouth, was depressing. Some people were still leaving for the countryside, but our family had all but resigned ourselves to staying, come what may. We were already living under Communist rule with pictures of Kim and Stalin on our front gate, as every household had been instructed to do. There seemed no real advantage to going to the countryside; it did not appear safer there. One of our relatives lost her husband, when he was killed by South Korean soldiers who insisted that he was a North Korean soldier. I heard my grandmother, mother, and aunt talk about so many killings, and I wondered if anybody would be alive when the war was over. "If we're going to die, we might as well stay home and die rather than get killed on the road," my grandmother said. Whenever I heard talk like that, I was sure I would never see my father again. But when my grandmother and mother said it was fortunate that my father was away, I had to agree with them. "Your father would have been among the first ones to be abducted and taken to the North," my grandmother said. "Unlike Teacher Song or Uncle Chang-Kyu, we could never have persuaded your father to hide." That was probably true. But now, sometimes when I thought about my father, I could not remember how he looked exactly, and then I would look at pictures of him to refresh my memory.

At home, the student Communists from my father's school

taught me several revolutionary songs, including the "Song of General Kim Il-Sung." They drilled that song into me so well while they stayed with us in Seoul that to this day I can sing the song by heart:

> Marks of blood on every ridge of the Jangbaek [Mountain],
> Marks of blood on every reach of Amnok [River].
> Still now over the blooming free Korea
> Those sacred marks shed brilliant rays.
> O dear is the name, our beloved General!
> O glorious is the name, General Kim Il-Sung!

Sometimes, when the student Communists were not around, I sang the song but substituted "O glorious is the name, General Kim Il-Sung," to "O, shithead is the name—Kim Il-Sung." There were two other verses to this song. Despite the horrendous lyric, the song's upbeat melody appealed to me; I still find myself humming the song once in a while even today in California, which shows that even the austere North Korean Communists could come up with a catchy tune.

☯

My father learned about the North Korean invasion halfway around the world in New York City. He was in the lobby of the International House at Columbia University on June 26 when the Reverend Jae-Kyung Hwang, who worked at the Voice of America, broke the news to him. Hwang was a humorist, better known to Koreans back home because of his informative and entertaining broadcasts than on account of his preaching.

The news did not surprise my father. He told me years later that he had been in a state of numbness for so long that nothing really shocked him. There had been simply too many horrendous incidents in his life beyond his control: growing up without his father, then seeing him return from prison a broken man, living under Japanese colonial rule (a liberation that turned out to be no liberation at all), leaving home to start the life of a refugee in Seoul, worrying about supporting the family. Absorbing the shock and becoming numb must have been the only way intellectuals of my father's generation had managed to keep going. Others, too, have told me about this wall of numbness that saw them through their difficulties without ever resolving the causes, which, of course, were unresolvable.

My father's first fear was that the North Koreans might try to protect themselves by using women and children as human shields against UN troops, most of whom were U.S. soldiers. With a young child and a wife in Seoul, he worried about that more than anything else. Then he fell once again into lamenting his fate and that of all Koreans, who were always caught up in the sweeping movements of world politics—a cursed fate, not much better than a dog's. He had been counting the days until his return to Seoul—originally scheduled for July 10—when the war broke out, and he had already shipped home most of his books, clothing, and gifts. Not surprisingly, they never arrived.

General MacArthur's Inchon Landing

In early September came encouraging news: the U.S. Marines were coming. For days we had heard the rumbling of cannons. I heard grownups saying that the UN forces under General MacArthur would overtake Seoul, and that once that happened, the Allied forces would go all the way and attack Manchuria north of the Yalu River as well. That alone would guarantee freedom under a united Korea to our people, they said. When they talked this way, they appeared almost happy—in anticipation of a liberated country. I did not know what was really happening, but the adults seemed so optimistic that I got caught up in their hopes, too. After a gloomy summer of discouraging news, we all needed a boost.

We did not know it then, but for weeks, MacArthur and the Joint Chiefs of Staff had been at loggerheads, squabbling about the general's plan to make an amphibious attack in Inchon, a port city about twelve miles west of Seoul, to force the North Koreans' capitulation. Everyone but MacArthur worried about the difficulties of putting an amphibious force ashore at Inchon, where tidal waves were known to be among the tallest in the world. Furthermore, implementing MacArthur's plan would require withdrawing from Pusan the marine brigade that was guarding the Pusan Perimeter, possibly risking a Communist attack on the only remaining Allied toehold. MacArthur got his way, and Operation Chromite, as the assault on Inchon was dubbed, proceeded on September 15 with two regiments of the First Marine Division, with a unit of the Korean Marine Corps in reserve. It was a success. Operation Chromite, executed at dawn on September 15, would go down in history as one of MacArthur's finest hours.

Following through with his plan, MacArthur sought to take over Seoul by September 25, three months to the day after the outbreak of the war. His troops headed north and seized Kimpo Airport, crossed the Han River, occupied Seoul, and then set up obstacle courses in a semicircle above Seoul. For more than a week before the Inchon landing, the Allied forces used diversionary tactics by bombing nearby areas.

North Korean units, taken by complete surprise, offered no resistance. Many surrendered and some took to the mountains. Then the marines, joined by South Korean soldiers and the First Cavalry and the Seventh Infantry, advanced north into Seoul on September 25, where determined North Korean units put up a valiant fight. The military and civilian losses were heavy.

On September 27, UN troops conquered the capitol building and hoisted the blue flag over it. Waving and applauding, we went outside and greeted the soldiers arriving in the city in their tanks and jeeps. The soldiers' pink faces stood out in my mind. Their arrival coincided with Chusok, the Harvest Moon Festival, so my grandmother collected rice she had hidden and made rice cakes to celebrate both occasions. To keep the sound of pounding rice with a pestle to a minimum, Grandmother put a quilt under the mortar.

Listening to the grownups, it appeared that the Communists were retreating and that even North Korea was being liberated. "We may be able to return home to North Korea, after all," my mother said. "It sure looks that way," my grandmother agreed.

On September 29, MacArthur flew in from Tokyo to turn the wrecked but liberated city over to Rhee. "By the grace of merciful Providence, our forces fighting under the standard of that greatest hope and inspiration of mankind, the United Nations, have liberated this ancient capital city of Korea," he said. Turning to Rhee, the general said: "Mr. President, my officers and I will now resume our military duties and leave you and your government to the discharge of civic responsibility."

With South Korean soldiers in control of Seoul again, life seemed—at least to my young eyes—to return to normal. On the battlefront, South Korean soldiers crossed the thirty-eighth parallel and occupied two major cities—Hamhung, my mother's hometown, and nearby Hungnam, while UN forces took Pyongyang, the North Korean capital, and headed all the way north to the Yalu River. It seemed only a matter of time before my father could return from America and we would all be able to go home to the North. "At this rate, your father may return directly to our home in the North from America," my mother said. The suspense was unbelievable.

But the situation reversed itself suddenly when Chinese "volunteer" soldiers joined the North Koreans in mid-October. By the end of October, Chinese forces had pushed back South Korean soldiers near the Yalu, fending off the Eighth Army and the marines who had successfully carried out the amphibious assault on Inchon. MacArthur accused the Chinese of "unlawful aggression," but to no avail. Until mid-November there were fierce ground and air battles over Sinuiju, a border town between Korea and China, and the U.S. Army Third Division arrived in Korea as reinforcements. On November 24, Mac-Arthur launched an attack and UN troops approached the Chinese border. The attention of the world was now fully on Korea, intensifying concern that this could lead to World War III. The Chinese counterattacked the next day, and from then on seemingly countless

Chinese forces followed, resulting in one Allied retreat after another until the Chinese crossed the thirty-eighth parallel on Christmas Day. On New Year's Day, 1951, the Communist offensive into the South began, and on January 4, UN forces evacuated Seoul.

Escaping the Oncoming Communists

This time, we knew we had to leave. A war with North Korea was one thing, but fighting China was something else. So, in early January, when North Korean troops were about to overrun Seoul for the second time in less than seven months, we finally decided to depart. Mother and Grandmother felt that the fall of Seoul and perhaps all of South Korea was becoming more and more inevitable. In only two months their high hopes and dreams of returning home had been dashed. The entry of China into the war changed everything. The image of millions of Chinese soldiers marching into our country until the last South Korean and American soldier was killed was too real to ignore. In these moments I dwelled on the possessions I had to leave behind. I thought about my jewel box, painted in yellow with a floral pattern with a mirror in front, that looked like a miniature dresser. My mother had given it to me for Christmas that year. I hid it in the attic above my father's study where Teacher Song had stayed during the summer. Perhaps, when I returned to Seoul, I could retrieve it, I thought.

We could not travel together as a family because there was no available transportation for everybody. So my mother and I found passage on a truck to the train station in Taejon, ninety miles south of Seoul, where we would meet Teacher Song's family. Whoever reached Taejon first was to wait at the station. There was room only for one adult on the truck, so I sat on my mother's lap. My grandmother and aunt would travel separately with Elder Kim's family and head straight to Pusan. (The Kims had returned from Pusan after Allied troops retook Seoul in September.) We would look for each other in a refugee settlement center. My uncle was drafted into the army by then, and my aunt's husband and Teacher Song, like all other able-bodied men, were conscripted as laborers to help move ammunition. I was bundled up in a heavy outfit made of American blankets bought on the black market.

From Taejon Station we took the last "freedom train" for Pusan. The only place available was the rooftop. I had protested vigorously about having to ride on the rooftop, but I gave in after I realized we had no choice. It was pandemonium. Had we hesitated much longer, we might not even have had the spot on the rooftop. Seminary students who had come all the way from the North Korean capital of Pyongyang were helping women and children get up onto the rooftop. They tied a rope around my middle and pulled me up like a package. Once we were settled on the rooftop, they helped secure us with ropes to prevent us from falling. I dozed off and on, as my mother held tight to the rope around my waist. Our worldly possessions on that January day consisted of an eighty-pound bag of rice and another bundle containing a change of underwear and kitchen utensils. I leaned against the rice sack for support, and my mother, holding me by the cord, sat next to me. With the orderly way my mother had arranged our space, there was enough room for the two of us and our bundles. I wondered what it would be like to travel on this long journey. I found out soon enough. The "freedom train" traveled all through the night, chugging away, sometimes whistling and passing what seemed like interminable expanses of farmlands and mountains.

Despite the layers of heavy clothing we wore, including coats and pants made of American blankets, the bitter wind seemed to go right through us. I wondered if we would make it to our destination without freezing to death during the night. It was too cold to talk. The only words I remember hearing from my mother were, "Don't fall asleep, you mustn't fall asleep." She said that all night long, like a lullaby, sometimes shaking me to keep me from nodding off. At times, the train stopped for what seemed like hours. I was glad when the train stopped, because the wind did not feel as vicious then. At one of those stops, I saw a small but brightly lit window far away, and I observed a piece of red cloth moving. The lighted window was conspicuous in the dark of the Korean countryside. I imagined a sorceress inside performing her rites behind the window, with a red kerchief. In the wind and cold I could almost hear her chants and gongs, and smell her incense burning. Perhaps the sorceress was working through the night to cure a sick child, or bidding a safe journey for an old woman who had died. The train would move again, and I would grit my teeth and pray that we would get to our destination without freezing.

Every now and then, the train went through tunnels. I was glad when it did, because while the train was inside the tunnel, we could get a momentary relief from the cold. I wished for more tunnels to go through, not knowing how easy it would have been for us to have been asphyxiated. Despite my mother's admonitions, I must have fallen asleep occasionally, because I only remembered parts of the long train ride. I never wished for the morning to arrive as much as then. That sentiment must have been shared by all of us huddled on the top of the train.

We greeted dawn with gratitude and relief that we were still alive. Our first stop was Gupo Station, where vendors were hawking pears as large as a child's head, which we bought and ate for breakfast. My teeth were chattering, and the juice from the pear was dripping over my red wool mittens. As I looked around, I could see that everyone on the rooftop of the train looked like soot-covered chimney sweepers. Gupo was more than four hundred miles southeast of Seoul. We had traveled two hundred miles during the night, and we had just one more stop before Pusan Station.

Besides my mother and me, our party consisted of Teacher Song's wife, her infant son, her sister-in-law, and their maid. Finally reaching Pusan, we found our way to a refugee settlement center, where we located my grandmother and aunt, who were there with Elder Kim's family. It was dinnertime and cooking fires were going when we arrived. The place was packed with refugees. Makeshift partitions of bed sheets and rags separated the living quarters of different families. The smell of people and food permeated the air. If our refugee life in Seoul was pitiful, living in the tiny rented room in

Chong-no, this was a hundred times worse. Children slept, curled up in fetal positions, but their parents dozed, snoring, sitting up, leaning their weary backs against their bundles. They looked like they had been there for many days. Here and there, laundry hung on straw ropes. The prospect of living there with all those strangers depressed me.

With careful steps, so as to not run into people, we went through the rows of makeshift partitions of blankets and sheets. I spotted my grandmother's corner. Next to it was Elder Kim's family, eating dinner.

"Grandma!" I was so happy to see her. "Baby, come this way," Grandmother motioned me to come toward her. "You've made it, baby." I squeezed myself between her and my aunt. I ate rice and boiled shrimp right out of my grandmother's aluminum bowls. My first hot meal in two days, it tasted so good. Afterward, Elder Kim and my mother went out with Mrs. Song to look for a place for the night. The influx of refugees irritated the residents of Pusan. Wherever the refugees knocked, they were turned away. Wretched and exhausted, their faces drawn with worry, the group returned late that night. We shared a small space in a corner against a wall by sleeping sitting up. On the following day, we managed to find some rooms. Teacher Song's family, my mother, and I shared one small room in a private home. My grandmother and aunt located a room in a different neighborhood. This was the start of yet another life in a strange place. I was eight years old.

Every detail of being a refugee the second time around is etched in my memory, like a video inside my head that never goes away. Even after forty-odd years, I can still taste every piece of food that my resourceful grandmother and mother provided. And the ordeal to survive: I still relive those days as if they happened only yesterday. In an eight-year-old's mind, uncluttered by other experiences, responsibilities, or preoccupations, living through a war does not go away. But so little of our hardship, and especially our life in Pusan, made any sense to me then. At least during the summer in Seoul, when I was guarding Teacher Song and Uncle Chang-Kyu, I had felt a sense of pride and accomplishment. But in Pusan, I could not figure out why I was there.

Within days after our arrival in Pusan, my grandmother, resourceful as ever, was peddling goods in a portable basket on the street. Just about everybody from Seoul—whether former schoolteachers, office workers, or well-to-do businessmen—did whatever they could to survive. The easiest thing was to put up a small stall and sell something.

Pusan was crowded and dirty. Homeless urchins in tattered clothes, with gaunt faces and lice in their hair, roamed the streets, carrying tin cans to collect leftovers. Sometimes they ran after American jeeps, which showered them with dust and dirt, hoping to get a piece of chewing gum or a candy bar. The American soldiers were not always kind, and they sometimes shouted "goddamn" at the children, which the youngsters, not knowing what the word meant, would repeat later. And for the first time in my life, I saw Korean women with heavy makeup and high heels walking with American soldiers. Sometimes children ran after them, yelling *"yang galbo"* (Western whore). To this day, Korean women risk being perceived as prostitutes or as barmaids when they are seen in the company of non-Asian men, except ones who are so prominent that people know who they are.

And so we settled into the life of a refugee family. My mother did the housekeeping, and my grandmother and Aunt Suk-Bin worked in their new trade as Pusan street vendors. Their inventory sometimes included American canned foods, which were a treat for me because I had never tasted any food from a can. Grandmother brought some of it home, and I had my first taste of canned Chef Boyardee spaghetti, which we mixed with rice. I loved it. My favorite was corned beef hash. I still like to eat it the way we did then—mixed in a bowl of hot steamy rice. It is comforting, in a way, reminding me of the mystery of life and of how people endure adversities.

Power outages and water shortages were routine occurrences. We used kerosene lamps and stood in line for hours with buckets to draw water from a public water pipe. People fought to get ahead in line. Sometimes we cooked food in water from the sea. We did our laundry with sewer water from a ditch that came out of a public bathhouse. And there was the nightly routine of de-licing ourselves, picking at the lice buried in the folds of our clothing like monkeys in a zoo, then wiping our fingernails clean with newspaper scraps. All of this made our life back in the North seem a distant fairytale, but my elders were tough and I, being young, was resilient. I even found a measure of excitement in this new, if tawdry, existence. I kept a diary and wrote poems on scraps of paper, then hid them so no one would find them. I dreamed of becoming a writer, although sometimes I considered becoming a college lecturer like my father. Many refugees pitched tents in the hills, but we were fortunate, at least, in having found a room in an area of Pusan called Yong-do.

Rereading the diary I kept at that time, I can see how confused and troubled I was, despite the new experiences. After taking a walk with Teacher Song and his son, Unju, along the seashore, I noted in my diary how refreshing the sea smelled. "Yet, I don't know why I am here," wrote the eight-year-old child I once was. "I miss Seoul. I miss my home. I wish we could end this refugee life soon."

I was busy back in those days observing this new life. Soon after we moved to another place, I was amazed at the people I saw. I wrote: "Another woman in the building goes out with American soldiers. Her eyelids are green, she has long fingernails, painted in red. She wears lipstick and her hair is curly. She sleeps during the day and goes out at night." And another time I wrote:

"There are also two sisters who live in the building. They work at the circus. I have never seen them in the circus, but they tell me about their work. They are supposed to juggle all sorts of things. Their life seems so interesting to me. They have beautiful long hair. They always take exercises. I wish I could be in the circus, too." All of that happened so long ago, yet is so deeply a part of me today. Sometimes I wonder how that child survived; maybe her diary helped keep her sanity.

Pusan was the only region that was not in an active war zone.

Millions of us, natives and refugees, lived in those few hundred square miles. Despite their good fortune, the locals resented all the refugees pouring and crowding into their space. Every spare room became a coveted rental unit. To my child's eyes it seemed they were the only ones who were profiting from the war.

January through March of 1951 saw bitter fighting in central Korea against Chinese troops. It was a deadly Korean winter, when temperatures often reached twenty degrees below zero. By mid-March, Communists had begun to withdraw on all fronts and the Eighth Army had regained Seoul. In early April, the Eighth Army crossed the thirty-eighth parallel into the North.

Frictions between the Truman administration and MacArthur on the conduct of the war came to a head in April 1951. Truman wanted to contain the war to the thirty-eighth parallel, but MacArthur wanted to drive back the Chinese from the Korean peninsula and cut off further access by bombing the border—if necessary, by using nuclear bombs. He argued that the Korean War was a showcase for Communist aggression, which had to be nipped soon. But neither officials in Washington nor their allies in Europe saw Korea as a worthy testing ground for containing Communism or a place worth risking an all-out war with the Soviet Union. Truman fired MacArthur.

MacArthur's dismissal shocked us all. Koreans admired MacArthur for his brilliance in Inchon. We had hoped that the American general would liberate all of Korea and push back the Chinese who had joined the North Korean forces. Koreans saw no sense in a limited war and viewed MacArthur's plan as the only one that made sense. My grandmother and my mother appeared almost as shocked with the firing of the American general as when they heard the news about the outbreak of the war. The qualities for which the general was criticized by Americans—his age (he was seventy-one in 1951), his enormous ego, his risk taking, and insistence on having his way, and his self-righteousness—were all ones that Koreans admired. Americans thought he was a tyrant; Koreans admired his leadership. The enormous statue of General MacArthur overlooking Inchon is testimony to the affection Koreans still have for him. He has long faded away from American memory, but not from Koreans'.

○

After about six months of moving from place to place, we were able to rent a three-bedroom house, which we shared with relatives, on a hill in Chwachun-dong. In its small front yard, there was even a persimmon tree, which I climbed often to peek over a wall and see who might be coming to the house. We lived there almost a year before we moved to Japan. But for the fact that my grandmother died in that house, this was a good place, one that gave me the stability that I craved.

Even during war, life must go on for civilians. The school for refugee children that I attended met in pitched tents where straw mats served as doors, and the playground was a muddy hill. We sang songs mostly about the bravery of South Korean and UN soldiers. We were instructed to salute if we saw a UN soldier on the street, and say "hello" and "good-bye."

My mother even had me take singing lessons, and the teacher formed a children's chorus. We gave performances in neighborhood theaters and schools, and before wounded soldiers in hospitals. On holidays we had our portraits taken at a photo studio; my mother and I always went to a beauty shop and had our hair curled with a curling iron before we posed for the camera. The portrait photographer had me clasp my hands like an opera singer and look straight into the camera. As we settled into refugee life, I felt like I now had two homes to think about—my ancestral home and the one we left behind in Seoul. I felt more keenly about the one in Seoul because it was the one I remembered and the one in which I had made an emotional investment. From the news that I heard from adults around me, the war progressed in a seesaw fashion, with the Allied forces gaining an inch, then losing it, near the thirty-eighth parallel. There was talk about a cease-fire. Some refugees even returned to Seoul.

It now appeared that we would be stuck in Pusan for a long time. I made new friends in school, and there was a semblance of settled life once again.

We had not heard a word about my father all this time. My mother kept in touch with families of other teachers who had gone to the United States. Nobody knew, for all communication had been cut off.

In early summer of 1951, we heard the news we had been waiting for. The Korean Red Cross contacted my mother and told her that my father was working in Tokyo. We were to learn later that he and his fellow teachers had been recruited by the U.S. Defense Department for General MacArthur's UN Command in Tokyo in August 1950. As soon as they arrived in Tokyo, my father and his colleagues placed ads for missing persons through the Red Cross. But Red Cross officials had trouble tracking us. It had taken months, and I still am amazed that they found us through all our moves. The very thought of my father in Tokyo, so close to Korea, was like a dream. I was so excited, I could not concentrate on my homework. I ran down the hill to the home of a classmate and told her the news. She seemed as excited as I. By the next day, the entire school knew because she had told everyone. Soon thereafter, letters from my father arrived, along with an official invitation from my father's employer, the UN Command in Tokyo, for us to join him there. Packages began to arrive from Tokyo, too. My father sent us beautiful fabric, purchased at a post exchange. My mother and I had new outfits made. We wanted to wear them for our trip to Japan, and this time we hoped to wear our new clothes. I felt like a Cinderella. The very thought of going to Tokyo to live with my father was so thrilling to me that I tried to picture what life might be like in Japan, so I asked grownups around me who had been there during the Japanese occupation. Japan sounded almost as nice as America, and I was determined to get there.

It would take another two years before a cease-fire would be declared in Korea. The first rumblings about a cease-fire were heard after the Eighth Army won a decisive victory over the Chinese

Communist forces in the area just north of the thirty-eighth parallel. By now, the morale of the Chinese soldiers in Korea was low, and they were running out of supplies and food. After all their successes of the winter, they were now compelled to confront the new face of the UN armies, the deployment of men and firepower which the Communists, despite their numbers, could not break through. But Washington and its allies had no inclination to move through the North and liberate the peninsula. MacArthur's successor, General Matthew Ridgway, in his memoirs, *The Korean War*, wrote: "We stopped on what I believe to be the strongest line on our immediate front."

On June 1, 1951, UN Secretary-General Trygve Lie declared that if a cease-fire could be achieved roughly along the thirty-eighth parallel, the resolution of the Security Council would have been fulfilled. Dean Acheson delivered a talk in which he reaffirmed the objective of a free and independent Korea. But he spoke of the prospects for peace contingent upon defeating Communist aggression and creating realistic assurances to prevent a repeat of another invasion. On June 7, the secretary of state told a U.S. Senate committee that UN forces in Korea would accept an armistice on the thirty-eighth parallel. The world was coming around to changed military and political realities in East Asia. On June 23, Yakov Malik, the Soviet delegate to the United Nations, extended an olive branch by suggesting a cease-fire in Korea. The Allies accepted it with relief.

But even after the decision to seek a truce, the UN side would learn the difficulty of dealing with the Communists. North Korea and Communist China were parties to the talks. Negotiations began on July 10, 1951, but the armistice would not be achieved for another two years. Discussions would begin, then be suspended, and the fighting would resume. Between July 1951 and November 1951, the UN Command suffered sixty thousand casualties, more than twenty thousand of them Americans. From late 1951 until the end of 1952, while the truce talks at Panmunjom dragged on, the U.S. Air Force waged a massive bombing campaign to bring pressure on the Communists.

The Korean War, or the "police action" as President Truman called it, cost 54,246 American lives and 250,000 American injuries; 8,177 Americans are still listed as missing. More than two million Koreans died. The United States was not prepared for the war. Its leaders had misunderstood the vital importance of Korea to the security of East Asia. History has certainly proved wrong the 1949 Joint Chiefs of Staff's conclusion that South Korea was of "little strategic value" to the United States. But then, Korea was not the only Asian country whose importance officials in Washington had miscalculated. In Japan, China, and Vietnam similar mistakes led to policy decisions that continue to affect American lives.

As for our family, we lost everything for the second time. But we were lucky to be alive; so many people we knew had not been as fortunate. Our material possessions were gone, but our indomitable Korean spirit was intact. I would not be in Korea to see the signing of the agreement on July 27, 1953. Eight months before the signing, when I was nine years old, my mother and I would move once again, to make another attempt to resume our lives. Like the journey on the rooftop of the train to Pusan, it would be an adventure— this time, however, out of Korea to Japan.

6. JAPAN

(1952–1958)

The mind is its own place, and in itself
Can make a heaven of hell, a hell of heaven.
—John Milton, *Paradise Lost*

A Jail Time

It was pitch dark when our boat pulled ashore. After a day of sea-sickness, it felt good to step onto land. During the twenty-four-hour crossing from Pusan to Japan on the East Sea, my mother and I each held a pouch of soil about the size of a cigarette box to our noses because someone had suggested that carrying the smell of the land with you was the best way to combat seasickness. The pouch did not help, but I kept it on my nose, afraid to take a chance. Our compartment was not much bigger than a car trunk, and my mother had to lower her head to sit up without touching the ceiling. We gave away the food we had brought for the journey because we could not keep any of it down. Later, when I became ill and crawled up to the deck, I met other passengers whom the captain of the boat had hidden in another compartment. There were eight of us altogether—three college students, two country women going to join their families in a Korean section in Osaka, the guide, my mother, and me. The college students in our party held onto me to keep me from falling off the boat when I threw up into the sea.

My mother and I wore moneybags around our waists. We each had twenty thousand Japanese yen, exchanged on the black market, and new clothes, wrapped in a large silk scarf, which we would change into as soon as we arrived in Japan. Mine were grape-colored wool pants and a yellow sweater, with small square designs in front and custom-made, dark-brown open-toed shoes that were in style in the early 1950s. My mother had beige gabardine pants and matching topcoat, complete with a maroon handbag, a gift of my father's from America, and a pair of matching pumps, custom made to resemble those in a Sears catalogue she had seen at a shoe store. With these clothes who would possibly suspect us of being illegals?

Several times during the voyage I thought our boat would sink. "There is a whale," someone yelled. "Look at that!" As nauseous and dizzy as I was, I got up from the confined space in the compart-ment and crawled up to the deck to take a look. I did not see any whales, but I did see huge waves. Our boat was alone on the sea, as far as I could see. The boat swayed side to side when waves hit it. Grownups said we were so fortunate that the weather was good and the sea was calm, but it did not seem calm to me. I wondered a few times whether we would ever make it to Japan.

On land, our guide, a Japan-born Korean college student, who my mother insisted looked and spoke Japanese like a native, led us up a slope, then over a hill to try to find a road. He was trying to locate a railroad station where he could leave us to continue on our journey. Since my mother spoke fluent Japanese and had lived in Japan while she received elementary school teacher's training in Okayama, we anticipated no difficulty. We would simply take the train to Tokyo and from there contact my father. But we learned later that the captain of the boat had landed at the wrong place, which is why our guide, who had successfully escorted other groups to earn his college tuition, could not locate the railroad station. We had landed at Karatsu instead of Hakata. We wandered in the dark for many hours looking for a place to spend the night, with the guide carrying me on his back because I could not walk anymore. We came across thatched-roof houses with livestock outside. Every time a dog barked, we cringed. We were startled a few times, too, when we ran into villagers in dark-blue traditional Japanese farmers' clothing, on their way home, perhaps from drinking at a village saloon.

Close to midnight, we saw a light and what appeared to be a paved road at a distance. Hoping we were near a railway station, we walked toward the light and passed by a small structure, not realizing that it was a local police station. Our guide, with me on his back, walked ahead of my mother and two others in our party who had fallen perhaps thirty feet behind. We had gone about forty feet or more when we heard a commotion and saw dark figures coming out of the station. Flashlights were directed up and down the road. My mother and the two others with her had been spotted by the police. The two students who had been walking with our guide quickly disappeared into the trees. But the guide, who was still carrying me on his back, went back and joined my mother and the stragglers who had been spotted by the police, even though he too could have disappeared into the trees. One of the policemen said something in Japanese, and we followed him inside. I was scared to death. Not understanding what the police were saying compounded my fear. I got down from our guide's back and stood next to my mother, holding her hand. What would happen to Mother and me now? I wondered. Will the Japanese police put us in jail? Will they put us on a boat and send us back to Pusan, where we would get into trouble for leaving the country? I did not know answers to any of these questions. At least one thing was reassuring to me: not once did I hear the Japanese policemen raise their voices.

I did not realize it then that not only had our guide sacrificed his own chance for freedom but his split-second reaction had also spared the others who had gone ahead and eluded the police. He had risked his own safety by telling the police there were no others in our party. More than four decades after that long night, I still think of the young man and regret that I was too young to appreciate what he had done; I had not even thanked him. Our mutual destinies had come together for that one night; we then went our separate ways, not even leaving a clue as to how we might meet again. How typically Korean! I think to myself now, for Koreans seldom ask for names, phone numbers, or addresses of people they meet. They meet and depart as if they were living in a Confucian village where they are sure to run into each other again.

Two police officers were on duty inside the station. We were obviously quite shaken, and, perhaps, to calm us down and to extend Japanese hospitality, they served us green tea in plain white teacups first. I could not imagine Korean policemen serving tea to people arrested for illegally entering their country. What a fine place Japan is, I thought to myself as I sipped the tea. While the grownups underwent questioning and the policemen filled out papers, I sat still and surveyed my surroundings. It seemed like an exciting adventure to me; I was too young to feel the weight of the journey's consequences. Before the night was up, I would find out, when we were taken to jail and put behind bars.

☯

By October 1952, when we left Pusan, the corrupt Rhee government was in shambles. Despite widespread poverty, high-ranking
officials, military officers, and others with connections lived well.
There was a word for this: *bbak*, an access to people with connections and privileges. With *bbak,* nothing was impossible, even in
war-torn Pusan; but without it, nothing was possible. My family
was among those without *bbak*, of course, because we were from
the North and had no ties except to my father's former colleagues
in the academic world. South Korean officials, many of whom had
been collaborators under the Japanese, stole from the foreign aid that
came into the country. Donations of food, clothing, and money that
were supposed to go to the general populace were siphoned off along
the way, so that about all that people on the street could count on
at distribution centers was powdered milk. This was unappetizing to
the Korean palate, so they mixed it into thin rice gruel that looked
like oatmeal with too much water. Every morning long lines formed
outside, and hundreds of orphans lined up with cans to wait for
the gruel.

The contempt for the South Korean government was high.
But, having seen North Korean atrocities against civilians during the
war, people grudgingly accepted the situation as the lesser of two
evils. A handful of the wealthiest or privileged ones managed to
smuggle themselves out of Korea to Hong Kong and Japan, but most
others were resigned to their fate.

As we prepared for our clandestine escape by boat to Japan,
my mother tried to explain to me how we had come to this: After
my father sent us an official invitation from his office in Tokyo, my
mother applied for a passport. But weeks, then months went by, and
all she got from sour-faced South Korean bureaucrats at the Foreign
Ministry was: "Come back tomorrow. The passport is not ready yet."

Several times I went there with her and saw the man at the
passport window in a dark suit. Even when the faces at the window
changed, the men behind it all had that sour look, the look of

someone with indigestion, which was the stamp of the South Korean bureaucrat. Sometimes the man did not even look up from the paper he was working on as he told us to come back another time. For an entire year, my mother made daily trips to the Foreign Ministry, and each day came back exhausted. While we were waiting for the passports, Grandmother Ke-Son had a stroke, and then, a few weeks later, a second and fatal stroke and died in April 1952. My father was able to get several days of bereavement leave from his office and came to Pusan from Tokyo on a big U.S. Navy ship for his mother-in-law's funeral. It had been more than two years since I had last seen him off at Kimpo Airport. It was like a dream. I felt a little shy when I saw him. My father looked like a foreigner in his smart American suit and a trench coat. He had packed his suitcases, with many gifts—clothes, candies and crayons, notebooks and pencils. His presence took an edge off the sadness I felt over my grandmother's death; my consciousness had never been without her, calling me "Earla-ya" ("baby" in the Hamgyong dialect) and squirreling away sweets that she pulled out of her pockets for me, her only grandchild.

Yet this was a happy occasion, too. By then, I had grown exhausted from waiting for my father, and his face had become fuzzy in my mind, so I would look at photographs to refresh my memory. With the house full of women—my mother, aunt, cousins, and friends—sewing white mourning garments that they would wear to the funeral, I felt consciously for the first time how happiness and sadness often come together. Grandmother's casket was in the main room of the house, and a stream of callers came to pay their respects throughout the day. Because my grandmother was active in the church and had been a deaconess, she knew a lot of people. The week my father stayed was gone in a flash because, with grandmother's death combined with his visit, his former colleagues, students, and friends all poured into our small rented home to pay respects on both accounts. I did not have much time with my father. But on the day of his departure, I got permission from my school to see my father off at Pusan Harbor with my mother. The ship my father was taking back to Japan was enormous, so I had this picture of my mother and me going to Japan in a big ship. My father was optimistic that we would be able to join him soon in Tokyo, and he urged my mother to press on at the Foreign Ministry. He was just as naive as my mother. In hindsight, I see how untainted and innocent my parents were. Having led sheltered lives in the North, they had never had to scrape to get ahead. They took people at their word.

Now that my mother was in mourning, she went to the passport office in white Korean mourning clothes with a small white ribbon in her hair. It was during this time that she met families whose husbands also worked for the U.S. government. As if she were going to work, she went to the passport office every day and waited in line all morning and sometimes until after lunch.

Rhee's bureaucrats issued passports to people whom they knew or who gave them bribes. My mother, cloistered in her home since marriage, was too naive to know how these things got done. Slowly she began to realize that even if she went to the passport office for another ten years, she would never get what she wanted. It was only after some people we knew had stopped coming to the passport office that my mother realized they had given up on the government and taken another route to Japan. But how? This information was not easy to obtain. After several inquiries she learned that there was a thriving underground business of smuggling people by boat to Japan. But which smuggler could she trust? What if they took our money, then dumped us somewhere? Or, worse, what if they took our money and then threw us in the ocean? She had heard some stories about that happening. Still, there seemed to be no other option. Only our immediate family—Uncle Suk-Hoon and Aunt Suk-Bin—knew of our plans, after arrangements were made with a go-between. My uncle even checked out the guide by inviting him to our home and spending some time with him, before we agreed to go with him. The cost of the trip was one million won, about five hundred dollars, which was a lot of money in 1952. My mother left her new Rolex watch, a gift from my father on his last visit, with my uncle so he could sell it and give the smugglers the balance. It was agreed that my mother would pen a note saying that she had arrived safely, and send it back on the return ship inside her Korean jacket, along with my old pants I would be wearing on the boat.

It was our bitter fate that, after all our trouble, we would arrive in Japan safely, only to be arrested. As the paperwork was completed, we were put on a van and taken to the local jail, where we surrendered our small bundle of possessions, including the moneybelt my mother carried. But I kept mine: they had not searched me because I was a child. Guards led us into a cell that was already occupied by a woman. Wearing a green dress and green eye shadow, she was dark complexioned and looked exotic to me. The woman greeted me with a friendly smile, and as an expression of her welcome, she broke off a large piece from the loaf of white bread she was eating and gave it to me. She sat on the floor of the cell, her back against a wall with a gray blanket over her outstretched legs, and nibbled away at the inside of the bread, leaving a hollow shell of the crust. How wasteful she was, I thought to myself, since poor orphans in the streets of Pusan would have eagerly eaten the crust she was discarding. A day or two later, I learned that she had been arrested for prostitution. My mother looked despondent most of the time and spoke very little. Sensitive to her moods, I did not trouble her with my questions about what was going to happen to us. If we were sent back to Korea, I just hoped that it would be on a bigger boat. I did not think I could endure another sickly journey like the one I had just taken.

On the following morning, I was awakened by the clanging of doors and the activity of inmates serving food. A prisoner who appeared to be quite old, with a graying crewcut and hairy arms, passed yellow chopsticks to each inmate, along with a dented aluminum box of rice mixed with barley and two pieces of salty radish pickles dyed yellow. This was our breakfast. I ate almost all of it, having had little to eat except the piece of bread from my cellmate the night before. My mother hardly touched hers. Perhaps she was worried, or maybe she was sickened by the smell of excrement that hung in the air from the nonflush toilet inside the cell. The cell was barely seven feet by seven feet. A lone naked bulb dangled from the ceiling.

The only other light was from the tiny window no bigger than two feet by two feet in one corner of the wall, through which I could see a small patch of sky.

After breakfast the male inmates went outside to the prison yard for exercises, which included jumping over long bamboo sticks. Since I was the only child in the jail, the prison guards were nice to me. They let me leave the cell freely. Needless to say, one of the first Japanese phrases I learned was "Please open the door!" which I said often. "Young miss, in one second," a guard would say. My mother and the other woman, however, remained inside the cell all day.

I passed my time watching the inmates do exercises. Some of them had tattoos on their arms, and their chests looked forbidding. I had never seen tattoos before, but when these men spoke to me, they were friendly and seemed good-hearted. One inmate was to be released in two days. I became a jail mascot, and the prisoners took pleasure in teaching me Japanese words and phrases. Among my new words was *irezumi* (tattoo).

The prison in which we stayed had a row of about two dozen cells facing each other, separated by a concrete corridor. Some of the inmates did chores, like the old man who served breakfast. He had an eye for my Japanese cellmate, who flirted with him from behind the bars. When he brought her breakfast, he lingered and spoke softly to her through the bars. I could not understand what they were saying to each other, but I had an inkling their acquaintance predated their jail time.

My mother and I soon learned that we were not limited to eating jail food. We could order meals from outside and buy fresh fruits, candies, and toiletries. From then on, we often ordered lunch boxes with food that looked pretty and tasted good. I had my first banana in jail, too. I thought it ironic that I would have to be in Japanese prison to taste a banana—the fruit Korean children of my generation only dreamed of eating, because they were not grown in Korea. We used to sing songs about bananas because we had heard so much about the fruit, and they were so expensive that only the rich ate them. A banana was described to me as being so sweet and tasty that it melted in your mouth, so I thought it must taste something like ice cream. I was disappointed when I bit into a banana and it did not melt in my mouth.

In Tokyo, when my father received a call about our arrest, he promptly called Byung-Chang Rhee, a good family friend and a former South Korean diplomat who knew his way around Tokyo. His wife, Duk-Choon, had been a colleague of my father's at Muhak in the late 1940s until she married Rhee and moved to Japan. Obviously, my father could not tell his superiors about our illegal entry and arrest to get time off from work, so he stayed in Tokyo. My father's visit would have been fruitless anyhow, since he did not know how to negotiate. Rhee assured my father he would get to work on our case right away and try to pull some strings. Within a week of our arrest, Rhee came from Tokyo to see us. He told my mother and me that he was working to get us out on bail and that it was only a matter of time before we would be free. During his visit, Mr. Rhee took me to an elegant Japanese restaurant where a beautiful geishalike woman in a pink kimono sat with us inside a sparsely decorated Japanese room and cooked sukiyaki at the table and then served us. Mother could not join us because she was not allowed to leave the jail, but she told me to hand him the money in my waist belt, so I gave it all to Mr. Rhee. He also took me to a big department store, the likes of which I had never before seen. I was dazzled by the friendly clerks, who kept bowing at customers, and the quantity and quality of consumer goods. I could hardly wait to return to the cell to tell my mother about what I had eaten and seen with Mr. Rhee.

A couple of days after Mr. Rhee's visit, my mother and I were taken out of the jail, and accompanied by a guard who, thankfully, did not handcuff my mother. We were relocated by train to a crowded, noisy detention center in Fukuoka where there were many young and middle-aged Koreans. Every person there had a unique reason for undertaking such a risky journey of escape from Korea, and some had been at the detention center for weeks without knowing what fate held for them. One woman we met had arrived with three children a day after we got to the center. She recounted the harrowing experience of her party after they were let off their boat at a remote island. "We walked all night. There was no water to drink anywhere except salty seawater," she said. "So we wet handkerchiefs with the dew in the grass and trees and sucked our handkerchiefs for moisture." After wandering on the island for a night and a day, she was only too glad to be rescued by police. "I never knew how unbearable thirst can be," she said. "You can live without food, but without water you can't even last a day!" Another detainee, who looked to be in his mid-twenties and who chain-smoked cigarettes, lamented that he was being detained even though his family had a pinball parlor nearby—"I can see it from here," he said.

About a week after our arrival, we heard the good news that we would be allowed to leave on bail. Mr. Rhee had worked it out so that my mother and I would be released to a private hospital nearby, where my mother would undergo minor surgery for a recurring internal ailment. Mother and I shared a single hospital bed. From the window of our room, I could look out to the street and a row of two-story combination residential and commercial buildings. For three weeks we shared the room with several different patients, most of whom had abortions or some complications involving pregnancy. One morning after breakfast I experienced something I shall never forget. There was a woman in our room who had aborted a fetus past six months and who regretted her decision when she saw it had a penis. "It was a little boy. It was a little boy," the woman cried. She let out excruciating screams and groans for the better part of the day, and I could not bring myself to look at her.

Sometimes I saw schoolgirls come to the hospital to get abortions. Although most of them did not stay long, one did. She was a tall girl, quite pretty, I thought, and she always wore a lovely kimono robe. She must have come from a rich home, because she had her own maid staying with her in a private room. One afternoon she fainted in the ladies room. I was shocked to see that she was not wearing any underwear under her kimono and she had so much pubic hair.

The most gruesome sight of all at the hospital was the large garbage can in the women's restroom. Like most Western-style toilets of that era in Japan, the women's bathroom had white tiles, scrubbed clean every morning. The minute I opened the door, the smell of cleaning solutions designed to lessen the smell of urine stung my nose. I could not decide which was worse—the smell of urine or of the cleaning solutions. At the entrance to the bathroom, I slipped off my regular slippers and put on woven straw slippers. To my left as I entered were two washbasins with a single cold-water faucet and a bar of soap on the side. Across the way, I stepped up a step to get to the two toilets—the squatting kind—which were enclosed behind light-green painted doors. Between the basin and a window stood a big garbage pail. Into it were thrown fetuses wrapped in yellow wax papers, like ordinary garbage.

I felt sick thinking that would-be babies were discarded like rotten vegetables. But no one ever talked about the fetuses in the garbage pail—not my mother, not the nurses, not the patients. It was as though no one wanted to acknowledge this horrendous activity. Korean children learn early not to ask their elders questions they know will be uncomfortable. We knew this instinctively because of the early training, so we accepted as a given that there were certain subjects we did not discuss. That was why I never asked my mother about the discarded fetuses. But I broached the subject once to one of the nurses, and all she said was that they were not yet babies. (This experience and the war affected my thinking and behavior profoundly: I am consistently pro-life—I oppose abortion, as well as the death penalty.)

Three nurses at the hospital took to liking me and let me inside their quarters, which intrigued me. They had an array of cosmetics in jars and tubes, small boxes containing costume jewelry and other accessories, and nice clothes that they saved for going out with their boyfriends on Sundays. Fascinated, I watched as they washed their faces and carefully applied makeup every morning.

The head nurse, whose name was Hatae, made a strong impression on me. She was stunning. Her skin was pale, the kind Japanese admire, and her exceptionally large eyes sparkled when she smiled. Hatae looked like an angel to me when she wore her freshly starched white uniform and a white cap over her wavy black hair. Her routine in the morning was to take a pink plastic washpan, fill it with cold running water, and then dunk her face, closing and opening her eyes several times in the water. That was the secret to her sparkling eyes, she said. So I mimicked her sometimes and found that it was not so easy to keep one's eyes open in the water.

After the nurses had put on makeup, they did morning exercises, accompanied by a seven o'clock radio program, which began with a cheerful child's voice singing a commercial: "In the morning everyone brushes his teeth. Even little boy Isopo brushes his teeth. A mouse brushes its small teeth." The radio exercise program was sponsored by a toothpaste company. Like clockwork the three nurses and I followed along with the male radio voice and did a ten-minute exercise routine. After this came a Japanese breakfast of rice, miso soup, an egg or a small piece of broiled fish, pickles, and tea. This was followed by cleaning and dusting their own room, the hospital lobby, and the doctor's examining room. Their final daily routine was to line up the sterilized instruments. A cleaning woman did the bathroom. All of this took about two hours, and when they were done, one of the nurses opened the doors to the hospital.

I began to study Japanese in the hospital. My mother first taught me the *hiragana* Japanese script, then *katakana*, which was more difficult. With native speakers all around me, I picked up Japanese quickly. My father called us frequently from Tokyo to keep us abreast of the legal work, which sounded complicated to me.

One evening, after the hospital was closed, the nurses threw a party. An American soldier and his Japanese girlfriend paid a visit with their baby. The woman had had the baby there a few months back and had returned to thank the nurses and bring them gifts. Music was turned up high, and the American soldier and his girlfriend danced. They were joined by the boyfriend of the second nurse, a plump and freckled woman, whose fiancé was a police officer. The officer came there regularly on Saturday evenings, and the nurse dressed up to go out with him. On that Saturday, with the American soldier there and the music from 78 rpm records playing on a phonograph, the nurse and the officer danced for a while too before going off on their own. I danced with nurse Hatae. Mother just sat in a chair and watched, amused by the activity.

Three weeks after our arrival in Japan, my father finally came to the hospital in a black carriage pulled like a rickshaw by a man on a bicycle to tell us we would be able to join him in Tokyo. He and Mr. Rhee had been in touch with a member of Japan's parliament, and we were granted temporary permission to remain in Tokyo while our case wound its way through the legal process at the immigration services office. I heard my parents talk about the huge expenses incurred and more to come.

The nurses gave us a warm farewell before we left the hospital to board a first-class train to Tokyo. What a comfortable change, I thought, from riding on the rooftop of the overcrowded train to Pusan just two years earlier. I watched tangerine groves, then Japanese villages, then towns pass by outside the window. I felt like I was dreaming. On the night after our arrival in Tokyo, I saw neon lights dancing up and down the streets of the Ginza. Tokyo seemed like another world. I had never seen neon signs until then, although I had been told there was one at Hwashin, the oldest department store in Seoul.

We went to live with the Rhees in the upstairs quarters of a Japanese-style home in an exclusive Nakano neighborhood, where the landlady taught young women to play the koto, the Japanese string instrument whose soothing harplike sounds I enjoyed. The abundance of food, the order in the streets, and the Japanese habit of incessantly bowing were all new experiences for an impressionable nine-year-old pulled out of war-torn Korea. The Japanese seemed to be always bowing their heads and saying, "Yes, yes." They were so different from the Koreans. When we gave our landlady even a small gift, she would bow half a dozen times and thank us for days.

We purchased tangerines by the boxes and kept them cool in an unused bathtub downstairs. I ate so many tangerines that after a few weeks my palms and the bottoms of my feet turned yellow. And, as if to make up for all the years when I was hungry, my parents continually brought presents for me. My parents appeared happy. And, for the first time in my life, we had family outings. With my father working just one job, we visited Hibiya Park on Sundays, after attending services at the Tokyo Korean Church. With the Rhees, we entertained and sent gifts to Japanese government officials to try to expedite our case.

After Christmas and New Year's, when we had been in Tokyo about two months, my parents began to worry about my schooling. Without proper legal documents, it would be impossible to enroll in a regular Japanese or American school, so I entered an ethnic Korean school, which lacked accreditation from the Ministry of Education. Korean boys wore generic black Japanese-style uniforms, and girls wore navy blue uniforms with sailor collars. Almost all the students were born in Japan, their parents and grandparents, in most cases, having been brought to Japan as conscripted laborers during the Japanese occupation of Korea. The children had both Korean and Japanese names and often talked of the discrimination they and their families encountered in Japan.

Even though it was a Korean school, the students spoke Japanese, even among themselves. Japanese, after all, was their first language. Classes were taught in both Korean and Japanese except for one by a Japanese teacher named Hayashi, a bespectacled, quiet man who sympathized with the plight of the Korean minority in Japan. Hayashi taught in Japanese. He subjected himself to considerable hostility, for the Korean students and teachers freely spoke ill of Japan and Japanese institutions. Most of the Korean teachers were pro–North Korea; they taught with the devotion and fervor of true believers.

Though I attended the school less than a year, a couple of teachers there made an impression on me. One was a music teacher named Park who wore a black velvet beret, a blue velvet pullover top with a sash around the waist, dark-brown pants, and dark-brown sandals, and he limped. He played classical guitar, and our music class was one of the most enjoyable hours for me. He told us about Spain and other faraway places and how important the guitar was to people in those localities. He grew his fingernails long on the right hand, saying that made it easier to pluck the strings. He wore tinted blue glasses, a rarity in those days. I thought Teacher Park looked like an artist. I had a crush on him; I even liked the way he limped.

Another teacher who moved me was an assistant principal named Cho, who doubled as a history teacher. His face looked burdened, as if he were carrying the weight of his peoples' wretched history on his shoulders. In his fifties at the time, he told us stories about what had happened to Koreans under the Mongols, the Manchus, and the Japanese. I remember him teaching history with a great deal of emotion, and his lectures piqued my interest in Korean history. We ten-year-olds cried as we listened to him.

It was 1953, before Korea and Japan had reestablished diplomatic ties, and relations between the two countries were strained. When Syngman Rhee drew what was called the Rhee Line to prohibit Japanese fishermen from fishing the sea near Korea, our teachers ordered us to various sites, including train stations, to hand out leaflets in opposition to Rhee's action. Left-leaning Koreans in Japan objected to just about everything the South Korean regime did, because they felt Rhee was a U.S. puppet who did whatever American officials told him to do.

As much as I tried to blend in, it did not take long before my teachers and classmates learned that my family was staunchly anti-Communist. They knew my father worked at the UN Command, but both the teachers and the students were good to me. Some tried hard to convert me with their anti-American propaganda. Looking back on that brief period I spent with the children and grandchildren of conscripted Korean laborers, I know the experience touched me deeply. I had a taste of Japanese brutality and its continuing unconscionable policies of discriminating against the very people they had forced to work for their country, only to let them out in the cold when they were no longer useful.

I wrote regularly to my uncle, Suk-Hoon, who had finished

medical school and had completed his compulsory duty in the army. He wrote us often. My aunt, who led a hard life as a street vendor, wrote only occasionally, usually at Christmas. My uncle's letters generally painted a rosy picture of what was happening there because everyone knew the South Korean postal service screened mail, especially international mail. As I began to speak Japanese fluently and adjusted to life in Tokyo, I thought less and less of Korea. As for my mother, with her siblings still in Korea, her mind was never far away from our homeland. Every time we went to department stores and saw beautiful merchandise, she got a lump in her throat thinking about her brother and sister in Korea. There was no way to send packages to Korea because they would never reach them—packages got taken by postal workers or anybody else who had access to them along the way. So, we sent along gifts through missionary or army friends stationed there or through people we knew from Japan who had business in Korea. My mother bought many things, as if to make up for the deprived years. She was caught up in building a home and in buying pretty vases, tablecloths, dishes and pans, and all the other things that we did not have after we left Boshigol.

When I graduated from the Korean Primary School in 1953, I attended a Japanese middle school near my home in Ikebukuro, a busy district in Tokyo. All my classmates were Japanese. I was becoming so Japanese in speech and mannerisms that my father became alarmed and decided to hire a Hawaiian-born Japanese American tutor for me and to enroll me in a private American school, the Christian Academy. Here my Americanization began in earnest. I had to drop a grade because of my inadequate English, but I gained it back when I transferred to the American School In Japan a year later. My inadequacy in English and unfamiliarity with American ways led to a humiliating experience at the Christian Academy that I still remember. My teacher criticized me in front of my sixth-grade home economics class for using Comet cleanser to wash the dishes. "Don't you know that Comet is for cleaning the sink?" she asked severely. Never having heard of Comet before, I did not. My mother always washed dishes in plain water, and I had no idea the Americans had special soap for dishes. I was banished from further participation in home economics because of my incredible dumbness—a trivial incident, perhaps, but just the kind of thing that sticks in your mind.

Because my father always said we would be returning to Korea, we lived like we had to be ready to leave on a moment's notice. In the early 1950s a person could buy a nice house in Tokyo with a small yard for less than three thousand dollars. He had the money, but my father preferred to rent. Deferring to the man of the house, my mother moved from one rental place to another. I was so unhappy about living in small rental units that I once knocked on a house with a For Sale sign and asked the owner to show it to me. I told her I wanted my parents to buy the house. To my surprise and delight, the old lady gave me (then twelve) a tour of the house and said to be sure to bring my parents. I said I would try. It was just the kind of house I wanted: it had a spacious Western-style living room with a fireplace, a Western-style bathroom and flush toilet, and a nicely mowed lawn. With excitement I went home and told my mother about it, but to no avail, since we could not get my father to look at it. We had a brand-new 1954 Dodge, but no house.

My main motivation for wanting a home was simple: I had been invited to classmates' homes, and I wanted to reciprocate. But I was too embarrassed to bring my American or European classmates to my home, because we were still living like refugees, with boxes stacked up and clothes hanging on a clothesline in one corner—ever ready, in case we had to pick up and move again. Fortunately, my best friend was a Korean girl named Chihe, whose family also attended the Tokyo Korean Church. To another Korean, the condition of our home and whether we owned or rented it did not seem to matter—at least that is the way it felt to me. Chihe was a year older, and she came to our home often. For almost five years, Chihe and I were inseparable. Though we lived in different neighborhoods and attended different schools, we visited each other on weekends. On Sundays after church, she came along with us to go to Hibiya Park or to play with me. Chihe and I also spent a lot of time visiting department stores, mostly looking at dresses and costume jewelry. We often wore identical dresses and pretended that we were sisters. Chihe visited us wherever we moved and never once mentioned anything about the way we lived. Eventually, sometime after the birth in 1954 of my brother, Emmanuel, the much-awaited heir to the Kang clan, my parents bought a house with a big lot in the heart of Tokyo. My father named his son Man-Yol, which in Korean means "overflowing with happiness."

I was so happy to have a sibling that I hovered around his crib and checked on him constantly. Being almost twelve years older, I was a devoted baby-sitter. Now the whole family's schedule revolved around this precious boy. When he got the day and night mixed, sleeping during the day and staying awake at night, my mother switched her schedule, too. I went to school without breakfast. And, my mother's personality changed after Emmanuel's birth. She became assertive and acted as if she now had her claim to legitimacy in the Kang household. The change was so apparent that I wondered why sons had such power. But I accepted the fact that sons were more important, because all the other families said the same thing. Looking back now, I see why the birth of a son meant everything to my mother. Having delivered an heir to the Kang clan, her place was secure, unlike with my birth. For all Korean women of my mother's generation, attaining their rightful place in the family depended on producing sons. So my mother fussed over her only son, as her own mother had done to her brother, devoting her every waking hour to him and spinning dreams about his future. I sometimes wondered, even as a twelve-year-old, who could possibly fulfill her expectations. My brother would be a handsome and brilliant Christian doctor who would play the violin and the piano as hobbies, and he would be a great humanitarian—this was my mother's plan for him. She had no dreams for me, so I created my own. I wanted to become a writer, a singer, and an actress, and fall in love and marry.

Now that my parents had bought one home, the decision to acquire a second home came easily. Using part of our sizeable lot, they had a second house built on it and sold the first home to a Japanese family. My father provided the money, but mother supervised the entire project alone and cajoled the team of carpenters and laborers. She enjoyed doing things like that far more than keeping house. Finally, my family had a dream home and I had my own room with a view of Mount Fuji. I loved this two-story pink house with its brick-colored tiled roof, pink and blue bathroom and kitchen, and an upstairs balcony. I covered the wall of my bedroom with pictures of James Dean, Elvis Presley, Sandra Dee, and Natalie Wood and sang along with my record player to "Love Me Tender," "Jailhouse Rock," and "Hound Dog." I was so wrapped up with my life in Tokyo that I did not think about Korea much. Whenever I thought of Korea, I remembered the freezing train ride, the squalid conditions of Pusan, and the South Korean government, whose refusal to issue us a passport—to which I felt we were entitled—had forced us to risk our lives to reunite with my father.

But my parents would not let me forget my Korean heritage. They had my uncle send Korean school texts, and I studied history and social sciences books at home. I also read in Korean *Gulliver's Travels*, *Heidi*, and many other American and European books at home. My Koreanness was so drilled into me that it became like a religion. My parents said it was a shame that Japan-born Koreans did not speak their ancestral tongue, and they were critical of parents who let their children forget the Korean language. They also preached Korean customs, which so often contradicted what I was learning in the American school. By junior high, my classmates were wearing lipstick and a little makeup, but for me that was taboo. By the time I was in the ninth grade, everyone was going to dances, but God forbid I should even ask. There was no question in my mind that there was a time for all these things, but insofar as my parents were concerned, that time was not now and I accepted it. But I did manage to buy a tube of lipstick and put it on during my trip to school on the train, and I carefully removed it before I got home. All the other girls were using it, and I could not understand what harm there was in wearing a little pink lipstick. When I was in the tenth grade, a very quiet and studious boy invited me to a dance. I turned him down without explaining why. He looked so hurt—he thought I was a friend—but I could not bring myself to tell him my parents did not allow me to date. I cannot remember his first name, but I remember his surname—Winslow. He had beautiful eyes and the longest eyelashes of any boy in class. All these conflicting values and notions were churning in my subconscious; they would manifest themselves in ways small and big in the years to come. I was Korean and Japanese, and about to become American, too.

So, in Tokyo, I went from a nine-year-old, so small that I was mistaken for a seven-year-old, to a fifteen-year-old, juggling three cultures and three languages and keenly feeling the conflicting pulls of each. And I kept dreaming of becoming a writer, singer, and actress, although I knew full well that no Korean from a decent family could aspire to sing or act. And I kept dreaming of falling in love and marrying, although I thought that I probably would not be allowed to go out with boys until I was away in college. But even as I dreamed these dreams in my upstairs room with pictures of American movie stars and singers on the wall, there would be yet another turn of fate for me. Our family would relocate again—this time, to Okinawa in the summer of 1958, when my father changed his job.

It was the year the movie version of James Michener's *Sayonara*, starring Marlon Brando and Miiko Taka, and costarring Red Buttons and Miyoshi Umeki, was a hit in Japan. I saw the movie once but read the book several times, reading it under my quilt late into the night. And I played Umeki's "Sayonara" album on my record player all the time and sang along:

Sayonara, Japanese good-bye.
Whisper sayonara, smiling as we go.
No more we stop to see pretty cherry blossoms.
No more we 'neath the tree, looking at the sky.
Sayonara, sayonara, good-bye.

I did not want to leave Tokyo, my second home where I had traveled from childhood through adolescence, and where my eyes had been opened to art, music, literature, a style of life, and sense of aesthetics I had not known in Korea. But fate was beckoning our family to move on. I was glad my family was intact, and naturally I had to go where they went, so for me, for that time, "sayonara" really was "sayonara."

7. FROM OKINAWA TO AMERICA

(1958–1967)

To see a world in a grain of sand,
And a heaven in a wild flower;
Hold infinity in the palm of your hand,
And Eternity in an hour.
—William Blake, *Auguries of Innocence*

An Island in the Sun

During our stay in Japan in the fifties, while we enjoyed the material comforts of Japan's booming economy and my father's paycheck in U.S. dollars, South Korea inched its way toward recovering from the war that had left much of the nation in rubble. South Korea was among the poorest nations in the world, and people grabbed any chance they could to get away from the place. Many of the country's elite sought to study abroad; others, whether government officials or businesspeople, welcomed even brief trips abroad as a respite from the corruption, moral decay, and cynicism that had enveloped the South Korean society.

Many visitors, mostly my father's former students and colleagues, stopped in Tokyo on their way to and from Seoul. Whenever my parents broached the subject of returning to Korea, their firm advice was to stay put: "Why would anybody in his right mind exchange this comfortable life for the wretched one in Korea?" People who lived by the government's rules had to be prepared to nearly starve, they said. As for me, I had decided that America would be the place to go for college. I was pretty sure that is what my parents had in mind as well, though they did not say so.

On the political front, the Syngman Rhee regime's main preoccupation was holding onto power. By August 1952, Rhee had been reelected because of a constitutional amendment, which he had railroaded through by declaring martial law and arresting opposition lawmakers. By a contortion of semantics he led the so-called Liberal Party. With his second term coming to an end in 1956, Rhee amended the constitution again in 1954, exempting the "present incumbent" from the two-term limit on the presidency. This, in effect, assured him life tenure, since he was almost eighty. In the 1956 election, Rhee won with only 55 percent of the vote, even though his chief opponent had died of a heart attack within days before the election. However, Rhee's running mate, his sycophantic former personal secretary, Ki-Bung Lee, lost to the opposition party candidate Myon Chang. That set off alarms in Rhee's quarters.

Rhee's followers became so driven by retaining power that they clamped down on all dissent, including criticism from the press. Branding opponents as Communists, Rhee's henchmen literally got away with murder. Remembering Rhee's patriotism of the past, Koreans were charitable and blamed his underlings for his misrule. Rumors were rampant that the octogenarian was senile and in poor health. I remember hearing some ranking government officials who were visiting us in Tokyo tell my parents about the extraordinary measures his advisors took so as not to upset Rhee. One ranking army officer told my parents how out of touch with reality the old man was. During his inspection tours of his soldiers, he would dig into his pockets and hand them a paper note, telling them to go out and have a nice lunch; the notes could not even fetch a bus fare. Such was the situation in South Korea, as my family moved to Okinawa in 1958, where a scorching sun greeted our arrival.

☯

It was August 3, 1958. I had never before felt a sun so hot or seen sunlight more bright; I could barely keep my eyes open. We had arrived during the hottest month of the year, and I could think only of wanting to return to Tokyo. My father, who had been there several months already while my mother tried to sell our Tokyo home, met us at the airport and took us to the Ryukyu Hotel, the only first-class hotel on the island of Okinawa at the time.

The imposing entrance to the hotel had a three-tiered glazed green-tiled roof and pillars of striking red wood. Two green glazed lions guarded the gates to keep evil spirits at bay. We had a spacious Japanese tatami room with a small low table in the middle and cushions around it. Quilts were neatly folded inside a closet. I liked the room. In one corner on a raised tatami mat was a simple flower arrangement, behind which hung a scroll; there was no other decoration. It made me feel like I still had a small piece of Japan with me. Eating Japanese meals, too, kept alive that feeling, which was important to me. Tokyo was my security blanket, the only stability I had known.

Our first night at the hotel was anything but restful. My brother, who was four years old, developed a high fever, and we called for a doctor, who diagnosed it as heatstroke. To make matters worse, our room was above the nightclub, and music from below kept going on through the night. A combination of my brother's crying, the unrelenting heat, and loud music from the nightclub below is what I remember of that night.

A woman with a pleasing voice but poor English pronunciation sang the Patti Page hits, "Tennessee Waltz" and "I Went to Your Wedding," along with "Blue Moon" and the theme song from the movie "Love in the Afternoon," while I tossed and turned in my hotel-provided kimono. I had an image of the nightclub below, although I had not laid eyes on it. In my mind it was dimly lit, candles glowing in red glass holders, wine glasses clinking, and people talking through rings of smoke curling up from cigarettes. I imagined the singer in a tight black satin dress with sequins, a red hibiscus in her long black hair, bejeweled hands, and eyes throwing come-hither looks. I fell asleep humming "It was fascination I know. Seeing you alone with the moonlight above . . ." and picturing scenes from a movie I had sneaked in to see with Chihe in Tokyo, in which Audrey Hepburn pretended to play the cello but was thinking about her new love, Gary Cooper. Thereafter, every night after dinner, I heard the music from below, capped by the singing of the popular songs. I wanted so very much to go down there and join the singer on the stage, but I did not say that to my parents. By the time we left the hotel after we bought a house, I had committed to memory the words to most of the songs in the singer's repertoire.

This time, my parents bought a house within ten days of our arrival—I could not believe it. Had my father at last come to realize how nice it was to have our own place? He admitted to becoming a convert. Okinawa was scenic and reminded me of Hawaii, based on the movies I had seen. But the heat and high humidity sapped my energy. Okinawa, the main island in the Ryukyu archipelago, is only seventy miles long and seven miles wide. In less than three hours we could travel from one end of the island to the other by car. Its small size and subtropical climate made me feel like I was trapped in a steam room.

The islands had a long and colorful history. Okinawans had their own language, music, and distinctive culture. Until the fourteenth century, when the archipelago came under Chinese domination, independent kings ruled the islands. In the seventeenth century, Japan invaded the Ryukyus, and the inhabitants were obliged to pay tribute to two masters—Japan and China. Then, in the nineteenth century, the islands were annexed and became part of the Japanese Empire. During World War II, Okinawa's location assumed strategic importance, and the invasion of the island by U.S. troops on Easter Sunday, April 1, 1945, marked the beginning of the bloodiest campaign of the Pacific theater. More than one hundred thousand Japanese and twelve thousand Americans were killed during this last major battle of the war. For the Koreans living under Japanese rule, it was the decisive U.S. victory that gave them hope. After the war, the Ryukyu Islands fell under U.S. administration, and Okinawa was developed as a strategic U.S. military base until the United States returned the islands to Japan in 1972.

The presence of U.S. soldiers and their dependents was overwhelming. It was a little America. Americans were everywhere; they lived like royalty because Okinawa was under U.S. administration. There was no shortage of "Ugly Americans"—a term in vogue in the fifties and sixties in Asia to describe Americans living or traveling in Asia who looked down on natives and their way of living. They gave other Americans a bad name.

I enrolled in an American school, attended mostly by military dependents, starting in my junior year, and I was determined to make top grades. On my first day of school that September, I was pleasantly surprised to meet Marsha, an American friend from Tokyo who was a native of Georgia. Marsha and I became inseparable. We had in common our love of singing and dieting. Though neither of us was fat, we looked at the pictures of models in *Seventeen* and *Glamour* and wanted to be as thin as they were. Marsha and I formed a duo called Teen Tops, and we appeared on the local armed forces TV station and at school functions. Twice, we sang at Fort Buckner's Officers Club, which was a real thrill; my parents allowed it because Marsha's father was the manager of the club. Wearing identical lavender dresses and cowboy hats and holding lariats, we performed the Kingston Trio's "Tom Dooley."

Okinawa gave me my first insight into American life—good and bad. For a long time, I was struck by the undemocratic behavior of a people who previously had embodied democracy and equality to me. For a time, a U.S. administrator of the Ryukyus ordered that vehicle license plates display the rank of both military and civilian personnel. The game of pulling rank to this extreme was years later declared unconstitutional by a court, but while the practice lasted for several years, it wrought needless humiliation to many, especially youngsters of fathers with low ranks. The Department of Defense was notorious in its blatant discrimination against its non–U.S. citizen employees. Though many of the noncitizen employees had superior education and work experience, they got paid less and did not receive retirement benefits. After spending a quarter century or more working for the U.S. Army, they received a small lump sum for severance when they retired or were laid off. Among those the army treated most shabbily were Okinawan employees. More than 15 percent of the Okinawans worked for the U.S. military establishment. America did not win friends through such behavior. These slights inflamed anti-American sentiment among Okinawans, who came to believe that being under Japan was the lesser of two evils.

But if those actions reflected negatively on America, I was touched by the willingness of so many American families to adopt Asian children who came from impoverished homes or were born out of wedlock. This humanitarian display made a deep impression on me, since Koreans rarely adopt children because of their emphasis on bloodline and pedigree. I was also impressed by American ideas of love: they married for love. I would see Americans marrying Okinawan widows with children and would be flabbergasted. In Asian cultures that rarely happened.

☯

After Tokyo, Okinawa seemed tame and unexciting. I felt isolated, not only because of the geography of the small island but because there were hardly any Koreans around. Nearly one million ethnic Koreans lived in Japan, but there were only a handful of Koreans in Okinawa, most of whom were affiliated with the U.S. Defense Department. My parents' emphasis on Korean was stronger than ever. My mother always spoke to my brother and me in Korean, and we ate mostly Korean food at home. Since there was no Korean church, my father and I went to an American house of worship and my mother to an Okinawan church nearby, since she did not speak English. Our social life was isolated, compared to that in Japan, with the family having to be a self-contained unit. Also, unlike in Japan, we lived in an American neighborhood. Okinawans lived in their own neighborhoods and were mostly poor.

I poured my energies into my studies, the school paper (for which I was the editorial page editor), and music. My piano teacher was a Japanese woman who was married to an American civilian, my voice teacher was a woman from Wisconsin who was married to an air force officer, and my classical guitar teacher was a low-keyed, polite Okinawan. I wanted to play pop songs on my guitar, but he would not deign to teach me chords I needed to know. Except for the times I spent practicing singing with Marsha or going shopping with her in downtown Naha, the Okinawan capital, I mostly studied. I wanted to get all A's—and get into a U.S. university. By the second semester of my junior year, I had received catalogues from dozens of American universities. Though my parents always told me that we would be returning to Korea, and that I must prepare myself for the eventuality by retaining my ability to

During a vacation in Puerto Vallarta, Mexico in November, 1982.

Even during our refugee life in Pusan, my mother made sure we dressed up and posed for a Lunar New Year's photo. 1951.

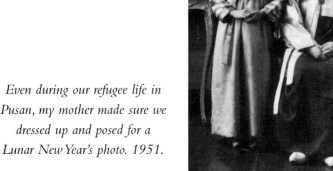

My parents and I spent Sunday afternoons after church
in Hibiya Park in Tokyo, 1953.

(Taken in April, 1952, on the
day my father left for Tokyo.) My
parents and I stand in front
of our rented home in Pusan.
My father, Joo-Han Kang,
had come from Tokyo for my
grandmother's funeral. My
mother, Sok-Won Choe, is in
white mourning clothes.

(Taken on the drawbridge connecting Pusan to Yongdo Island, 1951.) I'm wearing a dress made from the fabric my father sent from Michigan—the dress I never got to wear to the airport to meet my father because the Korean War broke out before he could return.

My elementary school classmate, Ji-Sook Tak (seated), and I performed Korean folk dances at a theater in Pusan. We attended a temporary school for refugees in a tent pitched on a hill. Behind us is promotional material for an American movie, "Beauty and the Beast." Our classmates are peeping out from backstage at left. 1951.

My mother took me to a beauty parlor to have my hair curled for this photo, taken in 1952. This was the outfit I was supposed to wear after we had smuggled ourselves into Japan. I never got to wear it because we were arrested for illegally entering Japan.

My family in my parents' San Francisco home in 1990. To my right is my mother. My brother, Emmanuel, and my father are seated in front.

Interviewing the wife of South Korean President Chung-Hee Park at the Blue House in 1968.

(LEFT) *Performing with Marsha, my Teen Tops partner, at the Sukiran Officers' Club on Okinawa during my junior year in high school in 1959.*

(BELOW) *This is the only photo I have of my family from North Korea. Taken in March, 1946, two months before I crossed the 38th parallel on my mother's back with my grandmother. I was three years old here. (Seated) my mother and my grandmother. (Standing) my uncle Suk-Hoon Choi and my aunt Suk-Bin Choi.*

I sometimes ran into these two North Korean officers when I was at the truce village of Panmunjom to cover Military Armistice Commission meetings. I'm wearing a blue press band, issued by the South Korean government to all foreign correspondents. Spring, 1988.

I was assigned to cover Prince Charles during his visit to Los Angeles in 1974. Here, I'm trying to catch up with his long stride at Universal Studios.

Having never owned a car, I have spent countless hours on public transportation.
For many years, I studied languages on my way to and from work.

This is Mangwol-dong Public Cemetery where citizens of Kwangju who
were massacred for rising up to challenge Doo-Hwan Chun are buried.
I visited the cemetery several times. This was taken in the fall of 1988.

speak the language and know the traditions and customs, I had an inkling that a big change awaited me in America.

I sometimes grew weary of Okinawa's sun, the unpredictable rain showers, the barren red soil that produced not much else than sweet potatoes, the meager-looking bananas and pineapples, the typhoons, and the poisonous *habu* snakes that kept men and beasts indoors at night. After sleeping under rocks and in the trees, these indigenous creatures, colored like the Okinawan earth, crawled out from their resting places at night in search of food. The only thing that could match the ferocity of the *habus* were mongooses, furry rodentlike animals that bit the snakes into pieces. People went to see staged *habu*–mongoose fights. They were as popular as cockfights elsewhere, but I never had the stomach to watch them.

Our white house was on a hill overlooking the East China Sea, and we had a picture-postcard view of the ocean, but I appreciated neither the view nor the slow pace of life. The relentless, muggy heat made my skin feel as if it had been smeared with syrup, it sapped my energy, overshadowing all my experiences there. But the weather did not bother native Okinawans, who resembled Pacific Islanders more than East Asians. Okinawans were easygoing and amiable and much like native Hawaiians in temperament. I was not surprised to learn that they have the longest average life expectancy of any people in the world—82.5 years—and many lived longer than that. The idea of keeping appointments was an alien concept. For instance, our newspaper delivery woman would often bring us a week's supply of the daily *Okinawa Times* all at once. "I'm sorry, I had a wedding and other family matters to attend to," she would say with a smile, and that would be the end of it. Because of my Tokyo-bred punctuality, I could not get used to such a casual lifestyle.

I was also well into my teenage years, and I wanted to get away from home, too. There was such a difference between my two lives—the Korean one at home and the American one outside. My biggest obstacle, though, was Syngman Rhee. I did not have a passport because his government would not issue one to me, which was why we had smuggled ourselves into Japan in the first place. Had my parents been more street-smart, they would have bribed Rhee's bureaucrats, but they played by the old rules, which did not work with Rhee's corrupt government. After illegally entering Japan, we were able to get permanent residence through influential members of the Japanese parliament, but we had surrendered our residency papers when we left Japan. I could remain on Okinawa as a dependent as long as my father was employed by the U.S. Department of Defense, but without a passport, I could not travel outside the island. Even almost a decade after we had left, South Korean officials continued to use the issuance of passports as a weapon to keep its citizens in line or to bring in payoffs, whichever was more expedient.

Then, a shocking event came to my rescue in the most unexpected place. South Korean student protestors toppled the Rhee government in April 1960, less than two months before my high school graduation. My parents had mixed feelings about Rhee's demise. Like most other Koreans, they were charitable, blaming his autocratic ways on his advisors. But I did not share that view. I was glad this old man who had inflicted so much suffering on his people and had blown the chance to bring democracy to Korea was no longer president.

Rhee may have studied the principles of democracy under Woodrow Wilson at Princeton, but when he returned home after his country was liberated from Japan's yoke and got in power, he dispensed with democracy and became a tyrant. He had fought Japanese imperialism and even wrote a scathing book, *Japan Inside Out,* but to get rid of his opponents and perpetuate his rule, he had retained the same police machinery and Japanese collaborators that his former enemy had used. More than three decades later, my verdict on Rhee has not changed. It was his personal tragedy and a tragedy for Korea that this man, who was so proud of his American education, could not practice its values. His immense ego and double standard had so blinded him that he had no vision; he could not distinguish a short-term gain from a long-term victory for his country and his people. Rhee's flaw was to surround himself with sycophants because he could not stand those who disagreed with him. In so doing, he smothered any chance for democracy in Korea. He had betrayed his freedom-starved peoples' goodwill toward him, and finally they—the young student generation—turned on him.

Though he was a self-proclaimed and devout Methodist, he had married an Austrian woman, Francesca Donner, even though he already had a Korean wife back home. It is true that some prominent Korean men of that era had done the same thing, taking on new wives in America and discarding the wife back home like an old shoe. But such a person, in my mind, should not become a leader of a nation.

Francesca Rhee was her husband's gatekeeper. Despite her ignorance of Korea and inability to speak Korean, she was in the center stage of the Rhee rule. As further misfortune for Korea would have it, she found as her confidant Maria Park, the conniving wife of Ki-Bung Lee, whose ambition knew no bounds. Maria Park had even talked the childless presidential couple into adopting her older son. Maria Park and her ambitions would be tragically ended in the hands of her own son, who later killed both his parents, then his brother, and finally himself in a family suicide pact after Rhee was forced to resign in disgrace in April 1960.

Less than a month earlier, on March 15, Rhee had been re-elected in one of the most fraudulent elections in Korean history. Rhee's Liberal Party had taken severe measures—including stuffing a third of the total ballots marked for the ruling party into polling boxes—to assure its victory. The election day was marred by violence, and at least ten people were reported killed in anti-government demonstrations in three cities.

Since the election, a series of demonstrations had taken place in the southern port city of Masan, an anti-Rhee stronghold. On April 10, during a protest, a high school student named Chu-Yul Kim, who had been out in the streets with the demonstrators, did not return home. Police denied that they knew his whereabouts, but two weeks later a fisherman discovered the boy's body with a fragment of a tear-gas canister still protruding from his head. As the word got around, angry Masan citizens demanded the boy's body so they could take it to Seoul and show it to the National Assembly. When the authorities refused, the crowd sacked city hall.

For the next two days the students marched with placards that read: "Down with Fraudulent Elections" and "Can Freedom Gained through Blood Be Taken Away by Bayonets?" By this time, as Keyes Beech of the *Chicago Daily News* reported, "only a spark was needed to ignite the flame." That spark was provided by the police force on April 18, when more than two score police-hired thugs attacked a group of Seoul's Korea University students who were returning to their campus after a peaceful demonstration.

On the following day, Tuesday, April 19, 1960, students from colleges and universities poured into central Seoul and marched toward the presidential mansion. They were met by a hail of police bullets, and 142 students lost their lives. To restore order, the government declared martial law. But six days later, university professors, joined by students and other citizens, demonstrated in front of the National Assembly Building. The soldiers refused to fire on the protestors. On the following day Rhee resigned and the demonstrations stopped. The old man left the country in exile to Hawaii to live out the rest of his days.

With the toppling of his government, I and thousands of Koreans throughout the Western world who were held hostage by the Rhee government finally were issued passports. I received my first passport—No. 23804, stamped with a red seal of Il-Hyung Chung, the foreign minister—almost a decade after my mother had applied for it in Pusan. I looked at the freshly minted document, black with a yin and yang symbol of the Korean flag in gold, over and over again, holding it like the most precious possession in the world. Now I could freely travel, like other peoples of the free world, no longer confined to the tiny island of Okinawa. Years later when I had become an American citizen and could easily obtain a passport, I could not help but reflect on how my freedom to travel had been held hostage for so many years.

But the passport arrived too late for me to enter college in America in the fall, so I postponed departure by a year and in the meantime took as many classes as possible at the University of Maryland's Far East Division in Okinawa to earn a sufficient number of credits in required subjects. I had decided to become a newspaperwoman. The *Morning Star*, the local English-language paper, was pretty dismal, but it carried Inez Robb, whose columns I read faithfully. I also read my father's *Christian Science Monitor* and *Stars and Stripes*, the army newspaper, printed out of Tokyo. I had picked the School of Journalism at the University of Missouri on the recommendation of a friend and colleague of my father's, Chin-Nam Whang, a gifted man who had quit the University of California at Berkeley in his senior year to work for the Korean independence movement in Shanghai. "Missouri is the world's oldest and best journalism school," Whang said when I told him I wanted to become a newspaperwoman. I took his advice without question.

By my junior year in high school, I knew I wanted to pursue journalism. Singing was fun, but realistically, I knew I had to choose something more respectable. Being the only one on the school paper who spoke Japanese, I often went to the Okinawa Times building, where our paper was printed, as the school's representative. My journalism advisor was impressed, and I got an A+. I wrote feature stories, in addition to editorials. I also wrote a novel the summer between my junior and senior years, which I sent off to Pearl S. Buck in Perkasie, Pennsylvania. She was gracious in her letter to me, and she returned the manuscript with an autographed picture of herself. She encouraged me to continue to write, though she said that a writer's first attempt seldom translates into print. Like Buck, who brought China to the outside world, I wanted to introduce Korea to English readers. It seemed nobody knew about Korea, much less about Koreans. And, I felt like saying, "Hey, Korea may be a small and poor country, but it's worth getting to know." So I wrote my first novel, set in Korea. It is still in my footlocker, along with many other attempts at fiction, poetry, and song writing. I used to send my songs off to outfits in Hollywood that I had read about in magazines. Little did I know then that I would be working in Los Angeles thirty-five years later.

In addition to journalism, my favorite subjects were English literature and languages. I took French, Spanish, and Latin, along with the required courses, including science and math, which I did not like. I did not do as well as I should have in physical education, but Mrs. Smith, my teacher, gave me an A. I had a sneaking suspicion she did not want to mess up my straight-A average. Report card days were happy days for me, because I got five dollars for every A. I saved my money to buy records—45s of Elvis Presley, Tommy Edwards, Johnny Mathis, Paul Anka, Pat Boone, Connie Francis, Rosemary Clooney, Miyoshi Umeki, and Doris Day, as well as some European singers I liked such as Tino Rossi and Edith Piaf. I also sang Japanese songs—my favorite Japanese singers were all women, including Misora Hibari, Eri Chiemi, and Peggy Hayama, who were top singers in the fifties and sixties. Since I had no access to new Korean songs, I sang the old ones from the times I was a child in Seoul. I had a piano in my bedroom, and I sang more than I talked in those days.

I taught a Sunday school class and sang in the church choir, whose members included soldiers stationed at nearby bases. I tried to keep my distance from them because I did not want to be invited out on a date. I did not feel like telling them that my parents would not allow me to go out until I was older.

Despite their restrictions on my wearing makeup and dating, my parents supported all my scholastic activities and hobbies. My father had always thought that a woman should know how to speak French, so I had studied French with a French tutor, Madame Calendreau, since the seventh grade. Occasionally, my father had mentioned that I might eventually want to become a simultaneous interpreter for the United Nations, but he never pushed. My mother—quoting the old Korean saying, "Clothes are wings"—bought me more clothes than I ever needed. When I wrote songs, my father ran them off on his office mimeograph machine so they would look professional. I did not even try to excel in sports because my mother said that "only idiots" could do sports. I could not even ride a bicycle, much less shoot baskets or play tennis. In running, I was the first to start and the last to finish.

But going to an American school with American kids, I got caught up in cheering at basketball and football games, and even acted as a substitute cheerleader, though I was not good at it. My life was totally American because there were so few non-Americans there. We did not have a chance to mingle with Okinawans—they were considered second-class citizens. Sadly, I did not even have a chance to acquire one Okinawan friend during my three years there. We followed American fashions as they came and went: bobby sox and white shoes with full skirts and petticoats, sack dresses, and tight black pants, and ponytails, beehives, and bouffant hairdos. And, occasionally, when I could get away from my studies, I watched reruns of *I Love Lucy* and *Ozzie and Harriet* on the local armed forces station.

My brother, onto whom my mother poured all her hopes, started his violin lessons when he was four, and piano lessons soon thereafter. He was only a first-grader when I left for college in 1961. Because of our age difference, I never really felt like I had a sibling. He probably felt the same, since his sister left home just as he was beginning to get to know her.

To America at Last!

I had a lot of time to prepare for my journey to America because of the long wait for the passport. The only friend I had in the United States was Janis, with whom I had gone to school in Tokyo. Janis and I wrote each other through all my years on Okinawa. Janis, who was from California, thought it would be fun if I could join her at the University of California at Berkeley, but I told her I was going to Missouri because of the school's fine reputation in journalism. She and her mother wrote me long letters about what to expect, what I should bring to school, and the kinds of clothes American college students wore. After living three years in a tropical climate, I had to get some cold-weather clothes, too.

For months before my departure, my mother and I commuted to our dressmaker to get my wardrobe ready, for casual, church, and party wear. My father, watching mother and daughter so obsessed with clothing, once remarked: "Are you going to America to study or show off your clothes?" To which my mother replied: "Clothes are wings—especially for girls."

I also talked to older sisters of my friends from school, who had returned home for the summer, to find out what college was like. Everyone seemed to say something a little different. For example, the ones going to Smith, Mount Holyoke, or other all-women's schools, told me they paid no attention to clothing because there were no boys on their campuses. I decided to leave with an ample supply of everything, since I had also heard that things cost more in the States.

❡

My journey to America took place the first week in September 1961. Friends and neighbors came to see me off at Naha Airport, as I was the first youngster in Okinawa's tiny Korean community to leave for college. I was busy thanking everyone, so the only comment I remember people making was, "We have high hopes for you." I wore a blue and white seersucker sleeveless dress, sewn by an Okinawan dressmaker who had left her husband and three young children to run off with a young American soldier. I carried a new white Samsonite suitcase and a matching overnight case, plus a large tan envelope containing a copy of my chest X-ray, as was required of all people coming into the United States who were carrying passports of the so-called developing countries.

When I was on the Pan American clipper, looking out the window, watching my parents and the well-wishers waving, even

though they could not see me, I felt a lump in my throat. And, as
the slow, noisy plane flew over the sea, and I watched the water
that looked like islands of blue and green opal, I felt homesick already
for my family and Okinawa. I had so often wanted to get away from
home, but now that I was leaving, I felt like a bird leaping out of
its nest. Similarly, however much I had not enjoyed being in Okinawa at times, I realized on the plane how stable my life had been
there during those three years. We had lived in a comfortable home
with a sweeping view of the East China Sea and bananas growing
in the garden, along with hibiscus, poinsettias, and myriad other
plants and shrubs in bloom throughout the year. On Okinawa, I had
received recognition for my academic performance, and my teachers,
especially Mr. Elliott, the principal, had taken a special interest in
me. I remembered what the people had told me at the airport, and
I resolved not to disappoint them or myself. Soon after we had a
snack and soft drinks, the plane landed at Tokyo's Haneda International
Airport. My childhood friend, Chihe, Mrs. Rhee, in whose home we
had stayed when we went to Tokyo in 1952, and her daughter,
Linda, greeted me with gifts. It had been three years since I had last
seen them. Our visit ended all too quickly; we promised to see each
other soon.

Back on the plane, now headed for Honolulu, I thought about
my journey. I was brimming with hopes for obtaining a good liberal
arts education, then training in journalism. I figured it would take
me seven years or so to complete bachelor's, master's, and doctoral
degrees. After that, I would return to Korea to make my contributions. Perhaps at that point I would marry a Korean, most likely a
college professor. This was an odd thing to think because I had not
been around any Korean boy during my high school days in either
Tokyo or Okinawa.

Arriving in Honolulu, I spent a night in a hotel room that
opened onto a balcony overlooking tall palm trees. The scenery reminded me of a Japanese movie about Hawaii that I had seen when
I was in Tokyo. I felt at home in Hawaii because it seemed so like

Okinawa; much to my surprise, I was not afraid of being alone. Because there were so many Asian faces, it did not even seem like part of America.

But my first night on the mainland in a Hyatt hotel room in San Francisco was frightening. I shivered because it was so cold— now I understood what Mark Twain meant when he supposedly said the coldest winter he ever spent was a summer in San Francisco. I also shivered because I was so nervous about being alone in this big foreign city with so many white people. I was so anxious I could not sleep. Tired but unable to sleep, I looked out the huge glass windows at streetlights and thought about home. Finally, I pushed a heavy armchair and all the smaller pieces of furniture against the door. But still I could not sleep. I was thankful when morning came and I could go to the hotel coffee shop and have breakfast.

On an American Airlines jet to Kansas City, Missouri, later that morning, I sat next to a California girl who told me she was also headed for Columbia. She was starting her sophomore year at Stephens College, an exclusive junior college for women. Her only carry-on luggage was a big stuffed dog and a stylish handbag in shocking pink that matched her shocking-pink and black dress and matching black jacket. I thought it odd that a college sophomore would carry a large toy.

Looking out the window, as the plane flew over the vast continent, I thought America seemed endless. Mountains stretched as far as my eyes could see, until the next cloud formation. They were big, rugged ridges, not the small ones I was used to in Japan. I remembered lessons from my geography classes and tried to match them with what I was seeing below. The idea that I was in a place different from anything I had known began to hit me as I looked down, fascinated by the scenery below. I wondered how I would adjust to my new life in America. Since San Francisco, I had begun to feel how being around Americans in Asia was different from being around Americans in their territory. I realized when lunch was served that I was already missing rice. I must have been preoccupied in my own thoughts, for I remember so little of my conversation with my seatmate.

From Kansas City, I switched to a fifteen-seater Ozark airplane that bounced in the turbulent air during the entire journey before arriving at the small airport in Columbia. I shared a taxicab with the Stephens College student and her roommate, who had come to meet her at the airport. They dropped me off at Lathrop Hall, where, with the help of one of them, I found my room, 919 B. The door to the room was wide open, as were other doors along the corridor. A young blonde woman was at a desk in the room when we walked in. Her side of the room was decorated, complete with a sticker from Louisiana State University, where she had completed the first two years.

Joann Upshaw, a soft-spoken daughter of a grocery store owner from Ruston, Louisiana, had mistakenly thought one of my Stephens College companions was to be her roommate. It had never occurred to her that she would be living with an Asian. Joann was a junior and had a beautiful singing voice. After we became better acquainted, she and I would spend many hours singing in harmony our repertoire of popular songs, among which Connie Francis's "My Happiness" and Andy Williams's "Moon River" were our favorites. I was happy to have a songmate right in the same room.

How strange everything felt to me—all these white faces everywhere I turned. As predominant as American influence and power were on Okinawa, it was still Asia, and Asians were the majority. Here I was definitely a minority, and an outsider—by virtue not only of race but of my lack of knowledge about the real America and Americans. Okinawa was an extension of America, but it had been skewed because of the miliary influence. I decided, when in Rome, do as the Romans do—and did. On my first evening in the dorm, I followed my roommate and the other girls from the floor to the Student Union for an early dinner. For some reason all the girls were ordering half a cantaloupe with a scoop of orange sherbet inside it. I thought it was an odd dinner—I could not imagine a meal without a bowl of rice—but since all the others were ordering the cantaloupe, I did the same. Students popped coins into the jukebox, and "Michael Row the Boat Ashore" blared. Someone else put another coin in and now it was "Never on Sunday." Some of my dormitory mates made dancing motions and twisted in their seats.

After that first dinner, my roommate persuaded me to join her and some of her friends who were going out to Woolworth's, where I caught my first whiff of a unique American aroma—the combination of nuts, candies, popcorn, shaving lotion, and perfume. I had never smelled this blend before, but I liked it right away. After Woolworth's we went to Howard Johnson's. Joann had driven her Plymouth all the way from Louisiana by herself. I could not imagine people driving all that distance, but I learned soon enough that Americans thought nothing of driving across the continent.

I had seen a few American high school students on Okinawa who drove their own cars to school, but here almost everyone appeared to own a car. The car was like an extra pair of legs, which they used just to go a few blocks. The parking lot in front of the dormitory was always full. It was unimaginable for Korean and Japanese students to drive cars to school. If they were that rich, they would have been chauffeured.

In my first letter home from Columbia on September 10, 1961, on the morning after my arrival, I told my parents about the high cost of food and the strange American custom of tipping. It really shocked me that an average meal cost $1.50 and that waiters expected to be tipped. I also wrote them about how talkative the girls in the dormitory were, and how relieved I was that my roommate was quiet and reflective, and that we could discuss Ernest Hemingway and Robert and Elizabeth Barrett Browning on my first night on an American university campus.

Sometimes, when I woke up in the morning, I felt as if I were dreaming, because it felt so strange to share a room with a girl with golden hair, white skin, and pink curlers in her hair. It was hard to believe that I was really in America. Everywhere I turned in the dorm, there were white faces, except for two black students who shared a room. Two days after my arrival, I was invited to a reception for foreign students. There, I met another Korean, Florence Lee, who was working on her master's degree in biochemistry. I would learn that thirty-six Korean students were enrolled at the University of Missouri that fall, all of them graduate students, except me. They had been attracted to the school because Missouri was one of the few schools that did not charge tuition for graduate students. Because of the South Korean government's tight control over foreign exchange, only the ones with connections could get money from home.

After spending a big chunk of my childhood and all of my adolescence in Japan, meeting Korean students with strong Korean identities gave me the oddest feeling. On one hand, it provided me with a connection to my ancestral land that had been missing during those formative years. But on the other hand, I knew how different I was from the other Korean students; my mannerisms were a mixture of the influences from my Japanese and American schooling. The Korean students were mostly in their mid to late twenties, while I was still in my late teens, and they seemed rather stiff and serious to me, with well-formed opinions. They all seemed very cynical, which I attributed to their having had to endure the hypocrisy and economic hardships of South Korea. Despite our differences, though, they treated me like a younger sister. They taught me popular Korean songs, jokes, and idioms then in vogue. So, in Missouri, of all places, my Koreanization began. I felt like a little girl relearning Korea from the real teachers. As much as my parents had tried, I knew they had been out of touch from being away for so long. Their feelings and knowledge about Korea had been frozen in their minds, and their value systems fixed in the pre–Korean War era. They had a tendency to look at Korea with nostalgia, remembering the good old days only and sloughing over the bad, as long absences can tend to do to one's heart and mind. Now, I was learning the real thing; these students had no illusions about Korea.

The Korean students mostly lived and kept to themselves. It was just more comfortable that way for them, I think. They could prepare their own food without worrying about the smell of garlic and other Korean spices offending Americans. It was also a way of keeping to a minimum the number of stupid and patronizing questions they were asked by many of the American students. It was hard enough just trying to follow lectures in a foreign language and keeping up with the schoolwork, much less coping with the alienating feeling that they were under a microscope. And, Americans certainly had an annoying habit, from an Asian point of view, of asking questions—all kinds—without thought to whether they might make another person uncomfortable. For Americans, no question was unaskable; everything was up for public discussion. This approach was their tradition and was what gave them a civic culture, but it could be irritating to people who were not used to that. Since these students were the elite of Korea, and they all planned to return home, it did not seem that important for them to become part of mainstream America anyway. The irony, of course, is that because of the series of dictators who ruled Korea, most of the students did not return home to contribute to their country's growth. Rather, they settled in the United States and became American citizens.

Life was especially lonely for male Korean students because there were so few female Korean students, so they dreamed up occasions to get together with them. My first birthday away from home was used as an excuse by a small group of male Korean students to get together with the girls. They threw a party for me in the Tiger Hotel in uptown Columbia. Ostensibly, the gathering was in my honor, but the occasion provided an opportunity for one or two of the fellows who had romantic interests in the other marriage-age female students. I grew up in a home where birthdays and holidays were generally treated as any other day, so I was quite thrilled to be the subject of this commotion. The host had rented a private room for the party, and we were served a fine dinner. I sliced a birthday cake and received a beautiful stuffed white Persian cat, which I carted around with me for many years, until it got lost during a transpacific move. The guys were drinking heavily, and one passed out. I had to be back at the dorm by the 12:30 A.M. curfew. All the partygoers got inside the host's Chevy, and while trying to bypass a car, he hit another car. The people in that car had all been drinking heavily, and one of the passengers in the car had passed out. The incident was written up in the local newspaper. I got grounded for several weekends for arriving after the curfew. I did not sleep much that night after they got me home, because I was worrying about their fate. I would never know the outcome of the case because the fellows would not tell me; they worried that I might feel guilty.

During the Christmas recess when the dormitory closed, I rented a room from a woman named Mrs. Brox, whose modest one-story home had a nice swing on the porch outside my window. Mrs. Brox's second bedroom had been rented by a group of Korean girls who also needed a place to stay during the holidays. Male Korean students gave me a ride to campus every day. One evening, shortly before Christmas, they were taking me home in one of the students' cars, when suddenly I wanted to get out of the crowded Buick: It was snowing, and there was no one on the streets. I had not seen snow like that since I was four or five in Seoul. While the driver moved slowly, we walked behind the car. The snow felt good crunching under my boots, and the cold air invigorated me. Singing "Silver bells, silver bells, it's Christmas time in the city," we walked all the way to Mrs. Brox's house, which must have taken us a good hour. Even today, when I hear that song around Christmas, I remember that night, and Columbia. How odd it must have seemed back then, to see a group of Koreans walking through the streets of Columbia, Missouri, singing gaily in the snow. But for me, it was just another bonding ritual.

I dutifully wrote home every day—even when I did not much feel like it or had little to report—because I considered it akin to a crime not to do so. That was due to my upbringing in a strict Presbyterian Korean home. And when this Presbyterian Calvinistic work ethic was combined with the Confucian fervor for education and achievement, the pressure was very nearly crushing. My father, like so many other people who have grown up in a fervent Christian home, was a quiet believer. As far as I can remember, he was always studying the Bible and reading devotional guides, and there were many books on religion in our home. But he never proselytized. Perhaps he had had his fill from his grandfather, the evangelist who went everywhere to spread the gospel, and who held a daily family prayer service at home. My father did not practice a daily family service, and this made my mother unhappy, for she was a vocal Christian who believed each person had the duty to spread the Good News. Our isolated existence in Okinawa only fed into my mother's religious zeal. A deaconess, she gave a lot of time to church work, volunteering her services and working with American missionaries. My religious life has gone through critical examinations over the years, so that while I consider myself a Christian, I can also say that I am a follower of Buddha and other great teachers who tried to show us a way to enlightenment. I believe a religion is a means to remind us of our potential good when good and evil are struggling for the upper hand. I wish we could know more and, as a result, become more tolerant of people whose beliefs we do not share. But when I was in college, I had been exposed only to Christianity, and I considered it a sin to even think that other religions had any merits.

Similarly, I felt it akin to a crime to waste time. Not that those words were spoken to me—I instinctively felt so. My mantras were: "Study, study, study!" and "Get straight A's." Was there life after good grades? I did not know. But I would remember my father clipping stories from Korean newspapers about students who had earned doctorates, and I would remind myself of the work ahead. One time, he showed me a picture of woman in a cap and gown holding her Ph.D. degree. With a smile on his face, my father said, "This Korean girl got her Ph.D. and she is only 18." I felt sick. There was no way I could get a Ph.D. by 18, no matter how hard I applied myself. I was already 15, and was only a junior in high school. I felt crushed at the thought of not being able to please my parents. My wily father had put his finger over her age to show only the numeral 8, but this I did not know until I grabbed the paper out of his hand and read the story myself and saw that she was not 18 but 28. "She is 28, not 18!" I shouted, in both anger and relief. "If I finish college in three years, and a master's degree in one year, then I can get a Ph.D. by 22 or 23," I told my father. So I studied and studied, not for myself but to live up to what I thought were the expectations of my parents. But what I really wanted to do was read books, write fiction, compose songs and sing them, and paint pictures. I wanted to become a Korean Patti Page or Edith Piaf. Even today, Korean newspapers routinely run stories about Koreans who have received doctorates. Whenever I look at those items, I want to pick up the phone and tell the editors of those newspapers to stop because they are unknowingly exerting pressures on young lives.

Throughout my high school years, I could not wait to get away from home—from all the strictures that made so little sense to me but that deep down I felt compelled to obey. This feeling continued even in Missouri. It was as if I had two religions: Christianity and Family Duty. It would take me years to peel away the layers to isolate this thing called Koreanness, in which the Confucian emphasis on duty to one's family comes before one's duty to oneself—in itself both a blessing and a curse. Part of my Koreanness was the duty to the family, the duty to bring honor to it. But the other part of it was going beyond my own Korean family to the conglomerate of Korean families and finding a connection, based on our ethos. The latter had been undeveloped while I lived in alien cultures. In Missouri, this part of my Koreanness was finally awakened and became validated in the company of these three dozen Korean students. That was immensely satisfying to me. I felt like I was onto something very important—discovering my identity and where I fit. This would sustain me.

The disruptions of my childhood—the memories of the refugee days after my family fled North Korea, the Korean War, our illegal entry into Japan, and the subsequent confinement and freedom—had cultivated in me a craving for stability and perhaps, as I was beginning to realize amongst these Koreans in Columbia, identity. But I got little of that at home from my parents, who, like other Koreans of their generation, were too numb from the turbulence they themselves had lived through to pay close attention to concepts as luxurious as their child's sense of stability and psychological comfort. For them, having enough food and a place to live was the standard, and everything else was extra. Only, I longed for more. In Tokyo, my family was always moving; between 1952 and 1954, I attended four different schools—a Korean one, a Japanese one, and two American ones. While we were in Japan, it was Japan itself—its aesthetics, mannerisms, language, and arts—that I could latch onto. But while the Japanese were attractive to me because they appeared to be so polite and accommodating, they also seemed superficial. Their constant bowing and gestures of gratitude over even a small gift, while charming on the surface, seemed basically artificial. Yet, the culture had an immense appeal to me, and I wanted to blend in and belong to it. When neighborhood children wore bright kimonos on New Year's Day, I, too, wanted to wear a kimono. I never dared to mention this to my parents, though. So I played *hagoita,* the traditional New Year's Day game in Japan, in my regular clothes while others wore their holiday apparel.

Embracing Japanese and American cultures, one after another, during my formative years left me feeling unsatisfied and uneasy—culturally adrift. And perhaps that explains why I responded as I did to the Korean graduate students, all of whom were older and possessed what appeared to me like a Made-in-Korea mark stamped on them. Their company, in the right doses, fed my soul. Had I not established this bonding with Koreans in my late teens while at college, I, too, might have gone the way of my Korean friends from Tokyo and the international schools, who today feel no deep connection to Korea or Koreanness.

I learned another aspect of Koreanness while in Missouri: the prevailing conditions for matrimony, which involved careful calculation far more than mere romantic attraction. Schools, hometown, family background, and social and financial status all were considered necessary ingredients in any romantic arrangement. The marriage equation would become so callous that by the 1980s, "three keys" for the bridegroom would become a popular phrase in Korean lexicon. To secure a promising doctor or lawyer for a husband, the potential bride's family has to provide three keys—"a key to a condo, a key to a new car, and a key to an office," people said. Since a doctor or a lawyer is a good catch, he can attract a woman whose family is wealthy. With those three keys a young man is ready to set up a medical or a legal practice and get busy on his career. He would have a leg up on his classmates. I finally understood the application of the old Korean saying "If you marry off four daughters, you can sleep without locking your gates": there is nothing left in the house for a thief to steal.

On some weekends, my Korean friends and I would drive one hundred miles to St. Louis or Kansas City to a Chinese grocery to stock up on bean sprouts and bean cakes, which supermarkets in Columbia did not carry. Despite their mothers' prohibitions against men entering the kitchen, some of the male students out of necessity became accomplished cooks. I had some of the tastiest meals of my years in Columbia in the roach-infested basement kitchens of these Korean men. I remember one in particular prepared by a graduate student who came from a well-to-do family. He and his roommate invited the three Korean women at Missouri and another at Stephens College, and served us an impressive array of Korean and Chinese dishes, including sweet-and-sour pork. I was impressed especially because of the traditional restriction against men cooking. Yet these men not only prepared their own meals but they invited women to share the meals with them. Things were certainly different in America. Or, America certainly made people change.

As was the case at other university campuses in the 1960s, male Korean students at Missouri outnumbered female ones. There were three women, including myself, and twenty-six men. Whenever a new female Korean student arrived, the word spread to colleges and universities in the area and in neighboring states. Male students drove hundreds of miles sometimes just to see a new face at a social gathering. In order to prevent any false rumors from starting, we girls were careful not to go out on a single date, and instead went to dinner or movies in groups. I still think of those poor fellows on limited budgets who took the three of us out every time they wanted to invite just one of us.

Since most of the male students were in their mid to late twenties, spouse hunting for them was a major preoccupation. Because of the shortage of female Korean students, some dated Americans and eventually even married non-Koreans, much to the disappointment of their families back home. One man told me why he had married an American woman: "Korean girls were all so stuck up because there were so few of them. So many girls also came from rich homes and didn't even deign to look at poor guys like me." Another told his graduate advisor he had to go home because his mother was ill, but actually he went to Korea to get married. His new wife joined him a few months later.

Because of the South Korean government's strict policy on foreign exchange, most Korean students struggled to maintain scholarships and to secure part-time employment. During the summer break, they all went away to big cities and resorts to work in restaurants and bars to earn enough money to see them through the year. Many also worked in libraries or dormitory kitchens, or mowed lawns. I was one of the few who received money from home and did not have to work. My father said no child of his would do menial work or be the recipient of a scholarship. "You devote all your time to your studies," he said. "That way you stand proud and tall." I felt guilty thinking of my father working so hard to put me through school.

On Sundays I would go to the First Presbyterian Church, where I sang in the choir, and afterward would go to one of my Korean friends' apartments for lunch. Reading my diary entries from this time, one would wonder if I had ever had even a moment of fun— even Sunday afternoons were marred by my feeling guilty about not studying. I seemed always to be berating myself for visiting with friends and spending a Sunday afternoon talking. If I were to attend a dance on a Saturday evening, I would be up at 5:00 A.M. that morning to study.

During my first spring semester, during what is called tornado weather in the Midwest, I encountered a strange American college custom. One night, I was awakened from a sound sleep by a commotion. A throng of male students were outside, nine stories below our windows, demanding women's underwear. "It's a panty raid!" my roommate said. "A panty raid?" I repeated after her. I had never heard of any such thing. Soon, I saw girls in the dormitory excitedly throwing their lingerie out the window. Perplexed, I did not participate in this strange American college spring ritual, but I observed the scene with fascination. A raid to capture panties? Was it a substitute for intimate contact? Freedom of expression in America was without limits, I thought to myself, as I tried to return to sleep several hours later. In the dark, the boys had not caught all the panties. On my way to the cafeteria for breakfast in the morning, I saw a few lying on the ground, looking forlorn and unwanted.

The Korean Students Association, to which not only the students but all Korean residents of Columbia belonged, sponsored social events, including an annual picnic at Cosmo Park. The single men and married students brought marinated beef for barbecue and sufficient supplies of rice, kimchi, and other items to keep us feeling full until the next day. We always finished social events by taking turns singing a song—a time-honored end to just about any gathering of Koreans. We sang about home, mother, and love—the most popular subjects for Korean songs. We sponsored a Korean Night of Korean songs and dances, and a traditional wedding ceremony. (This kind of tradition has continued so that even in the 1990s, foreign and ethnic student groups stick together, despite repeated efforts by university administrators to encourage broader mingling.)

Feeling the Long Arm of a Dictator

Though they were physically in the United States, it was Korea that was on the students' minds. Whether they read the *Columbia Missou-*

rian, the local newspaper, or the *St. Louis Post-Dispatch* or the *New York Times*, their eyes always turned to news about home. American newspapers hardly carried anything about Korea, and radio and television even less. Some students subscribed to Korean newspapers, and others went to the journalism school library, which received complimentary newspapers from around the world, to catch up on Korean news.

This was a period in South Korea when General Chung-Hee Park and the military were in tight control. Park had assumed power in a coup in May 1961, after overthrowing the democratic but ineffective government of Myon Chang, which had succeeded that of Syngman Rhee. During the ten months Chang was in office, South Koreans experienced their first taste of unhindered freedom. South Korean students, who had been instrumental in bringing in a new government, abused the freedom with protests of one sort or another nearly every day, making all sorts of demands on the fledgling government. The chaotic situation gave an opening for the military coup. The result was eighteen dreadfully long years of Park's rule, some of which I would later personally experience. What did Koreans do to deserve a dictator even worse than Rhee? Sometimes I thought we must be a cursed people. Park imprisoned dissenters, including opposing politicians, intellectuals, and journalists. It was the height of irony that Park, who had served in the Japanese Imperial Army and had been a key figure in the Communist-led Yosu-Sunchon rebellion against the South Korean government in 1949, would label people who opposed him as "Communists" and lock them up. Park changed the constitution to give himself lifetime rule. By the time his own intelligence director assassinated him during a drinking party in 1979, South Korea had been transformed into a country where materialism, the military culture, and power mattered most and traditional Confucian values mattered little.

All of us in America were aware of the long arms and ears of Park's regime while he was in power. We were careful not to criticize the government. South Korean officials, after all, could revoke our passports at their whim. The tradition, which had begun with

Rhee, became complete under Park. The Korean American poet Ko Won, who now lives in Los Angeles, told me he became a U.S. citizen because of Park: "That small man changed the course of my life. He is the reason why I did not return home after I received my doctorate."

☯

The School of Journalism attracted people from throughout the United States and the world, which gave the place an international flavor, otherwise lacking in Columbia, Missouri. I found theoretical classes such as ones on ethics, the principles of journalism, and the law of the press relatively easy; but instruction in the practical aspects of journalism, for which the school was known, was difficult for me. At the *Columbia Missourian*, a daily newspaper where all journalism students were required to work, I learned about bounties on coyote ears, property assessments, submissions of low bids for city and county projects, and probate court. I became acquainted with county judges who tried to be helpful to a foreign student, who must have appeared to them rather overwhelmed, as I tried reporting the doings of American city and county governments. During my reporting classes, I ventured to the other side of the railroad tracks where blacks lived, to interview a minister who had returned from Selma, Alabama, after participating in the civil rights demonstrations there with the Reverend Martin Luther King, Jr. Having never been to that side of town, I was apprehensive. I asked my friend Florence to go with me. The interview went very well, and I was excited to write the story up. Thereafter, I made trips to that part of town without any hesitation to interview many other people for stories. I got a dose of democracy in operation when I attended raucous city council and school board meetings that ran into the wee hours of the morning. These were eye-opening experiences for a young Korean woman, and they provided my first clues to what a career in American journalism might entail.

After completing my bachelor's degree, I went home to spend the summer of 1963 in Okinawa with my parents and brother, before starting graduate studies at Northwestern University's Medill School of Journalism. On my way home, I stopped in Tokyo briefly and saw Mrs. Rhee and Chihe again. At Naha Airport, many of the people who had seen me off two years earlier were there to welcome me home. The most noticeable change was in my brother, who had grown quite a bit and was now a third-grader. My parents looked much the same, and they treated me just the way they had treated me before I had gone off to America. After living away for almost two years, without anyone telling me what to do, their orders and meddling grated on me at times. Otherwise, it was life as usual, and I was being a dutiful daughter and a good sister.

I worked mornings at a summer activities center on one of the bases, where I took children swimming. In the afternoons I helped around the house and studied. When the initial happiness of being home wore off, the old feelings of being confined on an island and being under the watchful eyes of my parents started to irritate me. By the middle of the summer vacation, I was quite anxious to get back to the United States, be on my own again, and set my own schedule.

To economize, I took a propeller plane back to the States; it took me almost two days to get to Chicago from Okinawa. Only four Koreans—all graduate students—were at Northwestern that fall. There was no formal grouping, and I saw only two other female Korean students regularly. Medill had a reputation as a top journalism school, but I also had had romantic notions about Northwestern ever since I had read about the school in a famous Korean novel, *Sunaebo*, during my teens. I rented a room in a big house where thirteen other women lived, most of whom were working on their master's or doctoral degrees. There were two Anglos, two American Jews, one German, one French, one African from Sierra Leone, two Armenians, two Koreans, and two Cuban refugees, a mother and daughter, who were the only two not affiliated with the university. Mealtime created quite a mixture of aromas.

The most exciting thing about my one-year master's degree

program at Northwestern was practice reporting, akin to interning, in Chicago with established newspaper reporters. I got to see Mayor Richard Daley and a host of other Chicago politicians in action. I covered events and wrote about them, and later compared my stories to those written by real reporters at the *Chicago Tribune*, *Chicago Sun-Times*, *Chicago Daily News* and *Chicago's American*.

I got to know a group of reporters in the State Building press room who were very cordial and helpful. One of them, Fletcher Wilson, and his wife invited me to their home for Christmas dinner, and a reporter named Robert Hawkins wrote a story about me, "Two Worlds Unite for a Korean Girl." I sent a copy of the story to my parents in Okinawa, and they were pleased. Another reporter, Paul West, talked the head of the welfare department, Raymond Hilliard, into giving me an interview. This impressed my professor tremendously, since Hilliard was one of the busiest officials in Chicago at the time. During our Reporting Public Affairs class, which was conducted by Charles E. Barnum, who later became the executive editor of the *Quincy Herald-Whig* in Illinois, I got to meet more public officials. One of my more memorable classes was with Curtis MacDougall, the author of *Interpretive Reporting*, a textbook widely used in journalism schools, and an inspiring man. His lectures were extraordinary—more philosophy than journalism. The school brought in many well-known figures in journalism, including top editors and publishers with major news organizations. When there were important newspaper business events in Chicago, we were invited. It was at one of these editors and publishers' conferences that I met Al Neuharth, who later became the chairman of the Gannett newspapers, but who was then the general manager of the chain's flagship papers in its headquarters in Rochester, New York. He told me to contact him when I was close to finishing my studies. I had spoken with other newspaper executives, too, on that day. But Neuharth made an impression, so I made a note of that. The master's program at Medill was highly instructive, but grueling, and I was glad when it was over.

The program taught me that journalism is much more than stringing words together—it is being the public's eyes and ears. Along with the freedom of the press, there was also a heavy burden of social responsibility. I learned that journalism is physically and mentally demanding work, that remunerations are low, and that journalists who last must love the work. I liked it, and maybe even would love it.

I wrote Neuharth about two and half months before graduation and, to my delight, received a prompt response. He was interested in discussing possible employment with me. Soon thereafter, I received a letter from Norris "Red" Vagg, the managing editor of the morning paper *Democrat and Chronicle*, inviting me to fly to Rochester for an interview, and telling me to book myself first class. I could not believe my eyes. I reread the letter just to make sure, then ran a flight of stairs down to one of my housemates, Marleen Norman, and broke the news. Marleen, a theater major from Louisiana who remains a good friend to this day, gave me a big hug and congratulated me. That evening, we ordered out for pizza, bought a bottle of Chianti, and lit a candle to celebrate in our spooky basement kitchen, where the hip landlady, Ruth, had painted red handprints on a white brick wall. On the following day after class, I splurged and bought for the job interview a new black outfit with a white and black polka-dot blouse and a black and white hat at Bramson's, one of the more expensive stores in Evanston. Once I reached Rochester, the *Democrat and Chronicle*'s managing editor interviewed me, as did other executives, and then took me over to Neuharth's office. Soon thereafter, I was offered a job—at ninety-nine dollars a week. I was thrilled, and I promptly wrote home.

The next few weeks were very difficult. I had so many papers and assignments to complete, but my mind was spinning dreams of my first paying job as a newspaperwoman. My friend from Missouri, Florence Lee, came to my graduation all the way from Texas, where she was working on her doctorate, and acted like a surrogate mother, getting me to pose in many different ways for her camera. Unlike my bachelor's cap and gown, my master's outfit had a red velvet hood that I put around my neck, and it made me feel special. And, I had gotten a master's degree on schedule. Then, with Florence's help, I packed my books and clothes and flew to Rochester where I lived at the YWCA while looking for an apartment. The idea of living at the Y had been suggested to me by a woman from Rochester whom I had met on my flight there.

In the summer of 1964, I did not know of a single Korean working for a metropolitan newspaper in the United States. Koreans in America did not even think of going into journalism, which they had concluded was too exclusively a white man's profession. Later I would learn that I was not the first Korean to work in American journalism. A man named K. W. Lee, who was later to become a good friend and mentor, began his career in 1956 in Tennessee. From there he had moved to the *Charleston Gazette* in West Virginia, where he wrote stories that would lead to the integration of restaurants and hotels years before the 1964 Civil Rights Act was passed.

I considered myself very fortunate because I knew that a number of my classmates had not found work by the time of their graduation. Furthermore, the fact that I would be making a living as a newspaperwoman in my nonnative tongue gave me an added sense of satisfaction. But I was nervous, too—not only because English was not my first language but also because there were so many things about American life that I did not know. I resolved that I would work hard and learn, would prove that Koreans deserved to be— and could be—American journalists, and would be a good example for other Koreans.

I started work on June 22, 1964. It was the year the Gannett newspapers had won a Pulitzer Prize for a series on race relations called "Road to Integration." Spirits were high in the Rochester newsroom. As one of four writers in the Women's Department, I did my share of "brides"—write-ups of engagements and weddings— and spent the rest of the time writing feature stories. I wrote a story a day about everything from the local reaction to the Vietnam War to fortune-telling and interviews with visiting dignitaries. I put one copy of each in my scrapbook and sent one to my parents on Okinawa. My youth and foreign background elicited a great deal of attention and caring from my older colleagues, who extended innumerable invitations to dinner at their homes. I was exceptionally fortunate to be in such a nurturing environment in my first real journalism job.

After living almost three months at the YWCA, I rented a studio apartment in an old brick mansion called the Churchill Home at 249 Plymouth Avenue South that had been converted into apartments. It had a Pullman kitchen in the hallway with a tiny refrigerator, a small shower next to it, and a living room that doubled as a bedroom. It had been a drawing room in its better days, so the ceiling had a chandelier, and there was a beautiful mirror over a marble fireplace. This was my first residence as a working stiff. I was on my own, in a strange town, and I missed my old friends from Missouri and Northwestern. The house was in the heart of the Third Ward, an almost all-black inner-city neighborhood, and the scene of the first northern riots in June 1964. I was the only Asian in the neighborhood. When I went to the neighborhood laundromat, small black children stared at me. To those in the neighborhood, I became a "Chinese" along with the owner of Lin Far, then the only Chinese restaurant in downtown Rochester. I would have preferred to have been known as Korean, rather than Chinese, but I knew it was a losing battle to try to differentiate Chinese from Koreans or Japanese for Americans of that era. It was easier to be "Chinese" than to explain what I really was, which would have only invited other questions, like, "Where's Korea? What's Korea?" I had dealt with that plenty in the Midwest.

Rochester was the headquarters of the Gannett newspapers, so our offices were first class, or so it seemed to me. And since the Gannett newspapers were doing very well financially, there was never a problem taking taxis to assignments, which helped me especially because I did not drive.

I became hooked not only on journalism but on America. From doing interviews with the composer Howard Hanson to writing about the elderly fighting loneliness through dancing classes, from writing about teen pregnancies and about the Vietnam War, I gained a sense of America that I could not have had as a student. And, deep inside, I wanted to stay and continue what I was doing, but the idea of getting a doctorate gnawed at me. The subject came up from time to time in letters from home. A mere mention was enough to remind me that I was not free, yet. So I prepared to return to graduate school. Also, under the Immigration and Naturalization Services rules, a foreign student could work for eighteen months on what was then called practical training. After that, a student would have to get his or her employer to petition for a permanent stay. With my history of unfortunate experiences with South Korean bureaucrats, I was not sure whether I wanted to face American bureaucracy. Would it be any better? I was not sure. After debating, I decided that I should not get off the track. Getting a good education was paramount in my family ethos, and I should not stray from it, I decided.

☯

My colleagues gave me a farewell dinner at a fancy restaurant in Greece, a Rochester suburb, and a brooch of gold wishbone with a diamond on top. After storing my only piece of furniture, a foldaway bed, in newspaper colleague Kay Fish's attic and shipping twenty small boxes of worldly possessions to a friend in Columbia, I went home to Okinawa at the end of July that year. My parents were overjoyed to see me. By now my brother was in the sixth grade and was busy playing baseball, in an Orioles uniform. Except for my brother, Okinawa seemed to have remained just as I had left it. And, my parents continued to give unsolicited advice, despite the fact that I had been a working newspaperwoman for a whole year. After a month, I returned to Columbia, Missouri, to start graduate school.

I had been there only a few weeks when I had second thoughts about pursuing doctoral work. The rhythms of school seemed so slow and dull compared to those of the newspaper office, where every day we put out a new product. I did not like being back in

Missouri or at the school. The tedium of the academic work, especially in journalism, literally made me sick. So I did not pursue my studies and left in midcourse after failing a Ph.D. qualifying exam, instead of persisting like some would have. In the end, I simply could not motivate myself to do this for my parents, however much a doctoral degree might have meant to them, especially after I had tasted the excitement of daily journalism.

I had also fallen in love, and romance seemed far more important to me then than pursuing a degree. I had met a man, I'll call David, in a political science class. He was sharp and seemed to have a great deal of interest in Asian history. The attraction must have been mutual, because he asked me out soon after we had met. As we talked over coffee in the Student Union, I learned that he had been interested in Asia since he was a teenager and that he planned to specialize in Chinese studies. During both my undergraduate and graduate years before this, I had dated a number of Koreans rather casually, but none of the relationships amounted to much. With David, an American boy from St. Louis, something clicked right away. Through our months of courtship, I came to realize how American I had become. I found appealing the little things that Western men do, such as opening doors for women, and their sense of humor. By comparison, Korean men seemed so stiff and uncommunicative. And, when he proposed one evening after we had gone to see *Dr. Zhivago*, I said yes. I did not mention David in my letters home, however, but I had fully intended to tell my parents that I was engaged to be married when I returned home for the summer. When I got there and told my parents about what I planned to do, they exploded. Their reaction was no different from that of all the other Korean parents who disapproved of interracial and interethnic marriages. My mother was furious. "Did we send you to America and lavish our attention and hard-earned money on you so you can stop your studies midcourse and marry an American boy!" she fumed. My father did not use those words, but he was equally upset.

I had mistakenly thought that my parents, especially my father, would be more open-minded, since he espoused a liberal view about many things. But I realized that the Korean psyche prevented liberal ideas from going too far when it came to such close-to-home things as interracial marriage. Little did I know then the depth of conflict I would have with my parents or the Korean culture, or the hold my parents and culture together would have on me. Buckling under the pressure, I broke off the engagement and did not return to the United States that fall. Instead, I went to Korea to work.

8. GOING HOME

(1967–1970)

Squeezed between city and civilization,
We are a shattered people
That seek happiness bit by bit.

I ask my heart to put out its fire.
I spend many a night, hollow and vigilant.
Waiting does not tire me;
A promise is too precious to miss.
When the fallen leaves glow
In the bright autumn sun
We tell our old tales
On a street corner.
In the boiling hot summer
We endure good-humouredly
The long painful days.

—Byung-Hwa Cho★ (1920–), *Koreana*

★Translated by Peter Hyun

Rediscovering My People

It felt good to be among my own kind. I had not realized the extent of psychological comfort I drew from being part of the majority— among people who looked like me and shared a common history. There was no need now to explain things Korean to anyone. Hearing Korean spoken all around me, I wondered how I could have lived for so long without hearing it spoken. Korean sounded like music to my ears. People sprinkled their speech with a rich array of adjectives and adverbs, and the cadences of spoken Korean made everything I heard sound like poetry. Little things made all the difference, such as being able to eat Korean food at any time of the day without worrying about its pungent smell. And its aroma—ample garlic, onion, hot pepper, sesame seed oil, and soy sauce—added spices to my senses, which had for too long tolerated the unpleasant odor of cheese, milk, and ham. To be able to walk into any restaurant on the street and ask for a favorite Korean dish was a pleasure so new that at times I felt like a child in a garlicky Disneyland. My sense of belonging—a simple yet soulfully satisfying feeling—derived from these little things. My first few days in Seoul were truly exhilarating.

On the first morning after my return, I felt a lump in my throat when I heard a group of elementary school children walking to school in an alley singing songs I had learned as a four-year-old. They looked so secure in their surroundings; I envied them. How deprived and lonely my childhood had been, growing up among non-Koreans, I thought, as I watched the little ones in the yellow uniform of a private school disappear when they turned a corner. And later that day, when I heard the "crack, crack, crack" of a taffy man's scissors, I dashed outside and bought some candy as if to relive my truncated childhood. The taffy man wrapped the indigenous candy sticks coated with roasted sesame seeds called *yot* in an envelope made of newspaper. So little had changed, after all, I thought in that moment. A combination of nostalgia and the sense of rediscovering my native land was captivating; I felt giddy.

Fifteen years had elapsed since I was last in Korea. I had gone from a nine-year-old to a twenty-four-year-old newspaperwoman in those years. Koreans have a saying: In ten years everything changes— even the rivers and mountains. Indeed, much had. My odyssey had given me two other worlds in addition to my own, a formal education, a profession, and a taste of love. Perhaps, most importantly for the decisions I would make later, I had deeply experienced the cumulative weight of Korean culture, which seemed more powerful than love, or personal or professional aspirations. Having rebuilt from the ravages of the war, Korea had moved along and was striving to become a technologically advanced nation. Though it was still a poor country, and people envied those with American connections, a will to modernize permeated the air. In a way, both Korea and I were in transition. My father's high school classmate Hong-Soo Lee was a top man at the Ministry of Culture and Information, and one letter from my father to him had opened the door for me. It was my fate to return to Korea that fall.

Then I got my first dose of reality when I reported to work at my new job in the capital, three days after my arrival in Seoul. I had a fancy title: chief of the Asian Broadcasting Union's (ABU) Seoul office. I quickly learned that there was another, less rosy, dimension to being back home. Each encounter with a new person I met that day only enhanced the realization that despite our shared race and ethnicity, I was different. Here, among people from whom I had long been absent, the euphoria was quickly replaced with questioning and ambivalence. On one level I belonged, but on another level I did not. I wondered how I could put up with the dark-suited Korean male bureaucrats, whose stiff ways, chauvinistic mannerisms, ever-present cigarettes, and shiny, oiled black hair were so unappealing to me. I was missing America already.

The day had begun with the driver of the taxi I took to work telling me, "You look like someone who's had a lot of foreign water to drink"—meaning I did not look indigenous—and had ended with a middle-level government official telling me, "At a time when everybody is trying to get away from this awful place, why did you come back?" I began to doubt if having a Korean face—the wonderful feeling I had of blending in—was enough to slip back into Korean society. A prodigal daughter, I had learned in only one day, I was not.

I spent the first work day visiting different offices to present myself to high- and middle-level officials, most of whom turned out to be insufferable male chauvinists. As I went from office to office, accompanied by a superior who made sure he walked a respectable Korean male step ahead of me, I felt like I was watching someone else's day unfold. Everything seemed so unreal. As if playing their roles from an identical script, the men bowed and paid perfunctory respects in phrases punctuated with honorifics. Gestures and words appeared so exaggerated to me. And always there was an obligatory cup of instant coffee, which I was expected to drink, that had been prepared by a secretary who occupied a desk in the reception area and screened visitors to a ranking bureaucrat's office. The coffee was much too sweet, but Koreans liked their coffee with plenty of sugar. Sugar was considered a precious commodity. The bureaucrat's secretary was a combination receptionist and housekeeper. She kept an assortment of coffee cups, a jar of Nescafé, and a tea kettle on a small table by her desk, in an otherwise uninviting atmosphere of dull-gray metal filing cabinets and functional government office furniture of well-worn, dark-blue velvet. It was her job to answer the telephone, prepare coffee for her boss's visitors, and run errands. Although they were college graduates, secretaries were treated not much better than waitresses by their bosses, who spoke to them in a condescending and familiar way. I detected no resentment from the women, who at any rate would leave their jobs as soon as their families found the right suitors for them to marry.

I realized in my reaction to all this how Westernized I had become, for this was very much an accepted practice. The worst was yet to come. Women and men shared common lavatories in the showcase government office building. What that meant was that I, like other women in the building, had to pass by men, often colleagues and superiors, standing at urinals before I reached an enclosed squatting toilet beyond the urinals. After my experience in America, I thought the setup primitive and outrageous. What made things even worse was the way Korean males behaved. Truly unaware, some brazenly buttoned their flies as they walked out of the lavatory into the corridor. Regular residents of the lavatories included a couple of shoe-shine boys in their early teens, who had staked out a corner for themselves. Every morning they made their rounds collecting shoes, took them to their corner in the lavatories, cleaned and shined them, and brought them back. Since Korean office workers kept a pair of rubber slippers under their desks and wore them while working, the shoe-shine boys had plenty of time to take care of all the shoes. This was no doubt a mutually beneficial arrangement for the boys who earned their living at it and for the officials who could have their shoes shined without so much as getting up from their desks. How the boys kept track of the hundreds of pairs of similar-looking black shoes all the bureaucrats wore, I will never know.

My assignment supposedly entailed coordinating broadcast activities with other Asian countries and travel abroad, but I did not receive a single call from outside the country while I worked there, and I had no occasion to travel. Despite my title, there was no separate office for the ABU. I worked out of a large office that I shared with at least ten other bureaucrats. Our desks were laid out in a big U shape with workers seated with their backs against the walls and facing each other. At the center bottom of the U sat the highest-ranking man in the room, whose title was assistant section chief. His desk alone was detached, and his swivel chair was bigger and taller than the other chairs in the room, in a conspicuous display of his rank. From his vantage point, the man surveyed the room like a landlord checking on his tenant farmers, with his narrow eyes made narrower from squinting through the smoke from his ever-present cigarette. He hardly worked. From time to time he looked at a few documents and put his seal on them, and the rest of the time he sat in his chair reading newspapers. A work ethic was nonexistent in the South Korean government. It was all too common for bureaucrats to slip out to a bathhouse or get a haircut during the midafternoon. I was astonished to see some, their heads buried under newspapers, taking late-afternoon naps in their seats. I simply could not get over how little they actually worked. Everyone, from the secretaries to high-ranking officials, mixed work with play. They took long lunches and went to barbershops, beauty parlors, bathhouses, and tearooms during working hours. It was a way of life; there was no clear delineation between their personal and professional lives. One's colleagues and superiors became part of one's social circle, in a hierarchal way. Weddings, funerals, and a colleague's son's first birthday were office business, too, so attending funerals and weddings during office hours was an accepted practice. After work, all the men went out together to drink before heading home. Going out for a drink meant more than that—it also entailed eating out. It was such a contrast from my first work experience in America. There, most people went home after work. If they went out for a drink, it was literally that—a drink or two, and then they were off to their families. Those who hung around bars after work all night were either singles or alcoholics.

I sat next to a personable young man named Yong Yoon, who was not a typical bureaucrat. He was preparing to leave for graduate studies in the United States, and he studied English diligently during every spare minute he had. He often read aloud the front pages of English-language newspapers published in Seoul and consulted me about the correct pronunciation of English words. I spent my spare time studying Korean newspapers to improve my Korean. He answered my questions about Korea, and I told him about America. Considering the small salary we received, the equivalent of about $40 a month, I should not have felt guilty about not working all the time. But even here, my Christian work ethic influenced me, giving me no respite. When there was work to be done, it came in bunches and always at the last minute. Once I received a twenty-five-page radio script, which I was asked to translate into English as soon as possible. "To do this right, we need to spend at least a day or two," I said, to which my superior responded, "But we don't have a whole day to spend on it. We're entering it in a contest, and we need to mail it tomorrow." This was typical. Doing everything at the last minute seemed to be standard operating procedure.

I had been in Korea barely two weeks when I received a call from Kyoo-Hyun Lee, the managing editor of the *Korea Times*. "A fish has to return to its water," said Lee, teasing me about my job with the government. Lee said he was about to take a job with another newspaper, but he had made arrangements with his successor, Soon-Il Hong, to invite me to work at the *Korea Times*. Two weeks later, after completing a month as a government drudge, I moved across the street to work as a reporter for the *Korea Times*, one of the two English-language dailies in Seoul and a paper read by the capital city's international community and Korean intellectuals. The second English paper, the *Korea Herald*, was run by the government.

It was October and autumn was in full array. Koreans love autumn because we are romantics and fatalists. The autumn of 1967 was certainly the most beautiful in my memory, the best season in Korea, and everything that poets and writers said it was. The Korean skies were so blue and cloudless that they seemed to stretch infinitely to another world. Even the colors of the turning leaves appeared deeper and more beautiful in Korea than in Japan or the American Midwest. Ripening persimmons dangled from my neighbors' trees. Pears, apples, and grapes were so sweet that they felt like they were melting in my mouth. New-crop Korean rice hit the market, as it does every autumn, and it tasted good, too. I ate not one but two bowls of rice even at lunch. By changing jobs, I now earned a good salary by Korean standards—about $100 a month. Since I had a room in my parents' Seoul home—they had bought the house on an impulse during one of their earlier visits to Seoul, and it was being used by caretakers—I paid no rent.

Returning to journalism felt like escaping from a stranded island to civilization. It was fun rediscovering Seoul, whose population had more than tripled to five million during my absence. Yet, Seoul felt like a small town where everyone knew everyone else. Personal relations drove the wheels of Korean society. My family's connections were helpful, even though my parents still lived in Okinawa, and people referred to me as so-and-so's daughter. So many people seemed to know about my family. And, numerous ranking people in government and academia had been my father's classmates from school, former students, or colleagues. Knowing people meant everything at work, too. Mention a few names, and the Korean entanglement emerged to pull you in all directions. Similarly, because of my family connections, friends of the family imposed on me, too. Whenever people needed to write letters or fill out documents in English, my services were sought. I was everybody's English interpreter-translator. And, requests for my services typically came at the last minute. I had to juggle my own schedule to accommodate them, for it would have been a breach of Korean etiquette not to comply. I had to do this to save face for my father. It was a two-edged sword of obligations of favors given and favors to be returned at a later, appropriate time. Nothing came free in this Korean web of obligation.

Becoming a member of the *Korea Times* staff was like joining a big family. I was astonished by the lax atmosphere and the interest shown by staffers in each other's personal predicaments. Everybody minded everybody else's business, and I had mixed feelings about this. It felt good to belong to the big family, but I did not always appreciate unsolicited advice and remarks that freely came my way. When work had to be done, we all pitched in, even when the task was unpleasant. One Saturday evening, the entire *Korea Times* editorial staff was asked to stay late to black out a story about North Korea that had been inserted into *Asia Magazine*, a Sunday supplement for English-language newspapers in Asia. It was against South Korea's national security laws to disseminate information about its archenemy. Articles about North Korea or Communism under these draconian laws were banned because South Korea's authoritarian rulers wanted to block out any information about North Korea to sustain their propaganda campaign, which portrayed Il-Sung Kim and his men as demons without any redeeming qualities. South Koreans caught with books on Communism were hauled in for interrogation by the feared

Korean Central Intelligence Agency (KCIA) and punished. So we sat hunched at our desks, blackening out the story and accompanying pictures. We probably all were cursing our miserable fate of living in a divided country. No one said anything; we simply kept marking the pages with black ink. I saw a colleague named Seung-Hyon Kim looking especially glum at his desk. He was a smart and courageous man who overcame the obstacle of his less than four-foot height to enter the nation's most prestigious university and then become a journalist. Finally, unable to stomach the task anymore, Kim stood up from his desk and walked out of the room. Nobody said a word or tried to stop him as we watched his small figure exit, silent but loud in his personal statement.

Marriage was a preoccupation of the staff, who were mostly in their twenties and thirties. Nothing is more important to Koreans than marriage, since marriage is seen not just as a union of a man and a woman but as an alliance of families and clans. An elaborate send-off for the dead was also a social event, because a lavish funeral reflected on the living. Families went into debt because of weddings and funerals. I realized extravagance was a necessary ingredient of Korean life, but I had not been brought up to think that way. My parents had shunned ancestor worship, which they equated with idolatry because of their Christian beliefs, and they had never emphasized traditional marriage or funeral practices to me when I was growing up. Living in Japan and Okinawa had further deprived me of this part of being Korean; we were not a typical Korean family. Thus, much of this came across to me as excessive. With their obsession about marriage, some people at the newspaper thought that I had returned to Korea to find a husband. I was twenty-four and, of course, by Korean standards, was prime marriage age. I told no one about the complicated play of circumstances that had led to my homecoming, and I was amused whenever they discussed my marriage prospects.

Since everybody knew and conformed to the rules, people's behavior was predictable. Everybody understood about these social obligations, which had to fit into the work-a-day schedule; nothing was said about them. It did not take long for me to get used to these social rhythms and enjoy the pace. I, too, went to take a bath or ran errands during office hours, as did my colleagues. Occasionally, So-Yong Kim, the other female reporter, and I visited the fashionable Myong-dong, the Fifth Avenue of Seoul, to do window shopping. We would return to the office just before 7:00 P.M., when the first edition came out, to make sure our stories contained no mistakes.

Korean newspapers, both vernacular and English-language ones, had only four pages and almost no advertising. Stories had to be short and to the point. I wrote four or five fairly short stories a week. Since there was no such thing as a fairness doctrine in Korean journalism, news gathering took a lot less time. News stories often read like editorials or essays. Giving both sides to a story was rare. I would look at some of the stories my colleagues wrote and would gasp at holes in the story, but I did not say anything. I could not believe, for example, how they would simply take the word of a government official as fact and base a whole story on it. Nobody bothered to flesh out the story with others. Or, stories would be written based on nothing more than rumors and speculation from unnamed sources. Most of all, I was appalled at the coverage of crime stories. To become a crime suspect in Korea was tantamount to conviction. This was justice Korean-style, and the news media did not question it. But when it came to stories about the government, caution reigned. This was understandable, of course, as Korean journalists were always liable to censorship by the Park regime.

Six weeks after I got there, my wish to write a weekly column was fulfilled. I was able to prevail upon the editor, Soon-Il Hong, who had liked my stories from the start. "Seoul Carousel" ran on Sundays with my picture. It took off immediately and quickly became popular with readers. Along with the column, I usually wrote two or three stories every week. Tearooms became an extension of my workplace. I often felt more inspired writing in a tearoom than in the newsroom. I savored the charm and intimacy of a Korean tearoom, an institution that has no equivalent anywhere else. Every tearoom had a different personality, from its decor, music, and menu to the appearance and mannerisms of the waitresses. Each tea table usually had two or four chairs facing each other. Most of the chairs had velvet seats with high backs, but they all had white or chamois-colored seat covers to keep the velvet from getting soiled. But you could see the blue and maroon velvet peeping from the folds of the seat where the fabric was tied into little ribbons. Some had the modern appearance of a tourist hotel coffee shop with Renoir and Degas prints in gilded frames gracing dimly lit walls, while others had a more traditional look, complete with Korean landscape scrolls and rice-paper lanterns. Tearooms had regulars who left messages on bulletin boards. I noticed that some of the messages were in pink and cream papers, elaborately folded into shapes of small fans and stuck to the bulletin board with multicolored pins. They were probably love notes. Did operators of tearooms read those notes when no one claimed them? I sometimes wondered. There were hundreds of tearooms in Seoul in the sixties.

Within a few months, I settled on several favorite tearooms—all quite different from one another. After she found out it was one of my favorite songs, a young woman who was in charge of playing records at Kumran Tea Room flipped on Nat King Cole's "Rambling Rose" when she saw me walk in. I loved writing in smoke-filled tearooms, listening to Nat King Cole, Tino Rossi, and Andy Williams. I had the freedom not only in the kinds of columns and stories to write but in the way I wrote them. Sometimes, after an afternoon spent in a tearoom, I would produce not one but several stories. I enjoyed eavesdropping on people, because tearooms were places where Koreans got together to transact business—everything from matchmakers introducing prospective suitors to job interviews. At times I wondered if I would have ever developed this kind of journalistic freedom in America, for the newspaper business was much more disciplined there, with the tradition of news and features formats. For example, one would not find a short story or poems appearing in the *Los Angeles Times* or the *New York Times*, but Korean newspapers regularly serialized fiction.

English-language newspapers in Seoul had smaller circulations than the vernacular papers, but there was a distinct advantage to writing in English. This was the time when the authoritarian President Chung-Hee Park was clamping down on freedoms more than ever, and by writing in English, I got away with a lot more than columnists who wrote in Korean. Whenever I wanted to criticize the Park regime, as with some of its ridiculous periodic austerity campaigns which, for example, urged Koreans to eat less beef or less rice, I would write columns poking fun at the officials. I used many English idioms to elude the censors, whose proficiency in English was, thankfully, limited. I have never worked for a newspaper where I felt more relaxed than at the *Korea Times* in Seoul, even though we worked six days a week and had only three days of vacation a year. I looked forward to going to work because it felt more like going on an outing. Every day was a new adventure.

There was so much reaction to everything I wrote, because people noticed my byline and the simplicity and freshness of my prose, which differed from the more formalistic and stilted style of Korean writers who wrote in English. I became the subject of curiosity inside and outside the newspaper office. Requests for interviews, invitations to speak to students, and opportunities to write articles for magazines poured in. Discreet inquiries about my marital status were made through colleagues at the paper. Job offers came, too. With permission from the *Korea Times*, I accepted a teaching position at the Hankuk University of Foreign Studies, an institution founded by a couple of my father's former colleagues. I taught English composition and international relations twice a week, which opened my life to another facet of Korean life. Being with college students who had grown up in Korea during the years I was away seemed to give me a vicarious taste of what I had missed. They were so full of envy about my American education, and many of them said they wanted to go to America to study. Knowing English was so important to them, because it was a key to connecting with America. I enjoyed teaching at the school, and my classes were popular. Clutching copies of *Time* and *Newsweek*, my students sometimes visited me at the newspaper office to ask me questions that could not wait until the next class.

I also wrote and read over the air a radio program for the state-run Korean Broadcasting System (KBS) on aspects of Korean culture that was broadcast overseas. My salary more than doubled; at least on paper, I earned more money than a cabinet minister. I spent most of it on long taxi rides (I still did not drive, and even if I could, only the rich had private cars then) and eating out. Fluency in English was magic. It opened doors I did not even knock on.

From reviewing movies to interviewing visiting dignitaries, professors, street vendors, and orphans, each day was so fun that I did not think too much about the United States, though I did miss not having people with whom I could share that dimension of my life. After work, I went out for dinner, lingering afterward in tearooms or nightclubs to talk, then rushed to get home in a taxi before midnight. South Korea maintained a curfew until the 1980s, a carry-over from the Korean War days. I slept only four or five hours a night, but I had so much psychic energy, I do not remember feeling tired. On Sundays, to avoid the hassle of catching a taxi to go home at night, I stayed in my small room. About eight feet by eight feet, with white walls, it was furnished with a small bed made by a neighborhood carpenter, a low table that doubled as my desk, a coffee table, a cardboard box covered with silk scarves that served as my dresser, and a bookcase. The desk lamp with an emerald-green shade and small prints of Degas' dancers were the only distinctive features of the room. I did delicate laundry by hand because the maid for the house had a habit of beating on clothes with a washing stick, a carryover from the countryside where women beat dirt out of farmers' cotton clothing. Afterward, I read Albert Camus and T. S. Eliot in my room. In these rare moments of solitude, I was often struck by the paradoxical dimensions of my life—the hold of the West on my intellect and the deeper hold of the East on my emotions—and wondered how I might reconcile the two.

This hit me one evening when, after work, I was startled to

see a shamanistic rite in progress inside my home. I thought my
Christian parents would have a fit if they knew what was going on
in their house. The caretakers with whom I was living had called a
mudang, a Korean medicine woman. The husband had been ill for
some time from carbon monoxide poisoning caused by the briquettes
used to heat the Korean-style *ondol* (hot rock) rooms, which had flues
running underneath the concrete floors. The age-old prescription for
the poisoning is a bowl of juice from winter-cabbage pickles. But
the man was in his fifties and in poor health, so the effects of the
poisoning lingered for weeks. It felt eerie as I walked inside and saw
in the den next to the sick man's room a lacquer table loaded with
rice cakes, grilled fish, apples, pears, chestnuts, jujubes, boiled cow
hooves, dried pollack, and a pig's head. Candles flickered. The *mudang*, who appeared to be in her fifties, had sallow skin, small but
elongated eyes, a wide nose with large nostrils, and thick lips. She
wore a deep-blue silk Korean woman's skirt and a short white jacket,
and over those a gown and a headdress with a bird feather, under
which her hair was combed back into a knot and clasped with a jade
hairpin. She had a stick painted with bands of bright colors, from
which hung a gong. She beat the gong with a stick while chanting,
her body moving rhythmically. The *mudang* danced, sang, and wailed
with exaggerated gestures, accompanied by two female assistants. One
beat on an hourglass-shaped drum, while the other clashed large
cymbals. As the night deepened, I heard the *mudang* inviting different
spirits into the house and assuming their voices; she was communicat-
ing with them. I went to sleep uneasily in my room late that night,
hearing the drums, the cymbals and the *mudang*'s wails as she talked
with the spirits to purify the house and exorcise the man's illness.
All night long, as I heard the unique and spooky sounds, I phased
in and out of sleep. Once during the night I got up to go to the
bathroom and was startled to discover a stack of rice cakes on a plate
in the corner. At dawn, the *mudang* and her helpers vanished like
ghosts. The night of sleeping through the *mudang*'s rites was a Dante-
like journey into the inferno of Korean culture. During the following
day at work, I could not erase the sounds and images of the night

before. It was as though the night spent with the *mudang* had been a message to me about my irreconcilable conflict from having tasted the fruits of East and West. The torment of being an insider and outsider at the same time, and the greater torment of looking at my people and my culture with an objective eye, was a coming-home present I had not anticipated.

A Long Winter

Autumn ended all too quickly. My first winter in Korea, sixteen years since the fateful escape to Pusan on the rooftop of a train in the midst of the Korean War, greeted me with full force. With the first snow of the season, my thoughts turned to Columbia, Missouri, even though I tried not to think about America. But the snow made me recall, with poignancy, the plans David and I had made the previous winter—even picking out names of a boy and girl we hoped to have years later when we would be settled after he had completed his doctorate. I pushed David, his Irish good looks, and America out of my mind. I did not want to torture myself with what might have been or how much my life had changed—or had changed because I would not disobey my parents. Why look back, when I still had the wide future ahead of me? There would be others to choose from, I told myself, shutting the door once again to my first big love.

I spent the winter mostly shivering. With people burning briquette coals for heat, Seoul's air turned foul. Every home burned a minimum of two or three coal briquettes a day, and the smoke poured from the homes, offices, and commercial buildings. A white blouse worn in the morning would be dirty by midafternoon. Traditional Korean homes have no central heating; only the concrete floors are heated from underneath, and heat is transmitted through an intricate network of flues connected to various rooms from the central fireplace in the kitchen. This indigenous *ondol* system provides fire for cooking almost around the clock during winter, but people have to sit or sleep on the floor to benefit from the heat. After years of sleeping on a bed, it hurt my back to sleep on the *ondol* floor, which was nothing more than cement covered with layers of shiny oil paper, a sort of thin version of linoleum. Through the proper application of heat, the oil paper turned gold as the floor aged, so that it looked like a golden mirror. At first I had a neighborhood carpenter build a small bed for me, but when winter's freezing weather came, I resorted to the Korean-style sleeping arrangement, rolling out a quilt and sleeping on the floor to keep warm. Even when I was awake, I sat on the floor. This kept my lower body warm, but I had to cover the rest of myself with a comforter.

I did not fare any better at work. The *Korea Times* newsroom was so cold that I went to work wearing not one but two overcoats, which made everyone laugh. "You're wearing two coats," even a shy copy girl said, unable to restrain herself. "Better than freezing," I said. "But you look so funny," she said, covering her mouth demurely. "Better than freezing," I repeated. I figured they would eventually leave me alone and dismiss it as my idiosyncratic legacy from having had "too much foreign water" to drink, but they did not. Even the madames in the tearooms I frequented said, "You returnees from America are so soft." Finally, I did what everyone else did. I went to a market and bought thermal underwear, which came only in garishly bright red or off-white. I also had a pair of boots made. I gave the cobbler a picture from *Vogue* of the type I wanted. "Beautiful boots," the cobbler said, squinting his eyes and studying the picture. A few days later when I went back to the store, the cobbler proudly brought out the boots that looked just like those in the *Vogue* picture—only he had not put in any zippers. I could get into my boots, but to remove them, he had to help pull them off. "Not to worry. They'll stretch," he assured me. They did not. I gave the boots away to a relative, who had them cut to the ankles.

The coldest spot in the newsroom was the managing editor's corner, because his desk was farthest from the lone oil-burning stove in the room. I do not know how he kept warm, but I never heard Soon-Il Hong complain about the cold. Actually, the stove did little good unless you stood right in front of it. The situation was even more dismal at the university. Students and instructors worked in freezing classrooms with bare cement floors, with the wind slashing through broken windows and cracks in the walls, but still they seated themselves close to the windows in order to steal some warmth from the sun. Students asked me to call off classes and said some other professors had. I refused. Instead, I held one of my smaller classes in the corner of a tearoom across from the university. The students loved it, and the tearoom owner liked the extra business. But the word got around campus that I was conducting an English composition class in a tearoom, and to avoid drawing unnecessary attention to myself, I had to stop the practice. The only heaters to be found were in the teachers' lounge and individual offices of deans and ranking officials. So we struggled for another three weeks, until the schools closed in late December for almost two months of winter vacation. I learned why Korean schools have such long winter vacation; I could appreciate the custom.

Those broken windows were miraculously replaced in sunny May in anticipation of a visit from the first lady of the country. She hardly ventured beyond the auditorium, but all those windows that had been left broken through the winter were replaced. When I mentioned the irony of this to a colleague who had earned his master's degree in American literature in the United States, he simply said, "This is Korea. Different priorities, you know." Different priorities, indeed. It did not faze school administrators that students sat in overcoats and periodically put their fingers in their mouths to keep them from freezing, even when they took finals. Whenever I saw school administrators in their offices, with a large oil stove with a kettle of barley tea boiling on it, I was disgusted. I wondered how these administrators in their heated offices rationalized their decision not to spend the money to buy forty briquettes a day to heat the classrooms, but would not think twice about buying potted flowers to celebrate this or that special occasion throughout the year.

Shortly after the New Year, in January 1968, a male friend said he wanted to introduce me to someone he admired very much who had been wanting to meet me. The man—I'll call him Chan-Ho— had been following my columns and was curious about me. The three of us met after work one evening for dinner. Chan-Ho, who was well established in business, was older and sophisticated, had a sharp mind and quick wit, and was absolutely charming. He spoke English fluently, as did the mutual friend who had introduced us. We spent several hours that evening enjoying our meal and conversing in English. When they dropped me off at my home, I felt like I was onto something exciting. I hoped Chan-Ho would call, and he did the next morning. From then on, we saw each other every evening after work, dining at some of Seoul's best restaurants and, afterward, lingering in nightspots, where we danced late into the night. Chan-Ho was lavish and enjoyed buying gifts for me. This was a very different kind of relationship from the one with a fellow student in Columbia. Through Chan-Ho, I was discovering another aspect of Korean life—the relationship between men and women. But as the relationship deepened, I came to see the communication gaps. Despite his travels abroad and exposure to the West, he was a traditional Korean man. The difference in our age also had something to do with the gap I felt. During this period I met and became attracted to another man, an American journalist I will call Matthew. This added to my already conflicting emotions about Korea and America in things as important as what future husband to consider and as trivial as whether to have eggs and bacon for breakfast or a full-blown Korean meal of rice, soup, fish, and meat.

As days went on, my inner conflicts accelerated, and I encountered many gaping differences in outlook, as with gift giving. Among Koreans it was not the thought that counted so much as how much a gift cost. Every favor was noted and brought expectations of a return. The society had become so perverted by power and corruption that honest people were considered to be stupid. It took extraordinarily strong people of character to withstand the temptations not to seek power and money. While noting this aspect of Korean society, I discovered my own marginal place in each of my two worlds. I was more comfortable with Koreans when engaged in small talk, but when talk turned to deeper discussions, I felt frustrated by what I perceived to be a certain kind of Korean illogic. Koreans could not agree to disagree. Discussions ended rather quickly when differences emerged. Disagreeing publicly was tantamount to slapping another person in the face. So, no one said no, when that should have been said, and as a result, what was left unsaid left me with many unresolved ambiguities. This was the exact opposite of what I had experienced in the United States. There, small talk had been hard for me, but longer conversations and discussions had come easily. I attributed this to the fact that while my socialization had begun with my first language, Korean, my intellectual growth had taken place in English. And, I discovered that Koreans really do not have conversations. Because of the hierarchical structure of Korean society, where age and social position matter most, one either talked up or down to someone. Everyone had a title, and titles, not names, were used to address people, instantly putting the person with the higher title on a higher plane. How could there be an exchange of opinions in such a situation? A person with a lower title simply listened or took orders. Even within my world of the newspaper and the university, I had countless titles to remember. The only exception was among my childhood friends or old school classmates. Not having attended school in Korea, I lacked that important social network.

The sixties were perhaps the most intense period in South Korea's history because so many things were coming together at once, along with the incessant pressure to modernize and overcome the nation's inferiority complex of being poor and backward. After six years in power, Park was becoming more repressive and had his sights set on long-term rule. Soldiers, who previously had lacked social status, were now flexing their muscles because the military ran the country. Culturally, Korea was awakening. A resurgence of Korean classical music and dance was under way. After decades of Japanese colonial rule during which Koreans were indoctrinated into believing that their culture was inferior, followed by the American occupation, and the war, Korean culture was ready for a rebirth and reappreciation by its people. The Bando Hotel was the tallest building in Seoul, and its Skylounge on the tenth floor was the place to go. Its coffee shop attracted the well-to-do, or those who just wanted to be seen there. The rich arrived at the Bando in used American jeeps painted in black and reupholstered as "sedans." So few Koreans owned real sedans that the handful of people riding in black Japanese Coronas or Ford Cortinas stood out and were the targets of much envy. Only members of the diplomatic corps, U.S. military personnel, and the president of the Republic of Korea and his wife traveled in big foreign cars. Products from abroad, especially from the United States, were sought after. People paid exorbitant prices to buy American cosmetics, canned foods, and household goods sold on the black market.

Similarly, going to the United States was a preoccupation with Koreans. America was akin to paradise, Koreans thought, and the image of America they carried in their heads was exaggerated. They really believed everyone was rich and lived in big houses with winding staircases. I did not know how to begin to make my students at the university understand that what they believed about America was very different from what America really was. They were motivated to study English because they saw going to the United States as the best way to improve their lot. With an advanced degree from the United States, they could teach, go into government service, or work in private industry. Fielding their endless queries, I sometimes felt like a one-person U.S. Information Service. I tried to dispel their notions of what America was by saying that most people worked in uninteresting jobs to pay their bills and put their kids through school, but I do not think I succeeded. People want to hear only what they want to hear; it was hard to compete with the images of American life created by Hollywood.

And, socially, those were confusing times. I had a sense that the whole society wanted modernization, but without having thought through its price or its impact on the Korean way of life, which they cherished. My own confusion of awakening in this milieu was complicated by the fact that I was always comparing Korea to Japan and America.

Yet, some Korean ways were absolutely endearing to me. For example, on New Year's Eve, vendors shouting "pok-chori, pok-chori," the Korean name for a straw rice strainer that stands for good luck, would flock to the area. And there was the New Year's Day custom of visiting the homes of our bosses. Starting with the publisher's home, we went to the managing editor's, then the city editor's, to pay our respects. In return, we were fed scrumptious meals. These were Korean bonding rituals, where the lines of employer and employee were eliminated and we all became one big family—something that could never happen in America.

So began my love/hate relationship with Korea and things Korean. I had a strong emotional attachment to Korea on one hand, but I also had to grapple with an almost equally strong intellectual loathing for the rigidity of Korean society and the pervasive hypocrisy it engendered, because no human could live up to its rules. Hypocrisy was as rampant in America as in South Korea, but I felt it more in Korea because there were fewer jobs and resources to go around. Not only did this breed seething resentment and resignation among the have-nots, but it spawned the hit-and-run *hantang* philosophy— the idea that you take it while the taking is good, because another chance may never appear. The idea of doing one's best for personal satisfaction was a concept that no longer seemed to be valued, and there appeared to be no restrictions when it came to making money. Once wealth was achieved, the means used to acquire it were forgotten. Money bought just about anything—even respect. Or to put it differently, there was no real respect for anybody or anything because of the prevailing cynicism that one became rich not by working hard but by being lucky and grabbing the right chance. The Japanese colonial rule, the war, and two authoritarian presidencies during which collaborative, not conscientious, workers were rewarded had destroyed the old values. The double standard that divided the privileged and the poor, men and women, educated and uneducated was pervasive. The differences were so pronounced that people who did not have the desirable trappings were condemned for life.

My abhorrence of this hypocrisy and the double standard influenced most of my decisions, including those that changed the course of my life. In what seemed to be a fit of rebellion against my family and Korean society, I decided to marry Matthew. When I told my parents about my desire to marry, they promptly flew in from Okinawa to try to stop it. They objected to just about everything about the man—his Anglo ethnicity, social status, and religion, and even his looks. There was no way to talk to them. They locked the front gates of their Seoul home, my residence, and would not let me out. A houseful of people watched me around the clock, which only made me more determined. My parents, despite their many years of living abroad, never accepted the fact that their progeny could not grow up abroad and yet remain 100 percent Korean, as they had expected.

One morning, when I was arguing with my mother, I said I would find a way "to marry whomever I want no matter what you do." This prompted her to threaten that she would hire "goons" to keep him away from me. When I heard the word *goons*, it became no longer a matter of romance but a war of wills. I was not going to give in; I was determined to win. My parents already had succeeded in interfering with my romances, which I regretted having reported to them. All my honesty had gotten me was their meddling. This time, come what may, I was not about to let them interfere. My unannounced absence from the office prompted many calls to the house. Family friends and relatives came by as if we were in mourning, trying to persuade me to abandon this crazy notion of marrying an American. Did they not understand that love had no boundaries? What was so important about being pure Korean that united them in opposing my decision?

A few days later, I persuaded my mother to let me go to the office. I promised to return after work. I did not even get to the office. When I called Matthew from a pay phone to say that I had managed to get out of the house, he asked me to wait for him at our usual meeting place. When I met him at Kumran, he had a suitcase with him. "Let's get married now," he said. Though I had every intention of returning home after work that evening, and even thought about the promise that I would return, I could not bring myself to say no. I thought about the alienated protagonist in Camus' *The Stranger*, who is moved to do things as if he had no control of his will. I had always kept my word to my parents, but something bigger than reason was propelling me. I wondered why I was not saying, "I'll marry you, but not today." Then I thought of my mother's words about the goons. It was as though I had no will of my own at the time and was under a spell. We went to Seoul City Hall and took out a marriage license, then walked down the street to the U.S. embassy where we were officially married. I wore a black turtleneck and a taupe gabardine miniskirt, a gift from Chan-Ho—an irony that did not escape me even in those crazy moments. Had I thought I would be getting married that day, I certainly would have dressed more thoughtfully.

We exchanged rings in a taxi, as we discussed whom to call. We took a cab to his place, where I donned an Eva Gabor–style light-brown wig. A good American friend had given me her wig when I mentioned how difficult it was not to be noticed in Seoul when you were dating a non-Korean. I slipped my long hair inside the wig, adjusted it, then put on a pair of large sunglasses. The maid at his house stared at me curiously when she came out to lock the gate, though she did not say a word. Before we took off in a taxi for the countryside, I called my doctor's wife, a longtime friend of my parents, told her what I had done, and asked her to call my parents and take care of them. I was worried that my parents might get sick from the shocking news of my disobedience, inflicted on them in the way it would most hurt them. Fearful of my mother's "goons," we changed hotels several times during a week of the honeymoon. Our first stop was Onyang, a resort famous for hot springs. But I was in no mood to enjoy the cures of these waters, which Koreans have long praised and worshiped. No waters could cure the heartaches I felt on what should have been the happiest day of my life. Though Matthew had a way with words, all he could say to try to comfort me was, "You look so sad." My feelings went from hot to cold. At times I felt like saying, "You got your way, but look at the price I had to pay. I had not planned my wedding day to be like this."

How could I tell anyone why I had done what amounted to betraying my parents? How could I make anyone Korean understand the necessity of my defiance to the bitter end? The marriage and the escape were like a bad movie I was watching. The following day we continued our taxi journey further south and went to a tourist hotel within a stone's throw from Lake Susong, outside Taegu. The rural scene was so peaceful and indifferent to my predicament.

Love seemed to pale in the whirlwind of conflicts I felt. This was mid-June, and in the nearby fields, next season's crops were maturing. Rice, wheat, and barley grew in even beds of green, gold, and amber. Irrigation tunnels of water ran beside the beds and not far from small thatched-roof houses. It was a busy season in the countryside with everyone working, legs knee-deep in the mud as the people transplanted the rice with the hot sun beating down on their bent backs. Every now and then a car rumbled over the bumpy dirt road, leaving behind a whirl of white dust. It was so refreshing to feel the land still untouched by tall buildings and neon lights marring the night's beauty, and always the bustling people hurrying everywhere.

Climbing a small mountain by the lake on the following morning, I saw rice paddies spreading out before me like a thick green carpet that swayed in a gentle breeze. The farmers sweated to make sure that each grain of the planted rice produced many grains more. Women with white towels wrapped around their heads for protection from the sun helped their husbands and brothers, and children ran errands and helped with the work. As I surveyed the scene, I felt as if I could see generations of families before them who had used the same simple tools of excrement, cows, and grains of rice to produce new rice year after year, and in the fall, following a good harvest, had used the rice husks to rethatch their roofs. For a moment, I envied them and wished that I, too, could identify so closely with the land and be a part of it. The living worked side by side with the

dead, for there were small mounds of Korean graves—some with tomb-
stones and others with none—next to and in the fields. A man was
born, lived in his ancestral house, learned to work in the fields,
brought a woman into the house to be his wife and bear him children, help him in the field and see to it that his son, too, got married
when his time came, and the son, too, brought his wife to live in
the house. And when the man was old and could no longer work,
he could watch his grandchildren play, and enjoy the fruits of his
son's labor, and eventually his body would return to the land that
had given him life. It was a pattern, a way of life, obeyed without
question.

Looking all around me, I felt a deeper understanding of why
people had objected to my marriage. It was more than the act of
marrying a non-Korean; it was what that meant in every way. And
so this rural scene to which we had escaped gave me a frame of
reference to understand my parents. No matter how long they had
lived abroad, they would think and act like traditional Koreans, expecting their progeny to think and act their way. To my mind, it
was an unreasonable expectation, but to theirs, it was only natural
and perfectly reasonable. So the honeymoon was memorable for the
soul-searching I did and the tears I shed. I had gone against their
wishes in a public expression of defiance. I had won, but my victory
was so mixed with heartaches that I could not feel good. Returning
to the hotel, I drank a whiskey sour and fell asleep. When I awoke,
Matthew gave me this note to tell me what he could not speak:

> I feel so deeply the sadness of this woman I love. We have
> said so often that we feel part of each other. Usually this was
> in moments of love, or happiness. The cynics—and I must
> count a certain voice inside of me as one of them—might
> count this feeling of togetherness at these times as a selfish il-
> lusion—for who does not like happiness, even to the extent
> of creating for oneself the impression of becoming part of an-
> other person. Not so with sadness. No one would create this
> impression for oneself in order to suffer. Thus in this sadness

of hers which I feel, I know somehow we are part of each other—that to prick her finger is to prick mine, to tear her heart is to tear mine. Yet as much as this feeling reminds me of what we share, it also reminds me that still we are two, I am I, and she is she. For my own sadness—that stemming from the forces within my life—I know how to bear, how to cope with, how to salve. Hers I do not. This struck me this afternoon, lying next to her, I looked her full in the face and stroked her hair. If only holding her in my arms could be the answer, if only I knew the words that could—like some kind of magic—heal the wounds. Alas, this is not the case. And I fear I can help her little, bear little for her. But can only wait with her, sitting in this chair, writing in the light from the bathroom, slightly conscious of the drip from the faucet, but with most of my mind and all of my heart—directed toward that bed where she lies sleeping so fitfully . . .

The marriage was a scandal in Seoul. Everyone at the newspaper and at the university seemed to know about it. I tried to keep a low profile, but people gave me all sorts of unsolicited comments. One male Korean friend asked, "What did you see in him, anyway?" while another said, "You could have done a lot better."

I learned that after my parents received a call from the family doctor's wife about me, they contacted my editor at the *Korea Times*, who promptly had a city hall reporter check to see whether or not a marriage license had been taken out. When it was confirmed that the marriage license had been issued, someone at the paper suggested calling the national police to track us down. My parents chose not to go that far. My mother vented her fury by tearing into shreds some of my favorite clothes, including an apple-green silk dress with a mandarin collar, and went through my jewelry box and tore apart beaded necklaces. Our maid saved them and later showed me, asking if she could keep the beads.

My mother was obsessed about my elopement for many months. "I always dreamed of you marrying a fine Korean man and wearing a beautiful white gown with many bridesmaids at your side," said my mother, who loves pomp and ceremony. Even a year later, she could not accept the fact that her only daughter had eloped. I did not know until then that wedding ceremonies were really for mothers.

"You know that I never cared for ceremonies," I told her.

"I know," she said. "I cannot understand you. Doesn't every girl want to wear a beautiful wedding gown and a veil on the one special day of her life?"

"Not this one," I said. "I never wanted to put myself on display."

I could never make my mother understand that not every young woman wants a big wedding and to be the center of attention on her wedding day. Even as I got married, I was not sure that it would last "till death do us part." I thought it was quite possible that the marriage might end someday. How could I be sure? After all, people change and circumstances change, I thought.

My parents returned to Japan with their hearts in shreds, but from afar my mother hounded me for a year about having a wedding ceremony. Finally, unable to resist any longer, we had a formal ceremony a year later at a Presbyterian church and invited my parents' friends. I did not invite a single friend because the public ceremony was done to appease my parents, mostly my mother and her sense of saving face. I had caused enough turmoil and shame for my family, and I thought that was the least I could do. My mother assigned a relative, known for his photography, to take pictures. None of the photos came out because the film was put into the wrong solution at the shop. I heard that my relative was so upset with what had happened that he punched the person at the photo studio. I thought it was just as well that the pictures were ruined. How can you try to make something happen that did not happen?

We settled into the life of a professional couple and rented a two-bedroom apartment. I did not worry too much about domestic duties, because we had a housekeeper. But being married to an American thrust us more into Seoul's international set. Though Matthew had studied Korean diligently and spoke conversational Korean, he never became proficient enough to launch into deep conversation in Korean. Heads sometimes turned when we walked together because interracial marriage among people of my education and social standing was still uncommon in the Korea of the sixties. Eventually, people came to accept our marriage.

But the marriage changed the course of my life because it brought me back to America in 1970, for a second time. After several years in Korea, Matthew had come to the conclusion that he did not belong there—that his home was America. He had come to Korea after his tour in the Vietnam War and had become intrigued by it. Leaving a newspaper career in the United States, he returned to Korea to study the language, history, and culture. But there were limits as to how far a foreigner could be accepted in Korea. He had done about as much as he could when one evening after work in November 1969, he suggested that we return to the United States. We waited until I had completed the winter semester at the university and had resigned from a coveted tenured position as an assistant professor.

Little did I know when I got off the plane at John F. Kennedy International Airport in New York in January 1970 that I was joining a second wave of Korean immigrants, who in two decades would change the face of major American cities.

9.   BACK TO AMERICA

(1970–1987)

Until the peony blooms
I will be waiting for my spring.
The day the peony falls
I will be sunk already in the sorrow of a lost spring.
That day in May, a hot day,
The petals lay as they fell and shriveled.
No peonies anywhere,
My rising expectation crushed.
The peony gone, the year is over for me;
Missing it, every day of the year I cry.
Until the peony blooms
I will be waiting. Spring, sadness in splendor.
—Young-Nang Kim (1904–1950)★

★Translated by S. E. Solberg

Rediscovering America

Though I had been away just two and a half years, the America to which I returned in January 1970 seemed different. Perhaps that was because this time I had come to live as an immigrant, unlike in the past, when I considered myself a sojourner who saw the country through the eyes of an uncritical visitor. Whatever the reason, I saw harsher edges in the America of 1970 that engendered in me mixed emotions about being back. Sometimes I asked myself why I had not listened to my inner voice and remained in Korea. In my moments of discontent, I berated myself for making such a hasty decision to give up a coveted job at a major university, as one would discard a pair of old shoes, to marry and follow a man to his country. I had wanted to insist that I stay behind and perhaps join him later, yet for some inexplicable reason I could not bring myself to say that. Again, it could have been because I did not want to have to bare my soul by bluntly articulating what cannot be easily or fully verbalized. Perhaps, some of it had to do with not wanting to stay in Korea, where one's private business seems to belong to everybody else. When I did think about the consequences of my actions, I felt like I was observing someone else. Was this my destiny? Was it my fate to live away from my homeland? I found no easy answer from within myself. But leaving Korea just when my professional career had started taking off, I could not push out of my mind the many "what ifs" and the regrets that inevitably accompany such futile questions.

Some of the decisions, I explained to myself, were made because I was undergoing an internal revolution in my attempt to escape the lot of Korean women. There was no positive role model to follow, and plenty of negative ones not to follow. I had seen around me too many capable Korean women who were slaves to their husbands, children, and in-laws and who seemed, at least to me, to be caught in a living death long before their time. My attempt to mold my own life away from the strictures of Korean culture was the only thing that could explain why I had allowed myself to be pulled out of Korea back to America. Two and a half years earlier

I had let my parents talk me into not returning to America because of a man; now, I had let a man talk me into leaving Korea because of him, when I was not quite ready. My actions made me feel like a puppet. On the plane ride to the United States, I regretted that I had not tried to negotiate an agreement between us to stay behind, while Matthew got settled first. I regretted that I had not given myself a chance to remain alone in Korea, to weigh which was more important, my husband or my connection to Korea.

Matthew and I settled in Baltimore near his parents. We both quickly found work there, as reporters at the *Baltimore News American*, a Hearst paper. The city of Edgar Allen Poe and H. L. Mencken struck me as a dark, brooding place that appeared to lament the loss of better days. I shuddered when on my first night, looking out of a hotel window, I saw large men in police uniforms walking with German shepherds in the Civic Center. What had I done? Why had I come to live in a city that people called the murder capital of America? Beautifully decorated department store windows had no admirers at night, after people fled the central city at the end of their work day. Downtown was strewn with trash, and "The Block," a short stretch of bars and striptease establishments, added a tawdry air to this old, dark city. Dignified old rowhouses on historic Mount Vernon Square were marred by iron bars on their windows. I wrote features for the women's pages of the *Baltimore News American*, and lived within walking distance to work. My job took me all over the state and to Washington, D.C., where I covered women's issues. I hoped the work would plunge me into my present life and keep me from thinking about my displacement and about Korea.

The atmosphere in the all-white and female office of the women's pages was quite different from that of the Rochester paper of the mid-1960s, where I had felt only warmth and support. Here, for the first time I saw dimensions of American life that I had not noticed before. Baltimore was more of a southern city than anything I had previously experienced. Prejudice against blacks, about half of the city's population in 1970, was pronounced, even at the newspaper. I experienced this firsthand after I wrote an article about female cabbies. The story ran on the cover of the women's pages, with three good-size pictures of heavyset black women. Top editors hit the roof. Maybe one picture, but a page full of pictures of black women? The young woman who made up the page was told in no uncertain terms that this "mistake" must not be repeated. It was my first encounter with blatant racism at an American newspaper, and I did not like it. A few days after the story ran, I received a few unsigned letters from readers, accusing me of being a "nigger lover." Were these the kinds of people my editors feared? The very thought gave me goose bumps. Had I been more attuned to racism in the office, I might have anticipated the reaction. But until then I had no inkling that pictures of black women would cause newspaper executives such grief. After that I began to notice things I had not before. On the bridal pages care was exercised to disperse pictures of black brides. God forbid that their pictures run next to those of socially prominent white Baltimoreans, who lived in another world. The society editor and her assistant, products of private schools and colleges and known for their social connections, did not even attempt to disguise their prejudices. If they thought that way about blacks, I wondered how they really viewed me, the only Asian in the department. It was unsettling.

The office was not the only place where I felt unsettled, however. Juggling work and household chores, I felt ennui seeping into all phases of my life. The joie de vivre I had experienced in Seoul had all but dissipated. My continuing internal struggle with my guilt over the marriage and what that represented to the Kang clan gnawed at me, and with these feelings came increasing doubts that the marriage would work in a new setting. I found myself torn in many directions. The man who had seemed to me so liberated in Korea struck me as a chauvinist in America. The burgeoning feminist movement added to my dilemma and discontent because it articulated for me what I had thought on my own for so long. Sometimes I fancied returning to Seoul, only to quickly suppress the thought. Could I really stand to live in a society where men had all the privileges and women none? Could I be content to be an exception, one among

a small group of professional women who were treated with defer-
ence? I debated with myself, but in the end, I could not bring myself
to pack up and leave. So I continued to write my old weekly column
for the *Korea Times*, with the title changed from "Seoul Carousel"
to "The Carousel," and I sent it off from Baltimore to maintain at
least this one link with Korea. My former editor in Seoul had encouraged me to do so, and I had agreed; I felt it was my tie to
Korea, and that was important to me. My columns were mostly
cross-cultural pieces—long before *multiculturalism* and *diversity* became
common words in the American lexicon.

I had felt so American in Korea, but in America, I became so
Korean. My identity as a Korean took on far more importance than
I had ever imagined possible before. Here I was married to an American, with American in-laws, in the thick of upper middle-class mainstream life. If I did not put on the brakes, I might be swept away
into assimilation, which I resisted.

My weekly column for the *Korea Times* became a tool to maintain my detached observations of American life, rather than becoming
submerged in it. Writing the columns forced me to think about
Koreanness and to view America from that standpoint. In a way, I
was introducing interesting Americans and ideas to my readers in
Korea. My pieces were chatty commentaries and observations about
various facets of life in America—the women's movement, racism,
the plight of the elderly, or fashion. I was a combination foreign
correspondent essayist with unrestricted freedom to write—except for
pieces overly critical of the South Korean government. Nobody said
anything about that, but I knew just how far I could go on the
subject. With relatives in Korea, I did not want to cause trouble
back home unnecessarily. From time to time I also wrote about what
Koreans in America did. Whenever I traveled to New York City or
Washington, D.C., I made sure I wrote columns with a dateline
from those places. I tried to write them in an easygoing style, which
was my hallmark. The column writing on top of my busy job at the
newspaper gave me little time for other activities.

Not having a housekeeper meant most of the domestic chores

became mine. My in-laws were cordial and polite, and though they lived only an hour's drive away, they did not expect us to visit them all the time. We saw them once or twice a month and usually ate at their country club. Matthew's father had graduated from the University of Missouri School of Journalism in the 1930s and was an executive with a major corporation. His parents lived in a picture-book house where everything was in place. Matthew's extended family lived mostly in New England, and each Thanksgiving and Christmas brought three generations and assorted lifestyles together under the same roof. All of them made me feel welcome. And after my brother Emmanuel arrived to attend Loyola College in Baltimore in the fall of 1971, he, too, joined us in these family get-togethers. But one thing I never got used to was calling Matthew's parents by their first names, as they wanted me to do.

Within two years of our arrival in Baltimore, I began to have serious doubts about the marriage lasting. Romance, which had caused me to reject the restrictions of being Korean, now felt secondary. The repudiation now seemed too high a price, and in my resentment, I determined not to make any more concessions. Ultimately, it was my refusal to cut my ties to Korean ways—including my insistence on using my maiden name, keeping up with those columns, and paying an extraordinary amount of attention to my brother's and my parents' welfare (something far beyond the rationale of most Americans)—that put an end to the marriage. The price of making the marriage work proved too high for me. In the spring of 1973, carrying two suitcases filled mostly with newspaper clips, I headed to California to make a new start. If things did not work out in California, at least it was closer to Korea, I thought. And, I had long wanted to live in California. After I went there, my brother applied to transfer to Loyola Marymount University in Los Angeles in the fall.

I squinted at the sun while waiting for a taxi at the airport and instantly felt that I had come to the right place. In addition, Los Angeles provided what money could not buy—ever-present sunny weather which I grew to love. I also liked being at the edge of the

Pacific. Watching the surf from Ocean Avenue in Santa Monica, I felt better thinking that my ancestral home was just across that big blue sea. Under the shade of jacaranda and palm trees, I tried hard to be attentive to my heart and rebuild my shattered life.

Breaking five-year habits, I learned to eat and sleep alone all over again. I also learned to become my own best friend. Even as I walked to a corner grocery store, I recounted the joys and pains of love, asking myself if I would ever love again. I was not sure what I would do next, and I no longer seemed to have a blueprint of my life on the wall. Life thus far had treated me to a wealth of experiences. What was wrong with groping in the dark for a while, anyway? I told myself. One day, I would wake up with the sun in my eyes and the gloom would be gone.

With Korea only half a day away by airplane, I sometimes thought about returning for good, too. But now that my brother was in the United States, I thought it would be selfish to leave him behind, considering the way my parents felt about him, their only son. My mother had borne four children, but because of her difficult pregnancies, only the two of us had survived. When she was in the hospital to give birth to my brother, doctors told her at one point during her labor that they could save either her or the baby, but not both. My mother did not hesitate to tell the doctors if it were a choice between her life and the baby's, she would prefer to die. That is how strongly she felt about her responsibility to produce a male heir to the Kang clan. I was troubled to learn that my mother had been so willing to give up her life. What would have happened to me if she had died, leaving a baby brother? I closed my eyes and blocked out the thought. My brother was the center of my parents' universe, but I never minded it because I was happy just to have a sibling. Too, Korean girls of my generation were so indoctrinated about the significance of sons that we never really questioned the notion. I came to accept it, too. They felt better having me nearby to keep an eye on him. I put off a decision about returning to Korea, telling myself there would be another time. That just now it was not to be.

In 1974, the Department of Defense, as part of a reduction of forces, closed the office in Okinawa where my father worked as a foreign language broadcaster. My parents were in their late fifties, and I was thirty-one. My parents had the choice of returning to Korea or immigrating to the United States. Since they wanted to be close to my brother and me, they chose the latter even after I tried to discourage them. I told them that they should first come for a visit and travel around in the United States before making so big a decision. "America is not what you think," I wrote repeatedly in my letters to them. "It's not easy to start over again at your point in life." But my suggestions fell on deaf ears. It was understandable: Their marriage, like that of other Koreans of their generation, was centered on the children. I do not think they could bring themselves to face the prospect of moving back to Korea to live by themselves with their children so far away. Putting myself in their position, I could understand this, but my empathy did not stop me from feeling resentful about the curtailment of my freedom. If they immigrated, I would be committed to stay in the United States. I wanted to tell them what I felt, but I could not bring myself to do it. A combination of excuses prevented me—my sense of filial duty, an abhorrence at revealing my feelings, and my own uncertainty about returning to Korea. Besides, it seemed clear to me that their minds were made up. The only way to stop them was not to sponsor them, but my Korean upbringing would not allow me to go that far for the sake of my own freedom. My parents put their house on the market and said they would come as soon as it was sold. I had been in Los Angeles twenty-one months.

I proceeded with my prior plan to relocate to San Francisco and went for an interview, thankful that Larry Dum, then the city editor, agreed to see me on a Saturday so I did not have to take time off from work. I had long wanted to live in San Francisco because it was my favorite American city.

While covering the 1974 gubernatorial campaign that fall, I sat next to veteran *Examiner* reporter Andrew Curtin on the press bus that was following the Republican candidate Houston Flournoy in his contest against Democrat Jerry Brown. I happened to mention to Curtin that I wished I could find a reporting position in San Francisco. "Is that so?" said Curtin, who had the bemused, thoughtful look of a poet. Curtin, a quiet man and one of the finest writers I would know, had quickly mentioned me to his editor when he returned to San Francisco. And, that is how I was contacted by the city editor and hired. Dum and William Randolph Hearst III, then an assistant city editor doing the night shift, and now the publisher, took me to Mama's, a North Beach restaurant. They appeared easy-going and friendly.

When I returned from San Francisco on the following evening, I received a phone call from Chicago from my former Korean flame, Chan-Ho. I had not spoken to him since he had congratulated me about my marriage. He was visiting the States on business and said he was on his way to Los Angeles. The phone call sped my heart to happier times in Seoul seven years earlier. He did not say so, but I presumed that a mutual friend had told him about my separation and divorce. In an inexplicable intervention of fate—perhaps we were a family in another life—Chan-Ho and I would then meet every few years in Los Angeles or San Francisco or in Seoul. My other romances had clean breaks, but his Koreanness made him part of my Korean world long after the fire was gone. He was a piece of Korea, and I could not discard it because I could not discard Korea. Thus, on the eve of my departure for a new job in a new city, my emotions were turbulent, pulling me in many different directions.

I decided to keep my $165-a-month furnished apartment in the Mid-Wilshire District of Los Angeles for my parents. But at the last minute, instead of heading for Los Angeles where my brother was finishing his last year at Loyola Marymount University, my parents decided to join me in San Francisco. To say that I had mixed feelings when I went to San Francisco International Airport on the evening of June 2, 1975, to await my parents' arrival, would be an understatement. On one hand, I felt the excitement of our family finally reuniting after so many years of living apart; on the other hand, I was troubled by my family's future in America. I felt anxious and troubled about the heavy load of responsibility for the family that was about to fall on me—doubly so because I was not sure whether I belonged in the United States. I felt a pull of emotions, divided loyalties, and I felt caught in the tight web of the Korean family system and its accompanying entanglements. Even as I watched passengers coming and going—and wished that I, too, could fly away somewhere to get away from my immediate troubles—I was thinking about the Koreanness that had made it impossible for me to break off and do what I had wanted. I felt that the institution of the Korean family survived because it operated under one rule: We give you all and we want all back. The accumulation of obligations made it nearly impossible for the children to pry loose from the entanglement. Had I not been exposed to the individualism and freedom of the West, I might not have felt the rules of the Korean family system so stultifying. But now it was impossible for me to blindly follow Korean ways.

I had carried to the airport volume 5 of Anaïs Nin's *Diary* to read while waiting, but my mind wandered as I remembered my first sight of the airport on my way to Columbia, Missouri, in 1961. I fell into retracing the last fourteen turbulent years of my life since my first night away from home in a San Francisco hotel. I had traveled a long way, with many ups and downs. After having been in the dumps about my personal life, I was hoping to leave those wounds behind. In one sense I was dreading crossing a new threshold with my parents, who would have so many adjustments to make. This period back in America had been a difficult time for me—I had moved, had found a new job, and had recently gotten my divorce. The announcement over the public address system that a Pan American flight from Tokyo had arrived brought me back to reality. Feeling jittery with anxiety and excitement, I got up and headed toward the exit where international passengers would be deplaning. There were a lot of people, mostly Asians, waiting. I craned my neck to look for my parents. About half an hour later I spotted them coming through the glass doors with carts loaded with suitcases as they looked for me. "Father," I called out in Korean. "Mom," I yelled also in Korean. Their heads turned. My mother saw me first. She pointed to me, and my father saw me then. They smiled and looked relieved. My father was dressed casually in blue slacks, a shirt, and a tan cardigan sweater, and my mother wore a summer dress with a flower print. They had aged ten years since I had seen them two years earlier. My parents usually took care to dress fashionably, but there was no hint of that in their appearance now. I thought it odd that they had come looking as if they were just visiting a neighbor. Had they come that way, knowing that, as new immigrants, the decline in their social status would begin that very night? The ordeal of selling their home and preparing to come to the United States had taken its toll, I thought, immediately feeling guilty for all the unhappy thoughts I had entertained about their coming. I felt guilty, too, about not being able to welcome them with an untroubled heart. As I hugged them, I thought to myself, If they couldn't count on me, their oldest, who could they count on? My father was sixty and my mother was a month away from her fifty-seventh birthday.

Coming to America was a rude awakening for my father. A quarter century had passed since his last visit, when he had spent most of the time in the sheltered halls of prestigious universities. He had been treated like an honored guest then and had mingled mostly with the American elite. The America he remembered as a young man had completely changed. "Whatever happened to the days when university students wore sports coats to school?" he asked. "American students looked so smart as they walked to classes carrying books in their arms. There was a pride in the way they walked. Now they all wear ugly blue jeans." He could not believe what he saw. Having taught at Seoul National University and worked for the Voice of the United Nations Command as a translator and foreign-language broadcaster, my father had a wealth of professional experience, and he knew a dozen languages. But he quickly learned that at his age it was next to impossible to find a professional job in San Francisco. For my mother, it was doubly devastating, for instantly she had become a "deaf mute," as she put it. She had to depend on just one sense—sight—to get along. It was maddening for an assertive woman who was used to speaking her mind and often getting her way. Unable to speak English, she became a nobody, like so many other anonymous immigrants from Asia. Being plunged into that state was a perpetual reminder that she did not belong in America. Her frustration over her inability to communicate in English manifested itself in countless ways. It was often frustrating for us, too, because we had to interpret for her. My mother was long-winded, so she got upset when what she said did not produce an equally lengthy translation in English. "Why don't you just translate exactly as I say?" she said. "No American has that kind of attention span to listen to everything you say," I retorted. But she was not satisfied. "We should have listened to you and come for a visit first," she said. Then, she blamed my father. "Your father is so stubborn, he wouldn't listen. If we had come for a visit, I certainly wouldn't have moved to America." But it was too late for them to go back now. It was clear they meant to stay.

My Parents Begin Immigrant Life

For several weeks my parents and I lived in my small furnished studio apartment on Stockton Street on Nob Hill, not far from San Francisco's finest hotels and Chinatown. I slept in the walk-in closet, which was big enough to accommodate a bed, my mother was on a couch, and my father used a roll-away bed that my French landlord had loaned me. "I feel like I'm living in a tree house," my father said, looking out of my window to the peculiar San Francisco cityscape of hills and valleys, which cause the buildings to appear to be stacked on top of each other. "It feels odd to be suspended in the air like this." My father never quite got used to living in the small apartment atop a hill, with the clanging of the cable cars a block away on Powell Street as they climbed "halfway to the stars," as a popular song says. It felt strange to return home after work to the smell of my mother's cooking. Sometimes Mother went to Chinatown and bought a fish and broiled it in my small oven. I tried to introduce my parents to some of the sights of San Francisco, but they were not interested in playing tourist; they wanted to find a place and settle in. I got them as far as Ghirardelli Square, down near Fisherman's Wharf, once.

We were cramped in my studio apartment, but the thought of the family being together was reassuring. All three of us tried to be extraconsiderate in such a small space, and we did not have clashes. Within a month of their arrival, we moved to a two-bedroom apartment in a quiet residential area near the ocean, where we fell asleep listening to foghorns. This time we were on the top floor of a building whose rear garden was devoid of grass, flowers, or trees, but we had a view of the neighbors' better-kept backyards. My parents felt more at home here with a supermarket just two blocks away and the post office, shops, and banks within walking distance. My father especially appreciated the fact that the Lincoln Park golf course was just six blocks away. After two months of being unemployed, my father was anxious to work. "I can't stay idle much longer," he said, as he toyed with the idea of starting a business, perhaps a grocery store. "I didn't learn to grow bean sprouts for nothing," my mother said. She had learned to cultivate soybean sprouts, thinking the skill might be handy should we start a grocery store. "I don't think we can compete with the Chinese grocers," I said, to discourage her. I did not think my mother understood the amount of work involved in growing large amounts of sprouts by herself when they were being grown by big farmers who distributed them at low wholesale prices to Chinese grocery stores. Since she quit teaching after marriage, my mother had not worked outside the home.

After consulting with several old-timers, including pastors at the San Francisco Korean United Methodist Church, my parents mustered their courage and decided to buy a market at the corner of Twenty-sixth and Bryant Streets on the edge of the Mission District, owned by Mohammed, a Palestinian whose dream was that his son would become a fighter pilot and bomb Israel. With the help of Emmanuel, who had just finished college, my parents began their immigrant life in earnest in the fall of 1975. Emmanuel, who was undecided about his future and wanted to remain in Los Angeles and mow lawns to earn a living, instead was drafted into the family business. He resisted at first, but after days of arguments, he caved in to the family's pressure. He looked completely defeated. I had mixed emotions about his involvement. On one hand, it saddened me to think that my brother was being sucked into the web of the Korean family before he even had a chance to take his first step into society after college, but on the other hand, I was relieved that he was there to share the burden. My parents rationalized by saying that since Emmanuel had no firm plans for his future, such as going to law school or graduate school, he might as well make himself useful. They did not consider doing odd jobs while pondering his future a viable option for their son.

There was no way my parents could have operated the market without my brother's help. The work was grueling and boring. They worked twelve hours a day, seven days a week. My mother took Sunday morning off to attend church. Having never worked in business, we had to learn everything from scratch. My parents had never taken a drink or smoked, so learning the myriad names of the wines, liquors, and cigarettes in the store was a major challenge. Though my father's English was fluent, he found it difficult to react quickly to what customers wanted, because he had never done sales work. He would give butter to a customer asking for margarine, and he could not keep track of the different types of disposable diapers, toothpastes, soaps, and other sundries. My mother was quicker, but because her English was so limited, she had to guess at what the customers were saying.

My mother sold products that she had never seen before: mangoes, avocados, salsa and corn chips, half a dozen different types of butter and margarine, dog food and cat food, diapers, pantyhose, lightbulbs, and countless varieties of candies. In moments of panic she would speak to her customers in Korean, the foreign words tumbling out of her mouth as the customers looked at her quizzically. They would turn to my father or brother and ask, "What was she saying?" When told that my mother was thinking in Korean and so the words came out in Korean, the customers would inevitably smile. Some of them asked my father, "What language is your wife speaking? Chinese?" At the dinner table, going over the tragi-comedies of the day, I did not know whether I should laugh or cry. I wondered what we were doing in America in the first place. Sometimes I went to the store on weekends to pitch in, but my main weekend job was cleaning and doing the family laundry. After a week with Mohammed, my brother caught on to the business, but my parents had one problem after another. Making the correct change was a big hurdle for my father. For my mother, counting the change in English was difficult. One afternoon, my father gave a customer who had bought $8 of goods $22 as change for a $20 bill, instead of $12. The word must have gone out to the neighborhood. People kept coming in with $20 bills. "Imagine the kind of businessman your father is. He gave the customer $8 worth of groceries plus an additional $20. We lost $10 on that purchase," my mother said. My father was often more interested in practicing Spanish with his Latino customers than in doing business. Shoplifters took advantage of the situation when my father was preoccupied talking Spanish with his customers and when my brother or mother was not around. He was so immersed in brushing up his language skills with native speakers that he did not usually notice anything amiss until it was too late, but that explained why my father never found the work boring. "Your father," my mother said in exasperation, "is the most unlikely person to be running a grocery store anywhere—much less in lawless America."

Soon after we started our market, my parents also bought a small apartment building with the money they had from the sale of their home in Japan. I threw in my entire savings toward the downpayment and, with trepidation, agreed to manage the building. I was busy all the time. I put in long hours at the newspaper and often came home late in the evening. On weekends I cleaned the building, did the family laundry, cooked, and wrote my columns. I had very little time for any outside social life, which I probably needed more now that my lifestyle had been changed by my parents' move. Through my parents' decision to open a grocery store, we had become a typical immigrant family. It was such a change from their former life. I had never considered running a small market as an option for my family, and I felt depressed about it. But my parents, especially my mother, surprised me with their spurt of energy and will to survive in America. She seemed to take to San Francisco, even though she spoke little English beyond salutations. I had assumed the role of the eldest son because I was older and more motivated than my brother, who had been drafted into running the business and was not enthusiastic.

During our Mission District store days, we lived in a constant state of fear. Vandalism and shoplifting were rampant, and our store windows were broken several times. One night, unbeknownst to me, my parents spent the entire night inside the store after the alarm company had called them at home. We had some close calls, too, but always something intervened to keep us out of harm's way. Once, two young men came into the store at dusk. My brother had gone to the library, and my parents were alone at the store. My mother felt her heart skip a beat because of the hard expression on their faces and their refusal to respond to my parents' hello. One man lingered just inside the entrance, while the other one made a round in the store as if to pick out some merchandise. But he did not have the face of someone who was there to make a purchase. Then, my mother saw a handgun protruding from his waist. Shaken by what she saw, she quickly warned my father in Korean and started praying, but my father did not catch on quickly. She repeated herself. At the entrance, the second man kept standing in the same spot, as if he were acting as lookout. The man who had been walking the aisles approached the counter but was empty-handed. My mother was sure he was going to take out the gun and tell them to empty the cash register, or worse. So she prayed: "Lord, please help this young man change his heart." Just then, a police car pulled up in front of the store and two officers walked in. The two young men disappeared in a flash. After the police left, my parents hurried to close the business early, but the two men came back. This time, my mother was sure they would be robbed. All she could do was pray.

Out of nowhere the police car returned, and the same police officers were in front of the store. The two men hurriedly left. My parents locked up and headed home. The two men were later apprehended after they robbed another store.

All around us businesses were being held up, including a Korean-owned market two blocks away, on Twenty-fourth Street. Store owners kept each other abreast of these unfortunate incidents and warned each other. The possibility and the fear of being the next victim never left us. Neighborhood youngsters took advantage of my parents whenever my brother was not around. They would order a sandwich, and while my father or mother prepared it, they made the rounds of the store and stole things. Once, two high school boys came inside the store and fled with a case of beer. On a reflex, my father ran after the thieves, to no avail, of course. I urged my parents to give up the business, but they always said, "We have to make a living." "There has to be a better way to make a living," I protested. "How?" my father said. "How about a bookstore?" "We'd be starving if we had a bookstore," my father said. "You just don't know." We did not make much money. I calculated that on good days, my parents and brother, working full-time, earned $120. That came out to earning less than the minimum wage.

The strain of working long hours under the constant threat of robbery took its toll on the family. By the second year of the business, frayed nerves exploded into heated arguments. The dinner table sometimes became a battleground. I feared we would all fall apart if we kept this up much longer. I became a reluctant mediator in family disputes because I was the only one not directly involved in the day-to-day operation of the business. No family could spend twenty-four hours together every day and still get along, I thought. I felt the mounting frustration of being the only member of the family with mainstream connections—of having to bail them out whenever we faced a crisis but not being in a position to make decisions that would prevent them from getting into those situations in the first place. I grew weary of being the one who always could be counted on, so I often wondered how I might extricate myself from the situation and still remain a good Korean daughter.

In March 1977, a day after having an argument with my parents and me, my brother disappeared with the family car. My parents came home on the bus after work, carrying the day's earnings in a brown paper bag. With downcast faces, they ate the simple dinner I had prepared. When my brother did not come home even after midnight, we became alarmed. I called all the police stations and every hospital in the city to see if he had been in an accident. All night we waited by the phone for any word about Emmanuel. I urged my parents to close the store on the following day, but they would not hear of it. "We can't willy-nilly close the business. We have a responsibility to our customers," my father said. "They count on us to be there." After a few days of traveling on the bus without the family car, they rented a pickup truck. The thought of the two old people running the store without my brother distracted me at work. Days later, my brother called to say he was all right, but would not say where he was. I had an inkling that he had gone to Los Angeles. That weekend I flew there and with the help of a friend drove around the Loyola Marymount University campus, where he had gone to school, and located his car. We waited until he showed up. He had been living out of his car and sleeping on a couch in the lounge of his old dormitory. He looked exhausted and was ready to come home. After spending a night at another friend's home, Emmanuel and I drove back to San Francisco. He looked defeated. I felt defeated, too. His flight to freedom had not worked because he had not been prepared. Born with a silver spoon in his mouth, my brother had been pampered all his life until my parents started their immigrant life. When he was a baby, my mother carried a small container with cotton pads soaked in alcohol, which she used to wipe his hands to kill germs after people touched them at church. His birth had given her standing in the family, whereas mine had only brought her tears when my father refused to even look at me for two weeks. I saw her transform into an outspoken woman after she bore Emmanuel. She dressed him like a little prince, and he looked the part because he was so handsome and had a dignified air about him even as a child. People stopped to look at him. My parents had big plans for Emmanuel. But in their zeal, he was never given a chance to decide what he wanted to do. He had little time to be idle, because after his homework, he had piano, violin, golf, and karate lessons to take. He was a straight-A student and completed high school in two years. They thought he should study to be a doctor. My father and brother were sure he would get into Harvard or Yale without any trouble. After that he would go to medical school and become a doctor who was also a handsome and talented musician and athlete. My brother was crushed when he was not accepted into an Ivy League school. He had the grades, but in trying to get through high school quickly, he had not participated in extra-curricular activities—the kinds of things deans of admissions also take into consideration. My pep talk about being able to get a good education in the United States no matter where you went to school did not make an impression after all those years of the build up and expectations from my parents. So, on that night when my brother and I returned from Los Angeles, and they congratulated me on work well done, I could not fully share my parents' joy over the prodigal son coming home. Deep inside, I felt that however well-meaning they were, what made my parents happy was not necessarily good for my brother. Born and raised in Japan, but educated in American schools, he thought like an American. Yet because of my parents' extraordinarily strong Korean emphasis at home, Emmanuel had been unable to break away from the grips of Korean culture. If I felt marginal, he was a thousand times more so: he truly belonged nowhere. He did not even have points of comparison because he had never lived in Korea. He spoke the language because it had been drilled into him, but he felt no emotional attachments to the Korean ethos, and yet he was forced to live it. What a tragic figure my brother is, I thought as I watched my mother serve dinner, beaming at the sight of her only son safely under the family roof again.

And so countless times I thought it would be best for my

parents to return to Korea, where they had old friends and classmates, and leave their son and daughter to lead their own lives. But their desire to be near their children seemed to overshadow all other considerations. Their love was unconditional, and it was suffocating us. I did not have the capacity to make them understand why they had to let us go, and give us the chance to mess up our own lives, if that was our choice. Sometimes I even suggested that the whole family return to Korea. My mother liked the idea, but my father and brother did not. To my father, home was not Seoul but Boshigol in North Korea, to which he never could return as long as the Communists were in control. "If I can't go to my native place, I might as well stay in San Francisco," he said. My brother, having never bonded with things Korean, had no attachment to Korea. And, my parents were determined to continue the business and not be a financial burden to me. I admired their independent spirit, but I thought the price too high. I would have preferred suffering financially over living with the constant worry about them operating the market. It was not until our fourth year in business, after my brother fell ill and could not work for a while, that we got rid of the store. The Mission District store had exhausted all of us. We sold it at a rock-bottom price to an immigrant family from Hong Kong, who were still operating it with their children in 1994.

Relieved that the store was finally sold, and my parents and brother were home, I went to Paris for a vacation in September 1978. It had been some time since I last was in Paris, and I felt carefree for the first time since my parents' arrival in the United States. In my small room at l'Hotel Stella not far from the Arc de Triomphe, I felt the tension leave my body. I curled up on a soft French bed and slept for ten hours straight, oblivious to the traffic noise outside. When I awoke the following morning to the sounds of people sweeping the floor in the hallway, the last three years of my life did not seem like my own. Seated at a small table in my room, I figured out how I would meet the expenses of our apartment house. Satisfied that I could manage without the income from the store, if we did not have long vacancies that would interrupt cash flow, I went out for café au lait and French bread. I walked more than ten miles that day, writing down my thoughts in cafés and on park benches. I was thankful that at night I could return to my room and sleep without worrying about my parents. As San Francisco and the family diminished in my mind, I even lapsed into daydreaming about what my life might have been had I come to France instead of the United States for schooling. My French tutor in Tokyo, Madame Calendreau (see chapter 7), had so captivated me when I was in junior high that I had fancied myself studying art in Paris and wearing a black beret like hers. During my long walks by the Seine, I resolved to become more detached from my family and not get so embroiled in their problems.

I returned to San Francisco on October 2 to learn that during my absence my parents had located another business to buy. They were all set to proceed and were waiting for my return to complete the transaction. I could not believe it.

Were we back to where we had been three months earlier? All my resolve during my walks along the Seine to become detached from my family vanished in an instant. I became angrier by the minute, but I could not convey to them why I was so upset. As my mother told the story, the opportunity was the result of a fortuitous dream she had a few days after I had left for Paris. Without revealing the contents of the dream, she said she asked my father to go to a corner store and get a newspaper. Sure enough, they noticed an ad for a business opportunity that sounded too good to be true. It turned out to be a small cigar shop downtown on Third Street that also sold sandwiches, milk, fruits, wine and beer, and magazines. It catered to commuters and workers in nearby office buildings, and was open from 6:00 A.M. to 6:00 P.M., Monday through Friday. "Where can you find a business you operate only five days a week?" my mother said, happily. Even my brother seemed interested in acquiring the store. Apparently, when my parents had inquired somewhat disbelievingly about the volume of business, the seller had suggested that they find out for themselves. Turning over the key to my parents, he suggested that they work for ten days while he took his annual vacation to Nepal. My parents and brother took up the offer and discovered for themselves how profitable the small store was. "We would be kicking our good luck if we didn't take this gift from above," my mother said. They decided they could not pass it up. So, no sooner than we had gotten rid of one headache, we acquired another.

Watching my angry face, my father tried to smooth over things. "You don't understand what it's like not to have a job," he said. "Whether you teach at a university or run a market, the important thing is that you work. Don't underestimate the dignity of work." As soon as my father said his piece, my mother spoke: "While we were home without our store, I was counting every penny we spent. I was buying day-old bread. Your father and I went all the way to the greengrocery on Seventeenth Avenue to buy produce." I did not want to hear this. I wanted to scream, but what was the use? Unless I were a millionaire and could make them feel secure about their financial future, how could I stop them from wanting to earn a living? In the equation of my peace of mind and their desire to earn a living, I was compelled to give in. I tried to think like a Buddhist, telling myself that in my previous life I must have been deeply indebted to my parents, so in this life I had to repay the debt.

Juggling Several Worlds

I led several contradictory lives: There was my work life as a mainstream journalist, and one as an ethnic journalist. There was my life as a member of an immigrant family. And finally, there was my personal life, which was separate from the family and work. I also began to write fiction. And, when I could squeeze a little time out, I dated, although I felt ambivalent at the thought of marrying again. I did not have confidence that I could make a marriage work. Besides, the Korean family entanglement was so burdensome to me at times, I wondered if I wanted to create my own family unit. Why ask for more responsibility when I could barely handle what I had? I went out with men more to go to the opera or the symphony or to walk in the woods than to nurture lasting emotional involvement. Though women friends my age were talking about marriage and starting a family, I remained unsure. Not until I would meet the right man, I said. I wondered if I would ever find the right man, because I always felt huge gaps with non-Koreans I went out with, given their ignorance about things Korean. I certainly was not meeting eligible professional Korean men my age with compatible values and tricultural sensibilities in San Francisco. I also had several close American women friends, but with them, too, there was a limit to how much I could communicate. I was always longing to find people to share all of my worlds—something that would prove near impossible. My Korean women friends were far away, and even with them, I felt gaps because they had spent their formative years in Korea and I had not. Was I asking for the impossible, finding people with whom I could bear my soul? I would go to parties and come home, utterly disgusted with the time I felt I had wasted. What was the point of the small talk and laugher? Why had I not stayed home and curled up with Dostoevsky or Tolstoy, Camus or Sartre, Tennyson or the Brownings? My several lives were often incompatible, and I led a schizophrenic existence. I shut the door to one when I entered the other. Back and forth I traveled, sometimes within minutes of each other. At times I felt at home in all, and at other times I thought I belonged to none. Could I really find one world where my life's many components—now separated by languages, cultures, and sensibilities—could be integrated?

Just as I had practically no control over how members of my family made decisions that affected my life, I had little say in my corner of the mainstream American newspaper world, where white men of similar backgrounds, experiences, and sensibilities called all the shots. I liked them on an individual basis, but as purveyors of power and as members of a group, they manifested insecurities and posturing that repelled me. Underneath their smooth and polite facades, they were desperate for validation, always in a race with one another, competing for power. When they chose to hire nonwhites, they were usually those who talked white and acted white and laughed at white jokes. I did not take it too seriously, since I never aspired to get on the management track. It seemed like such a waste of one's energy to engage in and put up with the superficial, yet calculated, game playing just to get a title and more money. Managers of newspapers, too, were products of their backgrounds, education, and experiences, as I was of mine. How could I expect them to be otherwise? Besides, as long as I stuck to mainstream beats, such as government, law, and politics, our philosophical differences did not clash. I concentrated on my work in my small sphere and wrote extensively about issues pertaining to Asians, especially Koreans, for ethnic newspapers. I always had that outlet—the advantage of being a hyphenated American. So, even within my world of journalism, I lived in two: my regular mainstream job and my side work. With the influx of immigrants from Asia, I could not close my eyes to that side of my life. Koreans know me not because of my nearly three decades of work for American media but because of my many years of contributing articles to Korean newspapers.

In May 1975, I began covering the legal beat, an assignment that gave me an insight into the workings of judges and lawyers and how these powerful people and institutions influence our lives. Though my knowledge of the law was limited to a few law courses I had taken in graduate school and my brief stint covering the courthouse in Columbia, Missouri, during my senior year in college, I wanted to give it a try. The idea of covering the California Supreme Court appealed to me. But my assignment also entailed covering all the state agencies located in San Francisco, including the Public Utilities Commission, the attorney general's office, the appellate court, the trial courts, and the State Bar of California, the organization to which all lawyers licensed to practice in California must belong. This was a beat that reporters avoided because it was considered tedious. But I was intrigued by its possibilities, and I liked working on my own, outside the newsroom in a pressroom in city hall. I quickly learned why it was an unpopular beat.

Trying to decide what to cover and what to ignore was truly daunting. Had Michael Taylor, a *San Francisco Chronicle* reporter who was my competition, not helped me, I might not have survived those difficult first weeks on the beat. "The trick is to figure out which stories to kick," Taylor said in his wry, East Coast preppie way, meaning which stories to ignore or convince the city desk of their having no news value. I learned the beat from Taylor. Whenever he caught me looking dejected or lost in voluminous legal briefs and court decisions, he would light up an unfiltered Pall Mall cigarette and say, "Don't worry, it'll make sense soon." He was right. One day, the mystery of legal procedures and jargon disappeared. I could flip through a fifty-page state supreme court decision on deadline and call in a story from a pay phone. I counted my progress and celebrated those small victories alone to keep the pleasure to myself. I found covering the high court intellectually challenging, too. All the important issues of the day—social, financial, political, or eco-nomic—ultimately ended up before the court. The judiciary, not the executive or legislative branches, was the most powerful institution, I decided. These men and women in black robes ultimately made decisions that touched all our lives; the lawyers had made the legal profession an indispensable monopoly. I liked keeping my eye on them so much that I covered the courts for more than a decade, a record at the *Examiner*.

My ten years on the beat coincided with the last two years that Chief Justice Donald R. Wright was on the bench, and all of Rose Elizabeth Bird's years, when the state's first woman chief justice's administrative style and the liberal majority's decisions generated much controversy, in and out of the court. People were upset and concerned about Bird's managment style, and I wrote many stories covering this issue and the controversy surrounding the Bird court. Some of the powerful judges and lawyers in California who sup-ported Bird were upset with me. I had many sleepless nights over the stories I wrote, including one on Justice Marshall McComb, who was ultimately removed from the bench for senility. On two occasions, things became so harried that I even tried to prepare my mother that I might go to jail rather than reveal confidential sources. I could not make her understand why reporters might choose to do this. On several instances, powerful people exerted pressure to kill stories I was working on, and when that did not work, they went to my bosses to discredit me. I agonized over those stories, but the editors ran them and I survived.

☯

My fondness for San Francisco kept me there, despite opportunities to move to bigger newspapers through the late 1970s and 1980s. The old North Korean refugee in me was drawn to the City by the Bay because it seemed about as close to being in Asia as I could get in America. It was comforting to go to Chinatown for a bowl of noodles or Japantown to pick up a teapot, and to get lost in crowds of other Asians, some of whose ancestors had been in the United States since the 1850s. Still, through all the years in the United States, I could never quite quell my soul's longing to return to my native place to see whether I could adjust to living there. I had left Korea before I had had a chance to get sick of the place. My trips to Korea during vacations since my move to San Francisco had strengthened the longing, for one only sees the attractive things during short visits.

My opportunity to return came in 1987 when South Korean students put their lives on the line by challenging the regime of the notorious dictator Doo-Hwan Chun. Seoul would be hosting the 1988 summer Olympics, and brigades of foreign reporters and photographers were on hand to cover preparations for the games and many other aspects of the host country, including its so-called economic miracle. Radical students clashing with riot police, and the recording of these events by Western journalists, made it appear that the Olympics was in jeopardy. Night after night the images flashing across TV screens suggested that the whole country was going up in flames. When it appeared that there would be no letup, I received a memo from John Kirkpatrick, then assistant managing editor for the *Examiner*'s foreign/national desk. "I think we should be in Korea," he wrote, asking whether I would be willing to go. "Of course," I replied, promptly making arrangements to leave for Seoul.

10. REDISCOVERING THE REAL HOME

(1987–1989)

A single log bridge
of hate and love
across
lives' ash,
a bridge of no-return stands there.

Yet to meet again,
it's the waist of the human body.

Why don't we open the gate,
Panmunjom, Wood Gate Tavern?
On top of the hexagonal pavilion
with no guards around,
let's put up the same, one flag
with our hands
and not theirs.

—Ko Won (1925–　), *Some Other Time*

Koreans Fight for Democracy

The smell of pepper gas lingering in the languid summer air stung my nose as the taxi I boarded at Kimpo International Airport sped past the Yonsei University campus on the evening of June 24, 1987.

"There must have been another big demonstration today," I said to the driver. Like so many cabbies in Seoul, he looked over-worked and harrassed.

"We've had one almost every day since May," the driver said. "How long have you been out of the country?"

"Two months," I said. I had taken a ten-day vacation in Seoul in April.

"You were fortunate. It's pandemonium around here. I'm sick of the students; I'm sick of the government. I wish I could go some-place where it's not crisis every day."

Seoul always felt like a city in a crisis to me. Just being there made my heart beat faster. Tear gas, too, was part of Seoul's makeup.

During the more than a decade since my parents had pulled up roots and come to America, when I had been preoccupied with our immigrant life, much had transpired in South Korea. Koreans had the misfortune of living under two military dictators, one after another— Chung-Hee Park and Doo-Hwan Chun. After seizing power, the soldiers changed into civilian clothes and became presidents.

Park took control in a 1961 coup, capitalizing on the chaos that followed the student revolution that toppled the Syngman Rhee government (see chapter 7). He became increasingly more repressive, despite his pronouncements about creating a new society, free of corruption and graft. After getting himself elected in the October 1963 election by a mere 1.5 percent margin, he rammed through a new constitution that gave him the power to name the premier and cabinet members without the consent of the National Assembly.

Having lived through Park's rule between 1967 and 1970, I had a strong taste of his repression and hypocrisy. I still have a censored copy of the 1968 cover story I wrote about his wife for

Asia Magazine as a reminder of those days, when politics was the subject I discussed only among friends and in private places. Unlike her husband, the first lady was gracious and charming and was well-liked. In the spring of that year, the South Korean government had launched one of its periodic austerity campaigns. Mrs. Park herself urged female journalists to write stories criticizing Koreans who wore imported clothing, accessories, and luxuries such as mink, which was the most coveted luxury item in Korea in the late 1960s and early 1970s. Toward the end of my interview, I asked Mrs. Park if she owned any mink. She replied she had two—a coat and a shawl. "Why have we not seen you in one?" I asked. She explained that she wore furs and her jewelry only when she traveled abroad with her husband on state visits. I thought that was an interesting piece of information, so I put it in my story. But government censors had penciled it out, so the millions of English-language readers of *Asia Magazine* throughout Asia did not get this bit of news. As mentioned earlier, the Park regime had one campaign after another, from one urging consumers to eat less beef to another exhorting them to refrain from buying expensive imported merchandise. The irony, of course, was that high-level government officials were, by far, the worst offenders of his austerity movements.

Life became progressively more difficult for the average Korean. After nearly losing the 1971 election to opposition leader Dae-Jung Kim, Park tightened his control even more, smothering all dissent. He declared martial law, dissolved the National Assembly, closed all colleges and universities, imposed censorship, and suspended political activities. Then, he pushed through a new constitution that permitted him to succeed himself indefinitely, to appoint a third of the National Assembly, and to exercise emergency powers at will. The president would no longer be chosen by voters but by an electoral college of supposedly nonpartisan locally elected deputies.

When a wave of nationwide protests erupted despite the strictures, Park issued emergency decrees, which among other things made it a crime, punishable by not less than one year of imprisonment, to criticize the constitution or to report about it. The president justified the harsh measures by citing the need for national unity in the face of an alleged threat of attack from North Korea—an interesting twist for a man who had been involved in a Communist insurrection himself.

There appeared to be no end to the man's greed for power or his tricks to suppress dissent. To silence opposition leader Dae-Jung Kim, who waged anti-Park campaigns from abroad, Park had Korean Central Intelligence Agency (KCIA) agents kidnap him from a Tokyo hotel. And, when Dae-Jung Kim and former President Po-Sun Yun called for the restoration of democracy, Park had them arrested and sentenced to five to eight years in prison. Similarly, students, writers, and anyone else who dared to protest were all locked up.

When the opposition party gained a plurality in the December 1978 National Assembly elections, its leader, Young-Sam Kim, made a speech attacking the Park regime in the foreign press, charging that Park's emergency decrees were an unconstitutional suppression of human rights. The president had Young-Sam Kim ousted from the National Assembly. To protest Park's action, all opposition members of the National Assembly resigned on October 13, 1979. Less than two weeks after the incident, Park was shot to death by his own director of intelligence, Chae-Kyu Kim, during a dinner.

The end of the eighteen-year rule of the hard-drinking, womanizing little general from Kyongsang Province, however, left a huge political vacuum, since he had not groomed a successor. The vaccum was quickly filled by Chun, the head of the Defense Security Command, whose responsibility had been to investigate the presidential assassination. By December 1979, Chun and his cohorts had taken control of the army, and within four months the reins of the government. Chun, who like his predecessor was the son of a poor farmer from Kyongsang Province, ruled under martial law. Universities and colleges—the center of political dissent—were closed, censorship was imposed, and criticism of the incumbent and past presidents was banned. And, in what amounted to the absurdity of absurdities, Chun's decree also banned "the manufacture and spreading of rumors."

Despite his Martial Law Command orders, however, citizens of Kwangju—long the center of political disaffection in South Korea—rose up to challenge Chun in May 1980. Chun and Tae-Woo Roh, who would succeed him in 1988, put down the uprising by dispatching government troops. By official count, 189 citizens of Kwangju were killed, but residents believe the figure to be many times more. The United States played a role in Kwangju. General John A. Wickham, Jr., the chief of the South Korea–United States Combined Forces Command, had released South Korean soldiers under his command to help quell the uprisings. This unfortunate association of the United States with the bloody hands of Chun's men would plant a seed of anti-Americanism among students and intellectuals. America, which Koreans viewed as their savior for coming to their aid during the Korean War, was no longer so. Chun was not able to wash his hands of the Kwangju massacre, which dogged him throughout his eight-year rule. Less than three months after the massacre, on August 5, 1980, Chun promoted himself from lieutenant general to full general, retired from the army, and, like his predecessor, changed into civilian clothes and got himself elected president by the rubber-stamp electoral college.

If Park was bad, Chun was much worse. At least some had grudging respect for Park's intelligence and his economic policies that got South Korea into the twentieth century, but Chun was a laughingstock whom nobody respected. His appearance—bald head, plain face, and unrefined mannerisms—was the butt of private jokes. His wife did not help, with her loquacity and her relatives' involvement in major financial scandals. But unlike Park, whose relationship with the Jimmy Carter White House had been strained because of Carter's disapproval of human rights violations in South Korea, Chun had a friend in the new Republican administration. Chun was President Ronald Reagan's first official guest in the White House, which gave the South Korean leader a stamp of approval he needed, but which further alienated the country's students and intellectuals from America. Reagan bolstered Chun again by visiting Seoul in 1983. During my several visits to South Korea between 1981 and 1986, I could feel the sentiment against the United States growing among the ranks of my former colleagues in universities and in journalism. I met with dissident students and was chilled to see the scars on their bodies from electrical torture they had endured from Chun's agents. And, by the time of my visit in April 1987, even I was subjected to harangues from friends and former colleagues who lashed out at the hypocrisy of the U.S. government. Anti-Americanism had been extended even to Korean Americans; by virtue of being American citizens, we were guilty by association.

And now two months later I had returned to see South Koreans poised to risk their lives for democracy. The usually busy lobby of the Hotel Lotte in downtown was practically empty and reeked of tear gas.

"The smell of pepper gas is strong," I said to the check-in clerk.

"I must have become immune to it," she said. "I don't smell anything now. The demonstration was hours ago."

"Believe me, the smell is still pretty strong."

"I must have become immune to tear gas," she repeated, with an ironic smile.

Earlier in the day, a big confrontation had occurred between protestors and riot police around the corner from the Lotte, outside Myongdong Cathedral, the seat of the Korean Catholic Church. The cathedral was one of a handful of sanctuaries from the police.

From the window of my tenth-floor room facing the cathedral, I could see the ravages of the day's confrontation. Store windows in the busy Myong-dong shopping area were shut tight, and bricks, rocks, and spent Molotov cocktails, which demonstrators had thrown at riot police, were strewn on the street. Around the corner, four pale-yellow and green buses, which the locals called "chicken coops" because of the wire mesh protecting their windows, were parked at the entrance of Myong-dong. The temperature inside the buses must have been unbearable for the riot policemen who had to sleep inside in case they were suddenly needed.

I called the *Examiner* and talked to one of my editors, who filled me in on what she had read on the news wires since I left San

Francisco almost twenty-four hours earlier. We discussed our plans for the following day. With a seventeen-hour time difference between Seoul and San Francisco, even the best-laid plans could go awry by day's end in Seoul. I would be checking with the office at 9:00 A.M. and 1:00 P.M. Seoul time and filing stories no later than 5:00 P.M., which would be 1:00 A.M. San Francisco time. Before I left, I had submitted a list of a dozen stories I planned to write; it would be a matter of finding time to work on them while I covered breaking news.

After I hung up, I unpacked, took a bath, and called some of my contacts to confirm the appointments I had made from San Francisco. With the immediate chores out of the way, I tried to go to sleep but I was still feeling jet lag from the long flight and excitement about being back in Seoul. As I tried to sleep, twenty years of my life since I had first returned to work in Korea in 1967 flooded through my mind, like strips from a homemade movie. I'm always packing and unpacking, coming and going, I thought, as I slowly succumbed to fatigue. Where is my home? Where do I really belong?

I woke up at dawn with the sound of screeching cars below my window, a reminder of the harshness of life in the South Korean capital. Another hectic day was unfolding outside.

I began to call people shortly after 7:00 A.M. In Seoul, reporters had to reach news sources before they left for work or after 10:30 P.M. when they returned home. For the Korean male, so little had changed since the days of my great-grandfather Bong-Ho Kang, although the habit of staying out late was no longer limited to the idle elite class. Working men in Seoul also did not spend much time at home and went there mostly to sleep after drinking with colleagues and friends after work; this was (and is) the way Korean men rid themselves of stress.

As I called around, I was more sure than ever that South Korea was at a crucial turning point and I had come to witness history in the making. In the past, the silent middle class had not stood behind the dissidents in opposing President Doo-Hwan Chun. They had watched from a safe distance, because opposing Chun could mean only bad news. But now, the tide had turned, and they were not afraid to speak up.

What had tipped the scale was Chun's brazen decision two months earlier, in April 1987, to pick his cohort in the 1979 coup, General Tae-Woo Roh, as his heir apparent. They had made a deal back then that Chun would become president first and Roh would follow, and Chun was keeping that promise. Reaction was swift. Demonstrations erupted all over the country and continued for weeks. Images of firebomb-throwing students and riot police flashed across TV screens abroad and made it appear as if the whole country was burning up, raising doubts about whether South Korea could successfully host the summer Olympic games a little more than a year away in the fall of 1988. This was not good for Chun. The Chun regime, whose agents slaughtered and wounded several thousand civilians to stay in power, had staked everything on the Olympics. Chun had hoped to legitimize his rule and improve his tainted image by using the games as a showcase for his nation's economic miracle. South Korea's economic progress received plenty of attention, but it also invited concerns over the paradox of a thriving economy in a repressive authoritarian state. A dissident university student was killed during police torture, opposition leader Dae-Jung Kim was almost constantly under house arrest, and citizens' protests were routine. The economic miracle could not hide the fact that Korea was a police state.

On June 10, an estimated five hundred thousand protestors, including Buddhist monks, Catholic priests, and ordinary citizens, had taken to the streets in actions that stunned the world. Pictures of the mass demonstrations were played on the front pages of major U.S. newspapers and received top play on network news. It was into this charged atmosphere of mass demonstrations, firebombs, and tear gas that I returned to my native country, this time as a reporter from America, almost thirty-seven years to the day after the outbreak of the Korean War and twenty years since I had first gone back to work there as a young newspaperwoman.

Everywhere I went, I carried the gas mask I had purchased on the black market. In downtown Seoul, tear gas hung in the humid summer air for days. But the city's resilient residents went about their daily business, sneezing and coughing through their gauze masks, dampened handkerchiefs, and wash towels.

On June 26, the newly formed National Coalition for a Democratic Constitution, consisting of major dissident and religious groups, planned a nationwide "grand peace march" in a show of solidarity to pressure the ruling party into agreeing to a free presidential election. On the previous evening I had visited several university campuses and talked with students who were working late into the night, preparing placards, organizing teams, and planning logistics. The student command centers looked like bunkers with large supplies of instant noodles, soft drinks, and dried squid, the ubiquitous snack food. At Ewha Womans University in Sinchon in western Seoul, a junior English major told me she had spent the day knocking on seventy doors and passing out leaflets, an activity that could have led to her arrest. When I asked her whether she was fearful, she said: "At first I was scared, but as I went on, I became more brazen. I also felt encouraged. Everyone seemed very sympathetic—even grandmothers. It was quite infectious." But three of her friends were not so lucky. While I was on the campus, Sook-Hee Kim, a home economics professor friend of mine, received a call saying three of her students had been detained by police. At Ewha, many students spoke disparagingly of Chun and Roh when I solicited their opinion. "Roh Tae-Woo is Chun Doo-Hwan in a wig," one said, in reference to Roh's full head of hair and Chun's baldness. "They are one and the same bastard," she said. The comment elicited a peal of laughter from her classmates. Campus bulletin boards were covered with messages in black, red, and blue: "Down with Dictatorship," "How Are You Going to Atone for All Your Sins, Chun Doo-Hwan?" and, "Kill the Butcher of Kwangju," a reference to the May 1980 suppression of an anti-Chun civilian uprising in Kwangju.

On the day of the big demonstration, Yong Yoon, a former colleague from my days in the capital in 1967 who was now a university professor, called and said he would stop by to see me.

News sources seldom talked on the phones because they often were tapped. Over a cup of coffee in my room at the Hotel Lotte, he told me that that night's peace march would be a crucial turning point. He predicted more than a million people in Seoul alone would participate. We were careful to lower our voices when we brought up people's names, discussed sensitive topics, or made any reference to future appointments. We switched between English and Korean to annoy those whom we assumed could have wired the room, had they wanted to. "After a quarter century of military dictatorship, the Korean people are sick and tired of soldiers," Yoon said, as if he were addressing an audience and not just me, sitting alone across the coffee table from him. "This is our first real chance to show how united we are. This march is the culmination of years of hard work by students and other groups to bring together different segments of society to demonstrate our opposition to Chun Doo-Hwan." As he got up to leave, he said, "This is the day I've been waiting for. I feel very excited."

The demonstrations continued late into the night. I retreated to the hotel when the pepper gas became unbearable. Pepper gas was a repulsive form of tear gas that choked, blinded, and burned the skin of anyone caught in its path. I heard volley after volley of pepper gas cannisters go off outside the hotel. Yoon came to see me before he headed for his home. He looked exhilarated.

The "grand peace march" and the wide coverage it received had done the job. Finally, his back against the wall, Chun went on national television on July 1 and agreed to "take measures to promote democratic development and national harmony" by providing for the first direct presidential elections in sixteen years to pick his successor. The coming of the massive protests, with the Olympics looming in the background, had done more to speed up the democratic process in Korea than all the movements that had gone on in the previous four decades, I thought as I watched the glum face of Chun on the TV screen in my hotel room. All this happened, I also realized, because of the focus of the world press on South Korean dissidents— so different from the international community's neglect of the independence efforts eighty years before. The Olympics, which brought thousands of newspeople from around the world during the fourteen months immediately prior to the games, literally left Chun no choice but to give in, if he wanted to ensure that they would be held in his country. In the days immediately after Chun's announcement, there was much anticipation in the air, and everywhere I went, Koreans were talking about democratization.

A few days later, a funeral was scheduled in Kwangju for Han-Yol Lee, a Yonsei University student who had died after he was hit in the head by a tear-gas cannister during an anti-government demonstration. I went to Kwangju to cover the funeral. Tens of thousands of citizens had turned out to walk with Lee's body to Mangwol-dong cemetery, where many victims of the Kwangju uprising were buried. The burial under a full moon followed a three-hour procession after Lee's body was accompanied from Seoul on the train by Yonsei University students. Citizens lined the main streets and applauded as the funeral procession passed by. Some of them had waited for hours. Yonsei University students, wearing black and white mourning clothes, directed traffic. There were so many people headed for the funeral that we had to leave our cars a mile away and walk to the cemetery up the long, winding, unpaved road. During the walk, I met a young woman who told me she was Lee's childhood friend. Gwak-Suk Han, who worked at a café, said she left her job in the middle of her shift and took a taxi to the cemetery to say good-bye. She wiped her eyes as she spoke of her friend, whom she had not seen since they were children. After the burial she came to my hotel, shared dinner, and offered to keep an eye on the demonstration outside while I wrote a story in my room. She took my tear-gas mask and came back several times to let me know how things were going, until I had filed my story. When I went outside, it was nearing midnight and people who had gone to the cemetery had gathered in front of the provincial capital building around the corner from the hotel. They sang "Our Dream Is Unification," a song that Koreans of my generation had grown up with and one that had become a favorite ballad at protest marches of this younger generation. The protestors remained until the early hours of morning.

Later that morning, I headed for Pusan, South Korea's second largest city and a hotbed of anti-Americanism. I wanted to do a story for the *Examiner* on the growing anti-Americanism, which had become by then practically a subculture among students, intellectuals, and laborers. In Pusan radical students had set fire to the United States Information Agency. As I traveled south, I remembered my trip to Pusan during the Korean War on the rooftop of the "freedom train." Then, as now, my native land was at a crossroads. Then, it was Korea's survival from Communist invasion; now it was Korea's future and the aspirations of the nation's people. Having worked hard to achieve an "economic miracle" out of the rubble of the war, they now demanded a "political miracle."

Back in the early fifties, dusty roads were filled with fleeing refugees, carrying their possessions on oxcarts, and on their backs and heads. Hungry babies cried as they suckled on their mothers' dry breasts. Many of the women were too malnourished to nurse their young. There were few paved roads, and most of the roads were so narrow only one car could pass. Refugees were pushed aside into the ditches to make room for soldiers to pass. Koreans were so poor they ate "kkool kkool" gruel—another term for hog food—by making stew out of leftovers collected from U.S. Army garbage cans. The mountains were bald because people stripped them of trees for firewood, and the rivers and streams became bathhouses and laundries. And the smell of excrement, used as fertilizer, permeated the air. The sight of men carrying honeybuckets balanced on a pole on their lean and suntanned shoulders was as integral a part of the Korean scenery as the kimchi jars, used to preserve pickled cabbage, that were in the backyards of virtually every Korean home.

Now, thirty-seven years later, from inside my rented car, I saw mountains lush with trees. In the low lands, miles of rice fields stretched out like handwoven carpets in different shades of green. In the old days the farmers were mostly men, but now they were mostly women, because men were at the factories building cars, computers, and ships. And now those precarious narrow roads were hard to find. A modern highway had replaced the old road, next to the railroad tracks on which we had traveled more than a generation before. The new highway was lined with flowering acacias, poplars, maples, bamboo groves, and cosmos in pink, white, and lavender. Because of chemical fertilizers, there was no longer the stench of excrement, which Korean farmers used to call the "perfume of the countryside."

The Korean saying "In ten years even rivers and mountains change" rang true for me again. Indeed, everything had changed. I felt a complicated mixture of emotions—nostalgia for bygone days, happiness at the nation's prosperity, and fear of the indiscriminate acceptance of technological advancement. I do not think Koreans worried about that, but returning home from California, I wished that South Korea would not repeat the mistakes of other nations that had embraced technology to the point of polluting the environment. Faces I saw on this trip became superimposed in a collage in my mind's eye over old images from thirty-seven years ago. Everywhere I went, Koreans talked not about food and shelter but about freedom and democracy. Until recently, Koreans had been too busy trying to eke out a living and worrying about the threat from North Korea to talk about luxurious concepts like freedom and democracy. But now the emerging educated middle class longed for a democratic government. They were both embarrassed and angry that they had allowed democracy to elude them for so long. The talk in the streets and in their homes was that President Chun must leave office. So must Roh, the ruling party's presidential candidate. People held them responsible for the Kwangju massacre. "How will they ever pay for their sins?" asked Sun-Ak Koo, a forty-seven-year-old Kwangju mother whose son was killed by soldiers dispatched by Chun during the massacre.

There was another memorable face, that of the attorney Nam-Soon Hong, seventy-five, whom I interviewed for a story. Hong was sometimes known as the godfather of Kwangju's resistance movement, and the young dissidents worshiped him. He stood out because there were so few like him among his generation and social class. Long before it was fashionable, he challenged the government, risking his life, career, and personal comfort and that of his family. He had devoted the last twenty-five years of his life to fighting the government. In 1980 he received a life sentence for opposing the government, but after a long court fight, he ended up serving just two years in jail.

When I visited him at his home, Hong was sitting cross-legged on an *ondol* floor, covered with a pale-green bamboo mat. He wore summer clothing—long trousers and a long jacket of pale ramie. Hong, whose life spanned all of Korea's tumultuous modern history, told me he was "optimistic" about the future of his country and said if he lived another ten years, he would see democracy realized—that was his dream. He said he was happy that the Korean people's aspiration for democracy was being written up in American newspapers. "Help us," he said, urging me to come back and see him again.

In Pusan, Tae-Won Cho, thirty-four, a bespectacled man whose face reminded me of Jean-Paul Sartre's, told me he had been unable to lead a normal life or find decent work because of his involvement in anti-government demonstrations while attending Pusan University ten years earlier. Cho belonged to a new generation of Koreans who did not have a memory of the war and the starvation that went along with it. It was hard for me to believe there was a new generation that had grown up without experiencing the hunger pangs of those years. Cho and his friends told me that Koreans should be able to control their own fate. They said their elders were foolish to be so grateful to the United States, and to rely on the Americans. This is where my work and my personal life crossed. I could provide a personal look, an insider's view, because of who I was. Yet, had I not worked for an American newspaper, there would not have been the vehicle to tell the story. In these moments, I felt truly privileged, and my resolve to interpret and translate cross-cultural stories grew, for I would be reminded that I might be the only Korean American reporter who was in a position to do so. Thinking this put added pressure on me, but this, too, was part of my mission.

My journey south also took me to the coastal city of Chinju in the southeastern tip of Korea, the ancestral home of the Kang clan. It was dusk when I arrived. This was a side journey, made on the spur of the moment, yet it added to the story I wrote for my newspaper later, for it brought home to my California readers the connection between their reporter, a resident of San Francisco, and Korea. My first stop in Chinju was at a park carved out of a mountain, where I stood looking down at the city and the ocean, thinking of the old song about Chinju, and a long-lost native son who walks hundreds of miles to reach his beloved city after many years of wandering away from home. Every Korean schoolchild also knew about Chinju in another context, because of the city's beautiful *kisaeng* named Nongye, who in an act of patriotism in the sixteenth century, plunged into the water, taking with her a Japanese general she was entertaining. What a historic moment in my life, I thought. I was filled with excitement at the prospect of making some connection with my ancestors. More than six centuries ago they had left these shores for Hamgyong Province in the North in search of a better life. On that muggy summer night, standing on the hilltop, I imagined my long-dead ancestors walking on these same patches of deep-brown earth, growing rice, catching fish, and repairing their thatched roofs after the harvest. This city of the Kangs was known for upright and stubborn people. A few pointed inquiries brought me to an old wooden gate that was in need of repair. Was this the headquarters of the Kang clan? Obviously, the clan was not doing too well, if the sagging entrance was any indication. I pushed open the creaking gate and ventured inside.

Behind the old gate I was enchanted to find three traditional homes in the Chosun-era style, with slate-colored, upturned roofs worn with age. In the courtyard were pink balsam flowers, whose petals Korean girls use to dye their fingernails pink without using chemicals. I was overcome with a desire to spend a night there, though I knew I still had a long journey ahead and stories to write. But a light shone in the window of one of the houses.

"Is anybody home?" I asked, speaking in that direction.

"Who is here?" came a man's voice from behind the latticed doors.

"I am a person named Kang, too," I said. "I've come from far away."

As I approached the veranda, three people got up from what appeared to be an early evening nap and came outside.

The man who answered was wearing long summer cotton underpants that doubled as pajamas for older Korean men. A woman and a girl wore Western clothing. The man quickly pulled on regular pants over his underwear.

In the United States people would hesitate before knocking on a stranger's door in an unfamiliar city at night, but here I did not feel the slightest fear. I explained that I was on my way to Pusan to write a story for my American newspaper, and that I had stopped by because Chinju was the home of the Kang clan.

"Such a precious guest!" the man's wife said, bringing a fan out for me.

The man turned out to be in charge of the Kang clan business office. Sheepishly, he said that his name was actually not Kang, but Park. He promptly summoned Mr. Kang, the top officer of the Kang clan and a scholar.

Presently, Mr. Kang, who lived nearby, arrived. He was a friendly man who queried me about the names of my ancestors, and he instantly reminded me of my great-great-grandfather Soo-Il Kang as described to me. As my father was a modern man who subscribed to new thinking and had not followed the traditional style of naming his offspring, Mr. Kang could not readily deduce from my given name where I belonged. I promised to bring with me next time all the names of my ancestors, to enable Mr. Kang to better explain where I fit in the clan's genealogy.

Even as I listened to him, mosquitoes, fat as houseflies, feasted on my legs. I kept slapping at them in discomfort, but Mr. Kang appeared oblivious to such small annoyances. He was intent on educating me, this distant kin, and I was grateful. In the course of the evening, I learned that five thousand families named Kang lived in Chinju and that the Kang clan published a monthly newspaper. Every person mentioned in the newspaper was named Kang, which I found delightfully amazing. This was my other world, I thought to myself, happy at the discovery. More than 1.5 million Koreans are named Kang, the seventh most common Korean surname. When Mr. Kang learned that my time in Chinju was short, he led me to the Kang clan ancestral shrine, perched on a hill high above the city. "We're doing this especially for you because you've come from far away," the old man said.

Wearing a pair of tennis shoes, he walked up the steep hill with the energy of a young mountain climber. I could barely keep up. He did not waste a moment and talked all the while, explaining the history of the clan, as we climbed up the hill. When we reached the summit, Mr. Kang summoned a caretaker's daughter to open the gates and showed me into a huge hall, where a life-size color portrait of the founder of the Kang clan hung on a wall. I burned incense, but I did not bow to the picture. I slipped on my sandals and went outside to a breathtaking view of Chinju below.

A full moon shone through silvery clouds, adding a dreamy air to the scene. As I walked down the hillside with my newly-found kinsman, I promised myself that I would return to Chinju someday.

"When you come next, bring me the names of your ancestors," he said as he bid good-bye. "I can trace your roots back to the thirteenth century or more. Come back soon."

As I headed back to Seoul on the following evening, after meeting with dissidents and laborers in Pusan, I felt as if the Korean revolt of the summer, and my being there to report it, had been a journey of rediscovery for me. I had come not only as a Korean but as an American and a journalist. I was writing about the events that I cared about deeply, but with studied detachment, mindful of my readers back home. I could not let my emotions sway my reporting. During a few short weeks, I had witnessed pro-democracy protestors in Seoul force Chun to concede, and the euphoria in its aftermath. I had followed the movement, which was played out as much to the international media as it was to the people in South Korea. I had traveled to Kwangju for a spectacular burial of the university student who had been killed by Chun's riot police. The journey to Pusan brought back old memories and a frame of reference to compare where I had been since I had left that port city in a smuggled fisherman's boat on a moonlit night in October 1952. And finally, there was the trip to Chinju, which so richly reminded me of my roots and the migrations of my spirited and adventuresome people.

Returning to a cool and foggy San Francisco in late July, I felt like a faucet I could not turn off—I had so many stories to write. Sometimes, to find an excuse to write yet another story about Koreans, I connected them to Korean Americans here. By now, however, South Korea was firmly in the *Examiner*'s consciousness. In my spare time, I also wrote stories for Korean newspapers in Korea and in the United States.

As fate would have it, throughout this period executives at the *Examiner* were seriously considering opening a bureau in Asia. With San Francisco's significant Asian population—a third of the city's people—and its proximity to Asia and the growing trade, it made sense to have our own reporter there. As luck would have it, even after I returned in late July, many reporters from American newspapers were filing stories out of Korea. With the Seoul Olympics just around the corner, the amount of copy with a Seoul dateline was amazing. I made a proposal for opening a bureau in Seoul, complete with how much it would cost and why it was a worthwhile pursuit. Then, I waited for the top editors to decide. As I expected, they approved the decision to open the *Examiner*'s Seoul bureau. With the help of Tae-Yun Chung, the president of the *Korea Times*, I made arrangements by telephone and fax to rent an office in the Korea Times Building. Opening the bureau was a herculean task because of the South Korean government bureaucracy, but it was worth the hassle for what it meant for me. It seemed a dream come true—what more could I have asked for? I was excited at the prospect of living in Seoul again and writing about my native place full-time. My parents, too, were pleased about my move, even though my mother worried about managing our apartment building (see chapter 9) and the myriad other chores they had gotten so accustomed to my doing. My brother said he would help out. Had it been a move to Paris or London, my parents might have felt differently, I think. But through my assignment to Seoul, they were vicariously going to Korea, too. I decided this opportunity was a gift from God. I went to Saks Fifth Avenue on Union Square and bought a winter coat and cashmere-lined leather gloves—my first in fifteen years—and headed for Seoul.

Presidential Politics

The presidential campaign was in full swing in Seoul when I arrived in early December 1987 and checked into the Westin Chosun Hotel, a favorite with the foreign press corps because of its location and spacious rooms. With three main candidates named Kim running against Roh, in addition to several minor candidates, the entire city resounded with political loudspeakers every day. Opposition leader Dae-Jung Kim, a fiery orator, attracted huge crowds, and for a while it appeared that he would win. But the upper-middle class favored Young-Sam Kim because they thought Dae-Jung Kim was too radical. Then there was Jong-Pil Kim, a former colonel with a dubious past in the Park regime. Many were appalled at his candidacy: How dare he run for president! As the founder of the KCIA, he had been an integral part of the Park regime and his evil deeds. The KCIA was the South Korean equivalent of the KGB, notorious for torturing dissidents. But he had a constituency among the old Park supporters. The only issue was whether another military man would be elected.

On December 13, three days before the first free presidential election in sixteen years, I went to a public bathhouse in a Seoul neighborhood to learn what people were thinking. I figured no other foreign correspondent would go to a Korean bathhouse for a story. Even in this neighborhood bathhouse, the talk was about the presidential election. Han-Bok Shin, the proprietress I had known for many years—I had lived a block away from her place in the late

1960s—said she was disgusted with politicians as well as the students. Referring to the violence that had marred the presidential campaigns over the past several days, she said she was "ashamed to be a Korean." Shin said that with so much international coverage, she was afraid people abroad would get bad impressions of all Koreans. "I'm told all the eyes of the world are on Korea, and look what a mess these people are making," she said. "You'd think with the '88 Olympics, people would be a little more global-minded. Well, I tell you, Koreans will always be Koreans. Koreans can't handle too much freedom. That's my frank opinion, if you ask me. Sometimes I think we deserve dictators. To tell you the truth, we common people are sick and tired of demonstrations, violence, and confusion. Firebombs and tear gas are bad for people like us who are just trying to make an honest living." She berated students for demonstrating when they should be studying. As for the government, she said, for people like her, it did not matter who was in power as long as they could guarantee stability. She watched events on a color television set in the cubicle where she sat, collecting fees from her customers.

I took a taxi and went to Tonam-dong, another old section of Seoul, and to a bathhouse near my uncle Suk-Hoon's house. Here, too, politics was the order of the day. The television was turned up loud in the dressing area. And outside, you could hear loudspeakers blaring ads and speeches from the candidates.

It was hot and steamy inside the bathing area. As I soaked in the hot pool, I felt the weeks of accumulated tear-gas residue seeping out of my pores. I thought to myself that there was a good reason why Korean bathers spent an average of ninety minutes in the baths—and some, an entire afternoon. (Koreans use bathhouses the way Americans and Europeans use spas.) About five feet away from me, two middle-aged women were talking animatedly about the relationship between politics and food prices. The women were discussing the rising price of rice and their need to stock up on the Korean staple. That rice was still the yardstick for measuring the well-being of Korean households made an impression on me. So much money had been put into circulation because of the presidential campaign that inflation was rampant.

The events of that summer, autumn, and winter in Korea were of extraordinary interest to overseas Korean communities. U.S. editions of major Korean-language newspapers, transmitted via satellite from Seoul, were filled with political news from home. Perhaps more so than many other immigrant groups, Koreans lived with one foot in America and one foot in their homeland, because more than 80 percent of them were Korean-born and half of them had been in the United States less than fifteen years. They may have left Korea physically, but their hearts were still there. During those tumultuous weeks, Koreans in America talked as if they could almost taste and smell that tear gas. They raised money, lobbied the U.S. government, participated in partisan demonstrations in Los Angeles and San Francisco, and kept in touch with relatives, classmates, and friends back in Korea.

The December 1987 election was truly a historic occasion, the first popular presidential contest in sixteen years since Chung-Hee Park had done away with direct presidential elections. Also, this was the first contest in which presidential candidates were running seemingly viable campaigns against Chun's handpicked successor. But the outcome was disappointing. As expected, Roh won—by a plurality of 36.6 percent—because rival candidates Dae-Jung Kim and Young-Sam Kim split the opposition vote. For years, Koreans had fought and shed blood to end "military rule." Yet, when they finally got the chance, the rival opposition candidates, both of them eager to become president, refused to bow out to allow one a better chance at winning. I was disgusted with the two egotistical Kims, as were most people I knew.

South Koreans would have five years of yet another general-turned-civilian president in Roh before they would elect the first civilian president—Young-Sam Kim—in December 1992. He finagled his victory by joining the ruling party.

A few days after the election I found an apartment in downtown

Seoul within walking distance of many government offices, the American embassy, and major newspapers, restaurants and shops. I plunked down a $12,000 security deposit—called key money in Korea—high but typical in Seoul. In early January I returned to San Francisco to have some of my household goods shipped to Seoul, and then flew back. Though the *Examiner*'s bureau in Seoul had been officially open since November, I was now a full-fledged resident of Seoul—for the first time in two decades. It took me a while to get used to the noise. Seoul did not go to sleep. I would hear tipsy men singing or arguing under my second-story window until past two o'clock in the morning when the portable restaurants on wheels closed. Inevitably, road construction was done at night in downtown, around ten when I was getting ready to go to sleep. And, like all other residents of older apartment buildings in Seoul, I had a continuing battle with cockroaches, which were everywhere. The demand for "roach motels" with poisoned bait was so high that for a while there was a waiting list at a local supermarket. A friend on the *Examiner* staff sent a supply of Combat by express mail. Whenever I knew someone was coming to Seoul from the States, I asked them to bring Combat. Also, bathing in rusty water was the norm.

☯

In February 1988, a few days after the Lunar New Year, Roh was inaugurated as president. "An era of ordinary people has arrived," Roh declared at his inaugural ceremony. "From now on everybody will have a say in what is good for the country." I was one of twenty-five thousand people sitting through the ceremony on the vast grounds outside the National Assembly Building to witness this moment. A bitter chill was in the air, and my hands and feet were cold. He may be a former general, but still he would have to be an improvement over his predecessor, I thought. If nothing else, Roh had to remember the fact that almost 64 percent of the electorate had voted for his opponents.

Roh said all the right things in his inaugural speech and conveyed just the right style. He sat in an ordinary chair, just like other dignitaries on the platform, and there was no ostentatious display of flowers. Good gestures, I thought. Since his election, Roh's image-makers had gone to work, marketing him as an unpretentious, average man who carried his own briefcase, in an effort to set him apart from his predecessor, whose ever-present aides had not even let him light his own cigarette. As I listened to this former general speak like a champion of democracy, I was struck by the irony and hypocrisy of it all. "The day when repressive force and torture in secret chambers were tolerated is over," he said, in obvious reference to the previous administration, of which he had been an integral part.

With Roh in office, attention now turned to the April 26 elections for the National Assembly. There was a great deal at stake in the contest. For the ruling party, the National Assembly elections would provide a chance to extend its considerable power. For the major opposition parties, whose failure to unite in December cost them the chance to win the presidency, this was their last opportunity for five years to weaken the ruling party's influence. As the election day neared, fistfights, rock throwing, and even abductions occurred.

The ruling party failed to win a majority in the parliamentary elections. This was such a surprise that Korean newspapers dubbed the election results the "April 26 Shock." The Seoul stock market lost 24 percent of its value, rivaling the "Great Crash of 1979" on the day after Chung-Hee Park was assassinated. My disappointment with the voting was that not one woman was elected to the National Assembly. Fourteen women ran, and Korean voters turned down every one of them. When I mentioned this to some of my male Korean acquaintances, they said in their characteristic way: "Even some of the male candidates didn't make it, and you're worried about women candidates?" What more could I say to these Neanderthals, I thought, and did not respond.

I was glad the election was over; two elections in four months had been one too many. I could not wait for political posters to be removed from walls and lampposts, and for an end to violent scenes of campaign workers beating each other up. Because of the political activity, I had almost missed the enjoyment of spring. By the time the election was over, the cherry blossoms were gone. But forsythias and azaleas remained, and lilac blossoms still favored us with their perfume. So I savored what was left of spring.

Reunification Fervor

With the arrival of June, I had hoped for a little time on weekends to see old friends and even visit the beaches, but tension mounted again. People started talking about the reunification of the two Koreas, a subject that had been banned from public discussion under Park and Chun. As usual, students were in the vanguard. They proposed a meeting with their North Korean counterparts in the truce village of Panmunjom on June 10, the first anniversary of the eruption of 1987's month-long mass demonstrations that forced Chun to initiate democratic reforms. The proposed meeting was opposed by the South Korean government but endorsed by the regime in the North, which was always quick to take advantage of South Korean radicals and embrace them.

The South Korean government insisted that it had to be the "sole channel" for talks between the divided Koreas, and it declared that students would be blocked from going to Panmunjom, about thirty miles north of Seoul. But students said their "March to Panmunjom" would take place even if they were killed. With students and riot police headed for a major confrontation, Seoul was once again a boiling cauldron. The National Police Headquarters had already dispatched fifty-seven thousand policemen to Yonsei and other universities, and they lined all the roads leading to Panmunjom to stop the students. Government officials accused the students of playing into the hands of the North Korean propaganda machine. But student activists disbelieved everything the government said, because they had been subjected to years of government anti-Communist propaganda that made the North Koreans seem like they had horns on their heads. School officials, fearing the worst, installed nets and mattresses around the main library and student hall and cut off access to rooftops so students would not leap to their deaths—a very real concern. Already, four university students who were calling for re-unification had committed suicide by leaping off buildings or setting themselves on fire. Their deaths added a certain grimness to the debate. Ordinary people worried about the potential casualties and the discomfort of more pepper gas and traffic tie-ups, and merchants knew they would not get much business. As an observer, I could not help but see the absurdity on both sides. How could South Korean students undo what the superpowers had done? Yet, they were expressing the sentiment of every Korean—that this division was unnatural. And the students' passion for making a dramatic state-ment by jumping off buildings or setting themselves on fire seemed ghoulish to me. But I also realized that South Korean students had honed their skills in dramatizing their cause because they could not attract attention of the foreign press any other way. One thing the South Korean government did care about was its image abroad, espe-cially with the upcoming Olympics.

On university campuses, banners and placards reading "Let's go to Panmunjom and embrace our brothers in the North" hung from buildings, walls, and trees. Campus bulletin boards were filled with photographs of scenes in North Korea and angry messages condemn-ing America. On June 10, an estimated 17,000 students started marching toward Panmunjom. They were stopped by 57,000 riot police—29,000 of them in the capital alone. Parts of Seoul looked like a war zone, with stones, bricks, and broken glass strewn on streets and thousands of helmeted riot police, police vans, and buses everywhere. Many major roads were closed to all traffic. Riot police stood guard even in tiny back alleys. More than 100 people were injured. The student leaders vowed to try again on August 15, the forty-third anniversary of Korean independence.

That day I went to Yonsei University campus early in the morning to watch the proposed student march to Panmunjom. Red and pink roses on the campus were in full bloom. In the as-yet unpolluted air, I could smell their fragrance; in the trees, alongside the quadrangle, cicadas sang loudly in the already ninety-six-degree heat. Even though the school was out for the summer, several thousand students from all over the country were gathered for a rally before heading out the main gate to Panmunjom. Everyone knew the march would be blocked by the riot policemen surrounding the campus. But Koreans love spectacles, and there were a lot of spectators on the campus—even old women and young mothers with toddlers.

More than three thousand students, accompanied by a drum-and-gong corps, tried to march out of Yonsei's front gate, but were met by a blockade of riot police who fired volleys of pepper gas. Dense clouds of the choking gas enveloped the scenic campus. The students continued to inch forward, battling police for almost three hours. They kept their promise to remain nonviolent and did not throw firebombs at first. But as the clash became fierce and police began to beat them, students responded with firebombs and rocks.

"What a way to celebrate our Independence Day," said a university official with a sad expression on his face. "Because of the inability of our leaders, we are losing our youths like this."

As two months before, the students were no match for the riot police. The government had deployed twenty-two thousand policemen in Seoul and three thousand around the Yonsei campus. Hundreds of students were arrested, including the president of the National Association of University Students who had masterminded the march. It was theater of the absurd.

Projecting a Clean Image

With the Seoul Olympics just a month away, Olympic countdown fever began to grip the city. Radio stations aired English lessons several times a day for Seoulites to learn how to communicate to visitors expected during the Olympics. Taxi companies and department stores held English classes for their employees. Public service announcements over radio and television urged Koreans to "put their best foot forward" and to behave as a people worthy of an Olympic-host country.

To project a "clean" image of Seoul, thousands of street vendors, who scraped out a living by selling everything from magnifying glasses to barbequed beef, were ordered to leave town during the games, scheduled for September 15 to October 2. The vendors protested. Thousands of them staged a rally and demanded that the city "get off the backs of the poor."

"Which is more important—the Olympics or one's right to make a living?" shouted one vendor at the rally I attended. "We may be poor, but we want to live on what we earn." The vendors' protests inspired newspaper columnists on influential papers to come to their defense. One columnist suggested that the government capitalize on the vendors' street stalls by turning them into tourist attractions. But the vendors lost, and were banned.

Others lost out, too. Restaurants offering canine cuisine were ordered closed throughout the Olympics as a result of pressure from animal rights groups in Great Britain and the United States. In July and August foreign correspondents wrote so many stories about canine cuisine that it appeared from abroad that every Korean ate dog-meat stew three times a day. The controversy generated by these stories was substantial. Unfortunately, it also was one of the few stories my newspaper specifically requested me to do. I kept putting my editors off because the idea did not appeal to me. For one thing, it was another grating example of Western media zooming in on what to them was sensational exotica. I never found stories making fun of other people's cultures appealing. But stories about dog meat began appearing in major papers, including the *Chicago Tribune*. My editors faxed me those stories—a nudging reminder. Finally, I gave in, reasoning that at least I could write about the subject with a little more understanding than these Western reporters.

A couple of weeks before the start of the games, I went to the House of Happiness in an old section of downtown, famous among a select group of middle-aged Korean males I knew for its extraordinary canine cuisine. I asked a middle-aged male friend to go with

me, as I felt I had to witness the serving of a canine dish in order
to do the story. My friend said he occasionally enjoyed a bowl of
"Vitality Soup" after work when he felt run-down. He said he could
not understand why so many foreigners were upset. "Koreans don't
eat their pet dogs," he said, explaining that a special breed of large,
tan-colored dogs were raised especially for canine cuisine. "Besides,
people who eat cows and pigs and lamb are in no position to poke
fun at people who eat dog meat," he said. I agreed with him.

On the following day, I went to a big market where canine
meat was sold. I also interviewed the owners of several restaurants
where health stew was served, and consumers who told me why
they relished it. I learned that for centuries some Koreans have considered dog meat to have special curative powers, providing stamina
and strength. I filed a long story, complete with the fascinating history of how dog meat became a delicacy. But I still cringe whenever
I think about the story, because it was an example of American
journalism at its worst (not unlike the mass insanity of editors unduly
paying attention and allocating resources to cover the O. J. Simpson
double murder case in 1994 and 1995).

Government officials failed also in another hide-and-seek game
with foreign correspondents. The officials had decided it would be
a good idea to build a wall to hide a stretch of hovels along the
route of the Olympic marathon in the southern part of the country.
A British reporter discovered this and wrote a story poking fun at
the government. Soon, a legion of foreign reporters were on the
scene. They took pictures not only of the wall but of the unsightly
houses the government had wanted to hide.

This, coming after the controversy involving dog meat, angered
a lot of Koreans. "I don't understand what motivates foreign reporters," said a Korean reporter with a major Seoul daily. "What is the
purpose of those people going out of their way to uncover things
Koreans don't particularly want to show to the outside world?"

Dog meat and shantytowns notwithstanding, the twenty-fourth
Olympiad, an event that had been South Korea's official obsession

for six years, got under way at 11:00 A.M. on September 17. For South Korea, whose image to the Western world was that of war orphans and peasants, as conveyed in the *M*A*S*H* television series, the Olympics was an extraordinary undertaking that required extraordinary sacrifices.

After an overnight rain, the sky appeared clear and blue. A rainbow briefly appeared over the Han River—an especially good omen to Koreans. As one of the one hundred thousand spectators in the Olympic Stadium, I was witnessing this historic moment not only as a Korean, but as an American and a journalist. The opening of the games was a moving moment for all Koreans—in Korea as well as millions abroad.

"We did it; we did it," said a woman who was seated next to me during the opening ceremony. "I'm proud to be a Korean today. Through all the difficulties, we did it."

For millions of Koreans everywhere, September 17 was also an occasion to shed tears of joy. For Koreans, there is no such thing as pure joy. We cannot be happy unless we are sad, too.

Just about everyone I spoke with described their feeling as "overcome with emotion."

Many reporters from abroad had dubbed the Olympics as Korea's "coming-out party." It was indeed. The world had come to Seoul, and Seoul was reaching out to the world. As I sat in the 100,000-seat Olympic Stadium, made to resemble the shape of a traditional Korean urn, I felt uplifted. If the loudness and the length of applause were any measure, Americans still remained Korea's best friend. The entry of the 612 athletes of the U.S. team was greeted with more cheers and longer applause than for any other team except for the Koreans'. Anti-American sentiment may have been strong among radical students and intellectuals, but most other Koreans were still favorably disposed to Americans. When the Korean team entered the stadium last, with 467 athletes, a Korean grandfather, two seats away from me, nodded his head, tears trickling down his cheeks. Koreans were treated to a wonderful panorama of the world's citizens during the Olympics. The presence of so many people from around the world gave many Koreans a chance to feel the diversity of the global family for the first time in their lives.

Many were amused and amazed by all these different people. Newspapers ran picture pages filled with photos of visitors in all their variety of attire. A member of the U.S. Olympic team who had multicolored bangs was featured on the front page of a leading newspaper. Pictures of Western women in tank tops, short-shorts, and tights also attracted the attention of local photographers. The picture of a female Western photographer who wore a skin-tight outfit in a wild-animal pattern appeared in so many newspapers that I lost count.

Eleven days into the games, Koreans took time off to celebrate Chusok, the Harvest Moon Festival, their most important holiday. It gave them a welcome break from the mania of the Olympics and seemed to put everything in its proper perspective. Seoul's population of nearly eleven million decreased by a third as residents took off for their hometowns by car, bus, train, and airplane, carrying bountiful gifts to observe Chusok with their families. Whenever Koreans think about home, it is the countryside village of persimmon trees, pine woods, rice paddies, and brooks, not Seoul, where a fourth of South Koreans live. The absence of so many cars made it possible to feel the crisp autumn air and see the clear skies and mountains surrounding the old city. It felt almost like old times. If the gleaming Olympic facilities and glitzy tourist hotels showed a new face of Korea, Chusok represented the old. The two faces of Korea—old and new—lived side by side in harmony and conflict, I thought. But when Koreans had to choose between the two, they usually opted for the old. Choosing not to forget Chusok even during the twenty-fourth Olympiad gave us a chance to regain our equilibrium.

For South Koreans, the most important side effect from the successful completion of the games, for which they spent seven years and $5.5 billion, was that the Olympiad had put their country on the map. For the people, it was the exposure of their culture and arts that mattered the most. Koreans are obsessed about their culture, undoubtedly a legacy of having to fight to retain it under Japan's

colonial rule. Koreans rejoice when their culture is favorably publicized, and feel hurt when it is demeaned. For the government, the
biggest gain from the Olympics was in its diplomatic breakthrough.
The games gave South Korea its first contact with the Soviet Union
and other Eastern Bloc nations. Having hosted the games without a
major incident, despite threats from North Korea, which boycotted
the games, South Korea could stand tall, having joined the ranks of
the advanced nations.

Packing Up Again

With the Olympics over, I was to have only another six months
before my assignment in Korea ended. It had been, almost literally,
a whirlwind, as I was buffeted and blown by events from one end
of the divided Korean map to another. But it was unlike any other
assignment I have ever had; it had also provided me a chance to see
Korea through eyes that had become much more detached than
when I had gone back as a young reporter twenty years earlier. In
between, I had made numerous visits to Seoul, but I realized how
little I had seen during those trips. One cannot really know Seoul
by visiting; one has to live there. One has to breathe its polluted air,
smell the ever-present odor of its inadequate sewer system, and bathe
in rust-stained hot water from the old pipes in so many older apartment buildings to know. Its anomalies defy logic. For instance, custo-
dians of the apartment building where I lived turned off all but two
of the dimmest fluorescent hallway lights at night, so I could barely
see my way to my apartment door. But they turned up the heat so
high that I literally perspired even in winter.

But Seoul also gave me many simple pleasures. After years of
living as a member of a minority group abroad, I never stopped
appreciating the feeling of wellness that came with being a part of
the racial and ethnic majority. But that was emblematic of what I
realized was the difference between living in Korea as a member of
a totally homogeneous population and life in America, which was
often riddled with little annoyances caused by a basic, ongoing cul-

tural clash. The only way for Americans—of whatever race or ethnicity—to experience the feeling of being a minority is to go to a country where they are a minority and live there for a while. I felt a sense of belonging in radio and television programs in Korea, too. There was something soothing about seeing our stories told on the screen by faces with features like mine. And I felt physically safe: Even at night I could take a stroll without worrying about a crazy person attacking me in the city of almost eleven million people. In Korea, everybody knew the clearcut, unvarying rules, and each person could predict other people's behaviors. I enjoyed small things—like quick shopping trips to an outdoor market near my apartment to buy fresh vegetables and fish. I felt kinship with the old women who sold home-grown sesame leaves, onions, radishes, and lettuce, even though I had little in common with them. In this sense, I felt very much at home and "Korean" in Seoul.

But as in all other big cities, life in modern Seoul was so hectic, and obsession with materialism so rampant, I sometimes felt that Seoul had lost its soul. To feel Korea's heart and soul, I had to go outside Seoul to the countryside. There, I would be instantly reminded of why Koreans called their country Chosun, "The Land of Morning Calm." Mornings were still calm. I had gone to the countryside in spring, summer, autumn, and winter, and each season had rewarded me abundantly. In winter, rice fields were bare and brown, but there was the anticipation of spring planting just around the corner. Koreans would have their hope renewed in spring with the sight of new leaves sprouting and swallows returning from the south. In summer, rice fields were lush and green, and I could almost feel farmers counting the days until harvest in the fall, dreaming of delicious new-crop rice, succulent pears, and sweet persimmons. In autumn, after the harvest, rice fields were golden, with stacks of rice straw to be coiled into ropes—the kind that had been used to pull me up to the rooftop of the train to Pusan in the winter of 1951. And every yard had persimmons dangling like jewels from their branches, as if to invite me to share the satisfaction that farmers felt after a good harvest.

In Kangwon Province, there were villages with trickling brooks and houses with fruit trees in the yard. People walked and talked leisurely as if they were still living in a Confucian village. When an unfamiliar face such as mine turned up, villagers would gather with all kinds of questions. To them, America was still a faraway land. Mementoes from America were passed around like pieces from a museum.

During my stay in a remote village in Kangwon Province, watching me shampoo my hair became a spectacle. There was no indoor plumbing, so I had to wash my hair by a community well. Children gathered around me and watched. Some asked questions. Afterward, they followed me to my room, where they were amused to see me wrap a big towel around my head, then replace the towel with odder-looking things—curlers. They also seemed fascinated when I hung up my clothes to dry. My every move was followed and watched with intense curiosity. By the time I left the village, I think everyone in it knew all about me.

In Kangwon Province, I could still see an old woman walking with her goat on a leash, as one would walk a pet dog, oblivious to big rigs with choking diesel fumes roaring by. Farmers still trans-ported stacks of rice straw on oxcarts, just as their ancestors had done. Women gathered at streams to wash clothes and gossip, and they weeded rice fields by hand. Outside of Seoul, much of Korean life remained the same, except for TV antennae and telephones. Farmers had more machinery now, but the old ways of thinking and doing things had changed so little that I wondered whether Seoul really fit in with the rest of the country.

After my second winter in Seoul, and after covering President George Bush's trip to Korea in February 1989, it was time to prepare for a return to my other home in San Francisco, for a new assignment as an editor in the home office. I had a choice of going to Washing-ton, D.C., to cover politics and trade or starting a new project with a team of reporters to beef up the coverage of minorities. Both assignments appealed to me, but after thinking about it for a few days, I chose the latter because I wanted to remain in San Francisco and I saw possibilities of making a contribution by giving a voice to Asians, African Americans, and Latinos whose communities did not get the kind of coverage they deserved from the mainstream news media.

It was nice to have a challenging job waiting for me, but I had mixed emotions as I prepared to leave. On one hand, I looked forward to seeing my family and living peacefully in a city with wonderful parks, beaches, and air; but on the other hand, I did not want to lose this feeling of being part of the racial and ethnic majority. But I also knew that I would not miss student demonstrations, last-minute trips to the Ministry of Culture and Information on a Saturday night to pick up a press pass for this or that function, and those long exhausting trips to the truce village of Panmunjom, where South Korean and U.S. officials met with North Korean representatives for their interminable talks in smoke-filled rooms.

The last days before shutting down the bureau were trying. Closing it was just as complicated as opening it had been. The Olympics notwithstanding, bureaucrats at the Ministry of Justice had not changed one iota—that part of Korea, I would never miss. I had to remind myself constantly that I could not allow my dealings with some bureaucrats to befoul my otherwise eventful tour of duty in Seoul. After nearly two years of covering South Korea during its busiest period, though, I was so consumed by the boiling cauldron that is Seoul that I could not relax. I had caught Seoulitis—a condition of perpetual motion that afflicts eveyone who lives and works in the South Korean capital. I had reluctantly come to the realistic conclusion that it was good to go to Korea to replenish, to affirm and confirm my ethnic and cultural heritage, but that working there for a long stretch would be detrimental to my sense of well-being, which had been honed over the years on American reason and sensibilities. I had had to return to Korea for a second time to decide that home for me had become San Francisco—a realization that made me a little sad. But at least, I had resolved within myself where I belonged.

11. BACK TO AMERICA, AGAIN

O blue water flowing from the hill above me,

Be not proud of your speed!

For once in the green sea

Forever lost you will be.

The bright moon shines over the hollow hill.

O blue water, why do you not rest here?

—Chin-I Hwang (c. 1506–1544)★, *Koreana*

★Translated by Peter Hyun

Foghorns and Sense of Humor

After Seoul, San Francisco seemed almost too peaceful. I could not sleep on my first night back because it was so quiet. Where were the men who argued, shouted, and sang drunkenly outside my Seoul apartment? The only sounds I heard here were foghorns and an occasional "meow" of a neighbor's cat, and raccoons foraging through my garbage bin in the carport.

On the following morning as I tried to get used to my place, left vacant while I was in South Korea because my parents had moved some years earlier to a house a few blocks away, I realized that everything was just a little too tall or big for me—the toilet seat, cupboards, washbasin, and kitchen sink. When I put water on to boil, I noticed that the stove was at least three or four inches taller than the one in my Seoul apartment. The gas man who came to check my appliances and turn on the wall heater's pilot light walked into my apartment without removing his shoes.

These were reminders that I was back in the States. But so was the relative orderliness of auto traffic, which was so unlike that in Seoul, where aggressive driving was the rule, pedestrians and drivers were engaged in constant brinkmanship, and there was no such thing as standing in line and waiting one's turn. After Seoul, I felt as if even the earth under San Francisco seemed more stable, despite the San Andreas fault.

Sipping a cup of green tea and looking out the window at the Golden Gate Bridge, I felt more comfortable with the decision I had made before leaving Seoul that San Francisco was now my home. Korea *was* home; America *is* home. It had taken me twenty-eight years after first setting foot on American soil, and thirty-six years after learning English, to reach that conclusion. How many miles had I traveled through the highways and back alleys of my mind and heart to finally come to that resolution? And, was it a resolution for once and for all? I hoped so. Making myself another cup of tea, and noticing again the height of the sink and the stove, I was bemused by the irony that the home I chose was one in which, physically, I did not fit.

Since I had moved into my unit on the top floor of our apartment house in the mid-1970s, I had spent countless hours reflecting while looking at the Golden Gate Bridge, not once tiring of the view. It was like an ever-present friend to me. On a sparkling April afternoon the bridge shone in its bright red splendor like a giant sculpture; in the thick fog of July, the bridge played hide-and-seek; and on an early March morning, as now, the water beneath the bridge was steel blue, without a single boat disturbing its surface. I felt one part of my life was coming to a close and another one was beginning. My personal and professional lives appeared to be merging as I began to realize my desire to be a bridge builder between people from less well understood cultures to the dominant American culture. I had done this through the community news medium because the mainstream media's appetite for this kind of reporting had been minimal; but that appeared to be changing. In all of this, I felt a power beyond myself that was creating these projects for me. All I had to do was to follow.

The world of journalism is an odd place. Even though we journalists are supposed to communicate the lives of people and events around us, we seldom talk about the things that really matter to us all. During my three decades in the business, I can count on one hand the number of times I heard my colleagues reveal their own faith or discuss God. We use coins that say "In God We Trust," but the secular world has so permeated the newsrooms that even those of us to whom our religion is important do not talk about it—as if to mention it would undermine our credibility or impartiality. Yet religion has long been an important aspect of my life. I do not think one can come through the bombings and killings of the Korean War and not be thankful. I do not ever remember quarreling with God. The Creator has always provided for me—sending projects my way even before I thought about them.

And that is how I saw this new turn in my career. Heretofore,

I had concentrated on doing good work in high-profile assignments. Now I was going to bring visibility to those areas traditionally ignored by the media. After all these years, it was rewarding to see top newspaper executives across the country admit that they had done and were doing a poor job of reporting on their changing communities. Since beginning my newspaper career in 1964, when it was nearly impossible to find another Asian reporter on a metropolitan paper, I had to admit that there had been progress after all, and I felt invigorated at the challenge of helping produce newspaper stories that would more fully and accurately reflect minority communities. The more I thought about it, the more exciting the assignment seemed. I was glad I had chosen this over going to Washington. It was important for me to stay on the West Coast, where most Asians lived. But I knew my work would not be easy.

The one lesson I had learned over many years of working in metropolitan newsrooms was how insulated editors were. I would strive to be an intermediary bringing different perspectives into the American newsroom. After having covered a variety of assignments, this was the time to do it. Had I been younger, I might not have had the nerve to do this; had I been younger, I might also have considered this a thankless task, because newspapers always have considered foreign and national reporting assignments more important than local assignments. And among local assignments, or "beats," so-called minority or community beats were on the lowest rung. But at this juncture in my professional life, on the contrary, the most important thing I hoped to do was to foster understanding, tolerance, and appreciation for people's differences. I knew I would probably be a voice in the wilderness, but I vowed to be a strong voice.

With each passing day in the States, I felt the accumulated tension seep out of me, and with each breath of San Francisco's crisp air, I was sure I was ridding my body of the tear-gas residue and the nagging cough I had acquired in Seoul. Before retiring for the night, I stood on the balcony of my apartment, facing the amber lights of the Golden Gate Bridge, and breathed vigorously. After Seoul, I would never again take good air for granted.

My parents and brother were glad to have me back. It had not been easy taking care of the apartment building while I was away. They were only too happy to turn the responsibility over to me. "I really have an appreciation for what you've been through," my mother said repeatedly, about the unending chores that go with being a landlord in a city like San Francisco where city regulations are plentiful. "Not having you around was like losing my right arm and right leg at the same time," she said.

I returned to my routine as a working journalist and a landlady. I filled a couple of vacancies and thought about the number of toilets I had cleaned and the apartments I had painted myself after the tenants had moved out. I could only smile at the strange turn of destiny that had taken me on journeys I had never planned. Over the nearly two decades of taking care of the apartment house, I had seen dozens of people come and go, and had shown units to many hundreds of people of every description, background, and habit. But I could not complain, as I thought about my childhood in Tokyo, when I had wanted our family to have our own home so much that I had gone house hunting by myself. God had given me a lot more than I had bargained for.

As I settled back into San Francisco life, I rediscovered aspects of American culture I appreciated—especially the emphasis on humor. No matter how busy they were, Americans always found time to crack a joke. I had missed that quality in Seoul, where meetings were always deadly serious and no mechanism existed to break the tension or monotony. I also valued even more the American sense of fairness, of hearing the other side out, striving to reach an agreement through negotiation and mediation. The English language itself, with its lack of inherent class distinctions, was refreshing. The egalitarian pronoun *you* was applied to everyone—regardless of age, social status, education, or pedigree. I fell in love all over again with what *you* represented, after two years of having to use the titles by which Koreans are always addressed.

From being a member of the foreign/national staff, I returned to metro as one of several assistant metro editors. That merely meant that I was reporting to Jim Finefrock, the metro editor, instead of John Kirkpatrick, the foreign/national editor, and my salary came from another department's budget. I had performed some editing duties on nights and weekends before going overseas, but doing it full-time took an adjustment. I had a team of reporters to cover the Asian, Latino, and African American communities. Along with daily stories, we had ongoing projects on which reporters worked. It was hard to repress the reporter in me; my instinct was always to pick up the phone and start asking questions. Sometimes I helped with reporting when one of the reporters on my team had his hands full. It seemed like such a treat just to talk to a news source, instead of having everything relayed through someone else's eyes and ears. One of the more trying aspects of the job was having to work in the middle of so much commotion. The metro desk is the nerve center of any newsroom. It is noisy, phones ring constantly, reporters come up to talk to different editors, sometimes everybody is on the phone at the same time, and TV sets and police-radio scanners blare all the time. I longed for quiet so I could think before editing a story. Eventually, I got used to working in this condition, but not before it gave me a permanent frown line on my forehead from trying to concentrate.

There were rewarding aspects to being an editor, though. A reporter can only write one story at a time, which I liken to preparing just one dish at a time. But an editor can help prepare several dishes at once. One reporter might work on an appetizer, another on a main course, and a third on a dessert. After putting the dishes together, the editor has a full-course meal—a tasty one, if possible. That was the fun part of being an editor. But I did not look forward to attending meetings during which we had to peddle stories like salespeople. The idea of having to sell stories was abhorrent to me, but this was the way metropolitan American newspapers operated. If I wanted my reporters' stories to get on page one, I had to write a strong storyline in order to win the interest of higher-ranking editors who would determine how good a play the story would get—page one or inside—and make my arguments. We all went into the story meetings with a list. Some of our stories were accepted, and others were not.

My primary responsibility was to get more stories on ethnic minority communities into the paper. Although I was authorized to draw on various *Examiner* reporters in addition to the four assigned to me, some of my colleagues resisted parting with their people, and I sometimes went to Frank McCulloch, the managing editor, to intercede. McCulloch, who to me epitomized the best in an American editor, was always supportive, but I could not make a habit of marching into the managing editor's office for every story I considered important. A similar experience awaited me after I had spent weeks helping develop a minority source list in an effort to provide better and more sensitive coverage of the area's growing minority population. This list was made available to everyone through the computer and was also in a printed booklet. But despite McCulloch's endorsement and his urgings in a memo to the staff, I found that the list was seldom used. Reporters continued to use their usual sources, and readers were not introduced to the many nonwhite experts working at prestigious universities and hospitals and other institutions in the San Francisco Bay Area.

My efforts to increase coverage of minority communities had mixed success. I was the only ethnic minority member permanently assigned to the metro desk. During story conferences, informing my colleagues about issues and people they were unfamiliar with took patience and energy. Essentially, news was what editors decided to put into the newspaper. And no matter how conscientious and thoughtful some of them were, they were products of their own culture, social milieu, and life experiences. I know my mission was helped greatly by the support I got from McCulloch, who had spent many years in Asia as a foreign correspondent, and who felt that San Francisco was the Asian city of America. Some of the other editors empathized, but I could take them only so far. Editors are wedded to the notion that news is something out of the ordinary—natural disasters, violence, the bizarre. News may be all of those things, but I also happen to think we need to present a balanced picture of the world by presenting the good news, as well. News is about an arthritic woman who crochets Christmas decorations to raise money for the poor; news is the ninety-five-year-old former chef who always bakes a birthday cake for the senior citizen's group at his church—news is about ordinary people, too. I did not see eye-to-eye on some of the decisions that resulted from the story conferences, and I often left the room amazed at the similarity of the others' reactions to most story ideas.

Despite the odds, I did manage to sell a project I had been wanting to do for years. Since my college days, I had been troubled by the way minorities were portrayed in American history and social studies textbooks. Investigating this would be a project that would take a lot of time. Now, with a staff of reporters available to me, it seemed possible. I wrote a proposal, passed it around to my reporters, who added their suggestions, and eventually got the paper's commitment to do a series and to conduct a poll of the entire graduating class of the San Francisco Unified School District. The poll showed that the students themselves were largely aware that the standard history textbooks gave short shrift to African Americans, Asian Americans, Latinos, and Native Americans, except as victims or occasional heroes. The series ran while the state was adopting new textbooks, so we followed the process all year, giving an outlet not only to people critical of the new books up for adoption but also to the publishers and educators who approved them. No other paper gave so much attention to the adoption process or to the criticism that the new history textbooks, while an improvement, still did not adequately portray the important roles played in American history by racial and ethnic minorities. The newspaper also ran an editorial urging the state to reject the textbooks because of that failing. The textbook series, which generated a lot of statewide and national interest and controversy, gave me more satisfaction than any other project I was involved in as an editor. Just getting the series in the newspaper was enough to make all the other hassles of working on the metro desk worthwhile.

Being back in the States and concluding that I belonged here did not put an end to my connection to Korea. I read Korean newspapers and kept up with what was occurring in Korea. In June 1990, just fifteen months after the Seoul Olympics, San Francisco became the setting for a historic meeting between South Korean President Tae-Woo Roh and Mikhail Gorbachev. I was on vacation at the time, but was asked if I could help cover it with another reporter. I answered, "Of course." The Roh–Gorbachev meeting was the continuation of a breakthrough in relations between Seoul and Moscow that had begun with the Soviet Union's attendance at the 1988 summer Olympics. Though Gorbachev, who was already in the United States, was clearly the "star," Roh received his share of media attention by coming such a long way for a meeting with the Russian leader that lasted just fifty-five minutes. Before that, Gorbachev had Roh cooling his heels for several hours at his presidential suite at the Fairmont Hotel as he met with businesspeople in the hotel's ballroom to drum up financial support for his country. But the long trip and the waiting proved to be worthwhile, for the session with Gorbachev elevated Roh's stature at home and abroad. Who would have dreamed even six months earlier that the leaders of these two nations, which had been archenemies for more than four decades, would get together in the United States?

For South Korea, it proved to be a historic turning point: with Gorbachev's backing, South Korea would become a member of the United Nations the following year. For years, the Soviet Union, North Korea's mentor, had blocked South Korea's admission to the United Nations. Six months after the San Francisco meeting, another summit followed in Moscow, leading to the establishment of full diplomatic relations—a remarkable development, given the history of the two nations. The Russians needed South Korean economic aid and industrial know-how, while South Korea needed the Soviet Union's help in keeping North Korea at bay and in gaining international stature. This courtship of mutual convenience appeared to work remarkably well. In April 1991, Gorbachev became the first head of the Soviet Union to visit Korea. In return for Gorbachev's promise to support its entry into the United Nations, South Korea promised a $3 billion loan to the Soviet Union. A smiling Gorbachev, who had come from four days of grueling talks in Tokyo over the future of the Kurile Islands, told the Koreans upon his arrival on balmy Cheju Island: "I felt the cold wind in Tokyo, but here in Korea, like the warm breezes of Cheju-do, I feel only the warmth of the Korean people."

In 1991, Jim Finefrock, the editor of the editorial pages, asked if I wanted to join the editorial board. Becoming an editorial writer is how many journalists traditionally complete their careers. I would be the only minority on the editorial board. After a quarter century of varied, fast-paced assignments, I liked the idea of going down to the relatively quiet quarters on the second floor to reflect and to write opinions. With the *Examiner*'s editorial pages having undergone almost a 180-degree turn from conservative to liberal on many issues, I did not foresee any ideological problems. As it turned out, I was on the side of the majority in most cases. Our board meetings, during which we presented ideas for editorials we wanted to write and then discussed their merits—the pros and cons of each issue—were invigorating sessions. My colleagues seemed to value the different perspective I brought, and it was rewarding to write editorials on issues that otherwise might not have seen the light of day.

Mornings were usually taken up by our own meetings and then the almost-daily sessions with people who came to meet with the editorial board. Visitors represented the gamut—from supporters of the San Francisco Public Library to Zulu Chief Mangosuthu G. Buthelezi. The number of groups and people who wanted to come in to talk to us never ceased to amaze me. As a reporter, I had thought that editorial writers had all day to think and pontificate, but our deadlines and pressures were such that lunch was often a sandwich eaten in front of the computer. To my surprise, I found myself enjoying taking stands and writing them in a strong, forceful way. I wrote editorials supporting former Harvard law professor Derrick Bell's decision to protest the lack of minority representation on the law school faculty, an editoral criticizing the Japanese government's refusal to mention Japan's wartime crimes against its Asian neighbors in its social studies textbooks, and an editorial on the Lunar New Year, with a headline in Chinese characters—a first, I presume, for a metropolitan U.S. daily. My favorite was the editorial I wrote in which the *Examiner* apologized for campaigning to round up people of Japanese ancestry during World War II and put them in hastily constructed camps. The Hearst papers, as well as the *Sacramento Bee* and other papers in the McClatchy chain and the *San Francisco Chronicle*, had supported California Attorney General Earl Warren's call in 1942 to bar people of Japanese ancestry from living on the West Coast. The editorial, which received a lot of attention from our readers and from the news media, was the lead editorial in the February 20, 1992, issue of the *Examiner*, under the headline: "Learning the Lesson of Internment: The Internment of 120,000 Japanese Americans during World War II Was Wrong; An Apology Is Due." The editorial concluded: "Newspapers are products of human beings—reflecting all their shortcomings as well as their talents, their myopia as well as their broader vision. The lesson from this chapter in American history is to remind ourselves every day that the Constitution applies to all. We must make sure it always does."

I know the editorial would not have been written had I not been there. Writing it and getting it in print justified the loneliness of my being the only non-white at the table. I received so many calls the day after the editorial appeared that I barely had time to finish that day's work. I transferred calls from news agencies requesting personal interviews to a colleague who was sitting in for the vacationing Finefrock. I wanted to keep a low profile. I had done what I had wanted to do for a long time. Why ruin the effect of this quiet satisfaction by going public to explain my reasons?

☯

For many years I had resisted a professional temptation to move to Los Angeles, since San Francisco seemed like a perfect place for me.

I had worked on both the *Examiner* and the *Chronicle*, and I felt that I had a comfortable niche at the *Examiner*. For well over ten years, off and on, different editors at the *Los Angeles Times* had called me to discuss the possibility of my working there. Something had always held me back. Who would take care of the apartment house? How could I uproot myself when I felt so at home in San Francisco? Then, in 1990, I spent two days at the paper, talking with various editors and observing the operation. For about a year after that, Craig Turner, who was the metropolitan editor, and other editors called me periodically and apprised me of the paper's situation, then in a hiring freeze. In late 1991, Turner called to ask if I was still interested in working for the paper. I was the first one on his hiring list, he said, and he expected the freeze to be lifted soon.

I had hoped the *Times* would move slowly, in its characteristic manner, so I could take time off between jobs, but the Los Angeles riots intervened, moving up the timetable. So, in 1992, I moved to Los Angeles to join the *Times* metro staff. I had done almost everything I had wanted to do on the *Examiner*. My parents, of course, had mixed reactions. My father thought I should go, but my mother asked me why I would want to live in Los Angeles. She was also concerned about the apartment building. I explained that Los Angeles was only an hour's airplane flight away, and that it would be much easier to take care of the family affairs in Los Angeles than from Seoul.

I could not have picked a more tense time to move to Los Angeles. The six-block walk from my downtown apartment to the office meant my being accosted by a legion of panhandlers, some of whom spewed racial slurs as I hurried by. The animosity blacks felt against Asians was extraordinary. I have never heard as many racial epithets from people on the street as I did during those months after the riots. Friends told me I was crazy to live in downtown Los Angeles, but I could not see spending ninety minutes or more every day commuting to and from work.

I knew there was a reason why I was in Los Angeles and why I had chosen to go there at this point in my life. I would think about my mission whenever a tinge of regret about leaving San

Francisco crept up, prompted by the sight of an angry, disheveled
stranger on the street lurching toward me, as I walked at full speed
to work. But having made it to the office, and heaving a sigh of
relief that I was within its sanctuary, I would sign onto the computer
and see a parade of messages about the number of murders from the
night before. Was there any good news in Los Angeles? Mondays
were the worst. Messages, updates, and bulletins from the weekend
of maim and murder filled the screen. I knew not all of Los Angeles
was like this, but somehow, news gatherers—from the Associated
Press to the City News Services—had amassed reports on a collection
of miseries. Reading all this was a sobering way to start the day—a
jolting reminder that Los Angeles was vastly different from San Francisco. Here, amidst the flowering jacarandas and glamorous tinsel,
reality was living on the edge. Los Angeles, more than any other
American city, made me see how close we have come to the possible
end of American civilization. Unlike on the East Coast and in mid-
western cities, racial tensions in Los Angeles did not revolve around
blacks and whites; everybody—blacks, whites, Latinos, and Asians—
was vying for a piece of the shrinking American pie. Unlike San
Francisco, whose small size forced people to live in close proximity,
in Los Angeles a person could live without ever having to go to
South-Central or Koreatown. This allowed people who lived in sheltered, expensive enclaves to escape and ignore the miseries of the
inner city.

The Los Angeles riots of April 29 to May 3, 1992, devastated
the thriving Korean community in Los Angeles, the biggest Korean
settlement outside Asia. In one night, thousands of Koreans lost their
life savings and saw their many years of hard work go up in flames.
The immediate causes were easy to pinpoint. Korean community
leaders readily acknowledged that unpleasant encounters between
Korean shopkeepers and their customers had exacerbated tensions.
More importantly, they believed the negative portrayals in the media
of Korean merchants as rude, uncaring people were the main reason
that Koreans had been singled out in the looting and firebombing
during the riots. Interviewing and writing about riot victims, I often

recalled the Korean proverb about the "frog in the well": The riot victims I talked to had learned the hard way that it was not enough to work hard and mind their own business, viewing the world only from the vista of a deep well. They realized that they would have to expand their horizons.

Some during the riots took matters into their own hands. We will never forget the haunting television images of young Korean men, armed with semiautomatic weapons and pistols, positioned on the roofs of their buildings, ready to defend their property in the absence of any protection from the Los Angeles police. I cringed as I saw repeated television images of gun-toting Koreans. The images reinforced the problems that had preceded them—the lack of real communication with non-Koreans and the continued media representation of Korean store owners in an unfavorable light. The real story was the 2,400 Korean-owned businesses that were burned or destroyed by looters, and the financial toll that reached $400 million, not to mention fifty-three deaths and 2,383 injuries.

"The economic holocaust we experienced has affected every Korean in America and elsewhere," says K. W. Lee, the retired editor of the *Korea Times* English edition in Los Angeles whose observations of Korean American life span half a century. "The L.A. riots gave us a shocking recognition that we must make connections with other communities." The trauma of the riots and the legacy of anger, fear, and suspicion left by the looting and burning have become to Korean Americans what the World War II internment camps were, and still are, to many Japanese Americans.

Nearly three years later, TV cameras and reporters were no longer coming, but Koreans were still struggling to recover. Many who lost their businesses and livelihoods suffered from mental stress so severe that it was painful to describe, although I did so in articles for the *Times*. Others who managed to cope through financial hardship began searching for ways to ensure that the misunderstandings leading to the riots would never again occur. Hundreds of Koreans in the Los Angeles area enrolled in special classes designed to acculturate Korean immigrants to the realities of American economic and social life. Though they feel strongly that the media-reinforced stereotype of Koreans was unfair, their frustration has propelled thoughtful Korean Americans to come together and try to climb over the cultural wall that has made Koreans perhaps the most misunderstood of Asian immigrants.

"Learn to smile," they were told. Anytime I heard this, I thought, if only smiling at strangers were part of our culture! But by now, "smile, you're in America," became a new mantra, having replaced the one of "work, work, work." And they heard more messages: be cordial and friendly to your customers; cooperate with non-Koreans; and most importantly, accept the fact that now you are in America and this is your home—learn the language, learn the country, learn the rules.

I could not think of an assignment more challenging than explaining Koreans' outlooks and behaviors. When I was a young reporter, I might have felt typecast by being relegated to covering the Asian community, but now the Asian community—Koreans in particular—was so large and significant an economic force in Los Angeles that it was quickly becoming the tail wagging the dog, whether or not the mainstream media recognized this reality.

At the *Los Angeles Times* I was able to explore in print the cultural differences between East Asians and Americans much more than ever before at any previous newspaper. One of the highlights of my work in this area was a story addressing Confucianism as the basis of cultural conflicts between Korean immigrants and Americans. While the story focused on Korean immigrants' efforts to learn to smile and seek other ways of acculturating, I wanted to send the message that it was important to retain certain aspects of Korean culture, such as an appreciation for nonverbal communication.

Most of the stories about Koreans that I proposed to my editors in Los Angeles were readily accepted. For the first time at any American newspaper I had worked for, I was able to explore the everyday concerns of common American citizens and about-to-be citizens (who in this case happened to be Korean) and to display them, I hope, in their full humanity. My stories about the ninety-four-year-old owner of a Koreatown rice mill who still works twelve hours a day, seven days a week in keeping with his philosophy that "life without working is not worth living" brought countless responses from *Times* readers. And, my 1994 Father's Day story about an elderly black man who was raising an abandoned Korean child prompted such an outpouring of calls and letters that I literally spent days fielding queries.

At last, I was fulfilling my goal to introduce and interpret Asians to the non-Asian mainstream on their terms. And in doing so, I followed the lodestar of the sage Confucius by reminding myself that people's natures are alike, it is their habits that separate them. And, remembering the poet Robert Frost, we have miles to go before we sleep.

EPILOGUE

I cut in two a long November night
And place one half under the quilt.
Sweet as the spring breeze.
When he comes I shall take it out
And unroll it bit by bit
To stretch out the night.

—Chin-I Hwang (c. 1506–1544)⋆, *Koreana*

⋆Translated by Peter Hyun

It is Thanksgiving, 1994. Five and a half years have passed since my return to the United States. These have been defining moments for Koreans back home and in America, and for me personally.

In South Korea, for the first time in more than three decades, a civilian government, headed by Young-Sam Kim, a former dissident (see chapter 10), is in charge, and Koreans are enjoying more freedom than they have known except for the brief period after students toppled the Syngman Rhee government in 1960.

In America, the Los Angeles riots have given Koreans a searing experience of being at the flashpoint of racial and economic tensions. Their overblown expectations about life in America went up in smoke with their dreams. Through this baptism by fire, Korean immigrants have gained a much more realistic assessment of their limitations as newcomers in this country.

And, within me, the duality of being a Korean and an American requires me to continue the mental gymnastics of moving back and forth between these often-conflicting two worlds. The tensions of being both remain, but have eased. I am more American than Korean in my mind, but I am more Korean than American in my soul. As for my heart, it is split in half. Having chosen to live in America, though, I have a modicum of peace, a resolution at last.

That South Korea finally broke a dynasty of generals by installing a nonmilitary man in office in February 1993 was good news. Democracy, which has eluded Koreans for half century, may have finally taken root. I hope so.

The Korean road to democracy has been a long and tortuous one and still has a way to go. Given the backdrop of Korea's neo-Confucian social order, I doubt that Koreans will ever embrace democracy as we know it in the West. As long as Koreans address each other by their titles and speak a language that maintains layers of honorifics, the democratic premise that all humans are equal will be a challenge that I am not sure they can meet. Still, the political change is an advancement for a country where, until the late 1980s, getting a passport was a feat for the average person and citizens worried about their private telephone conversations being monitored.

Even from this side of the Pacific, I can feel this new wind of freedom. When I talk to relatives and friends in Korea, long pauses and silences no longer greet my queries, and words are not spoken ambiguously to get a message across without revealing too much. The Korean press is free, and people can speak without fearing retribution from the KCIA. South Korea and North Korea have been members of the United Nations for three years, and the issue of Korean reunification is being discussed in international forums. Like a large feuding family whose members have lived apart for a long time, the two Koreas have little in common. But reunify we must, so the seventy-five million ethnic Koreans can feel whole.

Since the death in July 1994 of Il-Sung Kim, North Korea's Stalin, I have looked at the old rusty keys to our house in Tanchon, which my family has carried through countless moves over the half century, to remind me that there is hope. Will the keys still open the doors of the house with the slate-colored tiles and upturned eaves? I do not know. But the prospect of the United States and North Korea establishing diplomatic relations excites me. Why must the Korean peninsula continue to carry the dubious distinction of being the last remaining legacy of the Cold War?

For Koreans in America, Los Angeles is the best place to be because of our numbers. I am reminded of this every time I go grocery shopping in a Koreatown supermarket. Trying to negotiate my cart around the bustling people with their loaded carts, hearing the din of Korean music and talk, and smelling the pungent odor of Korean spices, I momentarily can forget that I am in America. And, despite the lack of order and the pushing and shoving, I feel an inexplicable connection—a sense of Koreanness in a crowd. I feel the link when I tune in to Korean TV and radio stations, too. It is soothing to come home after a long day in the English-speaking world, turn off my cultural antennae, and turn on a Korean TV station and watch the news, then take in a soap opera or a miniseries to unwind and escape. On Sunday mornings when I cannot go to church, I can turn on the television and listen to the Reverend Hee-Min Park, the senior pastor of Youngnak (Eternal Pleasure) Presbyterian Church of Los Angeles, and hear his church's exceptional choir, in the comfort of my living room. Is there another place in the continental United States where I could make such choices on a Sunday morning?

America and Korea—each provides a mirror for me to look at the other more objectively and appreciatively. So I live with contradictions like preferring the smell of eggs and bacon and coffee in the morning rather than the aroma of a Korean breakfast, but I still have to think twice before addressing people older than me by their first name. And, when I am in the mood for kimchi, I bemoan the fate that keeps me working with non-Koreans. If I were around Koreans, I could eat kimchi anytime, but I ration my kimchi consumption for vacations and weekends. Yet, when I attend meetings and events in Koreatown after lunch and smell the overwhelming aroma of kimchi on peoples' breath, I'm tempted to admonish: "You really ought to save kimchi for dinner. This, after all, is America, and most Americans don't like the smell of kimchi on someone else's breath."

I like America in the spring, but I prefer Korea in the autumn. Like the swallows that fly to the south of the Han River, a child of Korea cannot help but look homeward toward the rabbit-shaped peninsula in the fall. Something about the skies of Korea, the chill in the air, the fruits and vegetables, the ondol room with a bowl of *soongnyoong* (the indigenous scorched rice tea), a plate of juicy sliced pears and sweet persimmons, a quilt, and a good book that stretched out into the night.

My father, who has lived away from Korea for forty-five years and has not returned except for brief visits, tells me he attends a Korean church because he feels slightly "more comfortable" in a Korean church than in an American church, as does my mother. But he does not feel completely comfortable in a largely immigrant Korean church, because he simply has had too much exposure to America and Western thought. So every now and then, he joins me in attending an American church, like Grace Cathedral on San Francisco's Nob Hill or Calvary Presbyterian Church in Pacific

Heights, because he has come to enjoy the experience deeply. I, on the other hand, regularly attend a mainstream church because I feel slightly more at home worshiping in an American church than in an immigrant Korean one. But every now and then, I do attend a Korean church, and when I do, I renew a sense of connection to my people. It also feels good to sing "How Great Thou Art" and "Amazing Grace" in Korean, and I find it a nice change to have rice cakes and barley tea instead of cookies and coffee when socializing after church service.

Often I have wondered if I am fated to lead a split existence, bearing the joys and burdens of having my heart in two cultures— hating and loving both. One way, however, I have remained Korean and Asian is in my outlook on humanity's place in nature. In Eastern paintings human beings are depicted as mere specks in grand landscapes, yet the great Western painters and sculptors have made the human form the center of their universe. I cannot help but admire their arrogance and brashness—it is that kind of humanistic ethos that underpins Western civilization. And, it was the Eastern attitude toward humanity's place that ultimately led Asians to try to insulate themselves from the encroachment of Western civilization in the nineteenth and twentieth centuries. But Western gunboat diplomacy was simply too powerful to push back, as first China, then Japan, and finally tiny Korea learned.

With the twenty-first century of the Pacific Rim upon us, we hear people say that it is time to learn from other civilizations, to cull the best from each. Obviously, that is easier said than done. There are simply too many inherent contradictions and conflicting values between West and East. Take, for instance, the idea of communication. Western culture is verbal and prizes assertiveness; in the Confucian cultures of East Asia, the situation is reversed. "Speak up, speak up," Americans are prone to say. But in a culture where "speaking up" is impolite, doing so is offensive. Belatedly, after many unfortunate experiences, Asians learn that to an American "No, thank you" means just that, not just a polite way of saying "Yes, please."

And, more than a century after the United States established diplomatic relations with Asia, Americans are just now learning the nuances of communication with Japanese, Chinese, and Koreans.

There are metaphors galore on both sides. In the West, the squeaky wheel gets the grease. But across the Pacific, the nail that sticks out gets pounded down, and trees that stand tallest catch the most wind. Here, one has to toot one's horn to be heard. In the East, only a half-baked fool would boast, because people in positions of authority are presumed to recognize a person's qualities. In the West, a man who speaks well of his wife outside the home is considered a good spouse. But in the East, nothing could breach social etiquette as much as bragging about one's spouse beyond one's family. In the West, particularly in the United States, people communicate by explaining their views. Among Koreans, important communication is often nonverbal, and sometimes what you say may be just the opposite of what you mean. A Korean of sound mind could not imagine holding up a placard saying, "Hi, Mom," and waving into a TV camera—especially on an occasion as auspicious as the Seoul Olympics. Yet, to his American counterpart, no occasion is so dignified that he cannot send a message to his mother. Even on the most august occasions, Americans take the time to kiss and hug, and Europeans have made such gestures an art form. This is the way they show their feelings. Koreans transmit their feelings silently. They will send a son off to war, and not touch him one last time.

I have kept in mind always, when comparing Americans and Koreans, the story of the famous Korean General Yu-Shin Kim. The general was leading his troops as they passed through his native village. In front of him stood the house in which he had been born. If he had only knocked at the gate, he could have seen the face of his beloved mother, whom he had yearned so long to see. Instead, General Kim had his soldiers go to his house and bring back some hot bean-paste sauce. He remained on his horse and tasted it. When he confirmed that the bean paste was as he remembered it, he knew that his mother was well, and the general left without a word.

Whenever I think of the story, I can imagine the general's mother, tears streaming down her wrinkled face, wondering whether she would live long enough to see him again, but bound to our timeless cultural code. I know these Korean mothers. Koreans love this story, but Americans would probably think how silly he was to have been at his mother's doorstep without going inside. In Hollywood Westerns, the cowboy rescues his love and they ride off into the sunset. In Korean movies, mismatched lovers part because they must yield to society's demands.

That difference between the two scenarios is what makes living in America both an exhilarating and an exhausting challenge for Koreans. Korean women adjust more easily to American life than do Korean men, because America is liberating for the women. But it has an opposite effect on most Korean immigrant men. Since most Korean women have not worked outside the home, they are more willing to take any job—in sewing factories, Asian restaurants, Korean groceries, laundries, and manicure parlors. But the entry of Korean women into the workplace and their ability to earn money have created tensions in the home. Korean men, being so used to having their wives waiting on them, find their self-esteem plummeting in America. It is hard on the macho Korean male ego to become suddenly crippled by language, cultural barriers, and the inability to find professional work of the type they believe they deserve. The feeling of inadequacy depresses them. With so many of the roles reversed, Korean women, too, are overwhelmed. The high divorce rate among Koreans in the United States—double that in Korea—reflects the stress of immigrant life.

Starting from the bottom up in America has contributed to deep psychological problems for Korean immigrants, too. Overcoming the frustration of feeling like nobody in America is a struggle for both men and women, though the situation has been especially difficult for educated Korean men. Away from the society where they were on a pedestal, Korean men find the American culture of "ladies first" hostile and grating on their nature. In this new land, their children take on inordinate importance. The fathers may work as janitors, run liquor stores and pump gas, but their children will go to top schools and will achieve the social status here that their parents were denied as immigrants. The pressure on Korean youngsters to fulfill their parents' ambitions is enormous. I should know. Reading over the pages of my journals from college days, it is a wonder that I did not break down under the pressure of my family. The cumulative effect of centuries of poverty and hunger on the Korean psyche is so pervasive that immigrant parents cannot fathom why their children complain when their stomachs are full. What could be easier than studying when you don't have to worry about where your next meal is coming from? is what the parents think and say.

My transcultural journey of four decades has led me down many roads my culture would never endorse. At the same time, I have been unable to break away from the innumerable intangible constraints of my culture or from family entanglements. But Koreanness is like being a member of a big family. You rejoice, fight, and sometimes stop talking to each other for a while, but the sheer effort of keeping the family together gives you this thing called *cheong*—"love," Korean-style. *Cheong,* a complex emotion encompassing love, closeness, affection, affinity, trust, and loyalty, is at the root of Koreanness. To Koreans, there is no such thing as love at first sight. Love, Korean-style, is like embers in a smoldering fire; only betrayal can end it. *Han* is the other side of *cheong.* It is this indescribable fate that Koreans feel in the depths of their hearts and deepest recesses of their souls. It is that inexplicable Korean belief in everlasting grudges, everlasting sorrows, everlasting regrets, everlasting woes, everlasting wishes, and everlasting hopes—rolled into one. The divided Korean peninsula best expresses on a large scale the collective Korean *han,* a sense of incompleteness and unfulfillment. On a personal level, *han* is the Korean tenet of an eternal woe, unrequited love, and unending hope and wishes.

It is because of *cheong* and *han* that Koreans cannot agree to disagree. *Cheong* and *han.* Koreans esteem *cheong* and *han* as much as Americans revere the ideals of liberty, justice, and the pursuit of happiness. *Cheong* and *han* make Korean life both meaningful and wretched. They create entanglements that prevent us from keeping our emotional drawers neat and tidy.

☯

I do not believe we Asians can assimilate in America because of how we look. The melting pot was possible for non-English-speaking Caucasians from Europe once the second generation spoke English like natives. But with us, it does not matter how long our ancestors have been here and how well we speak English. Even a fourth-generation Chinese American whose great-grandparents came to San Francisco in the 1850s will still be considered a "foreigner" in America.

For this reason, I believe maintaining our collective memory and bilingual and bicultural identity is essential. I do not accept the American proposition that once you come here, you have to burn the bridge behind you and rid yourself of your cultural memories in order to become a good American. On the contrary, we become better citizens with a greater appreciation for America when we know who we are, where we came from, and why we came. A strong identity is not only crucial to our well-being but will contribute to making the great American experiment work—and everybody has a stake in making the experiment work. I think Americans of Italian, Greek, French, German, Swedish and all the other cultural backgrounds ought to speak their ancestral language in addition to English. The American preoccupation with monolingualism is laziness bordering on arrogance. To know another language is to discover another world. To know another world is an asset, not a liability. All of us—yellow, red, brown, black, or white—can only gain by such knowledge.

One of the saddest sights I have witnessed is American-born Asian youngsters who cannot talk to their grandparents. I think we can have both heritages—Asian and American. We will be richer for it, as will the country in the long run. Those who do not know their ancestral language, culture, and history are "cultural eunuchs"—a term coined by the Korean American thinker K. W. Lee to describe Asians without memory. But knowledge can sustain us because it is powerful. I think of the Dalai Lama, the spiritual leader of Tibet, who talks of confidence by quoting from the ancient Sutra of Vajra Banner: "When the sun rises, it shines over the whole world, regardless of people's blindness or mountain shadows." Knowledge is like the sun, I think.

So, I look back to where I came from. I hope my ancestors, asleep in the family orchard behind our home, are not cross with me for neglecting the duties of their progeny. Living nine thousand miles away in the United States, I feel sorrow at my destiny, which will not allow me to visit their resting places, to put flowers in front of their gravestones, and to pay them the respect they deserve. It is my fervent hope and prayer that these days of separation will soon end.

SUGGESTED READING

In writing this book, I depended not only on my own observations and research, including interviews with hundreds of Koreans, but also on the studies of a vast number of Korean and foreign scholars, writers and journalists. They are too numerous to list. For those who want to read more about some aspects of Korean life I touched on in this book, there are many books available in English, though more narrowly focused works still remain accessible only to those who read Korean.

Allen, Richard C. *Korea's Syngman Rhee: An Unauthorized Portrait.* Rutland, Vt.: Tuttle, 1960.

Baldwin, Frank P. Jr., ed. *Without Parallel: The American–Korean Relationship since 1945.* New York: Pantheon Books, 1974.

Boettcher, Robert, and Gordon L. Freedman. *Gifts of Deceit: Sun Myung Moon, Tongsun Park and the Korean Scandal.* New York: Holt, Rinehart & Winston, 1980.

Burge, Frederick, ed. *North Korea: A Country Study.* Washington, D.C.: Government Printing Office, 1982.

Carpenter, Frances. *Tales of a Korean Grandmother.* Rutland, Vt., Tuttle, 1973.

Choy, Bong-Youn. *Koreans in America.* Chicago. Nelson-Hall, 1979.

Chung, Donald K. *The Three Day Promise: A Korean Soldier's Memoir.* Tallahassee, Fl.: Father & Son Publishing, 1989.

Chung, Henry. *The Case of Korea.* New York: Revell, 1921.

Cook, Harold F. *Korea's 1884 Incident: Its Background and Kim Ok Kyun's Elusive Dream*. Seoul: Taewon, 1972.

Crane, Paul. *Korean Patterns*. Seoul: Royal Asiatic Society, Korea Branch, 1978.

Cumings, Bruce. *The Origins of the Korean War: Liberation and the Emergence of Separate Regimes, 1945–47*. Princeton, N.J.: Princeton University Press, 1981.

Dallet, Charles. *Historie de l'Église de Corée*. 2 vols. Paris: V. Palme, 1874. Reprint, Seoul: Royal Asiatic Society, Korea Branch, 1975.

Daniels, Michael J. *Through a Rain-Spattered Window*. Seoul: Taewon, 1973.

Daniels, Roger. *Asian America: Chinese and Japanese in the United States since 1850*. Seattle: University of Washington Press, 1988.

Dean, William F. *General Dean's Story*. New York: Viking, 1954.

Dennett, Tyler. *Americans in Eastern Asia: A Critical Study of the Policy of the United States with Reference to China, Japan and Korea in the Nineteenth Century*. New York: Macmillan, 1922. Reprint, New York: Barnes & Noble, 1963.

Deuchler, Martina. *Confucian Gentlemen and Barbarian Envoys: The Opening of Korea, 1875–1885*. Seattle: University of Washington Press, 1977.

Gale, James S. *Korea in Transition*. New York: Laymen's Missionary Movement, 1909.

Gardner, Arthur L. "The Korean Nationalist Movement and An Ch'ang-Ho, Advocate of Gradualism." 1905–1945. Ph.D. diss., University of Hawaii, 1979.

Gardiner, K. H. J. *The Early History of Korea: The Historical Development of the Peninsula up to the Introduction of Buddhism in the Fourth Century A.D.* Honolulu: University of Hawaii Press, 1969.

Goodrich, Leland M. *Korea: A Study of U.S. Policy in the United Nations*. New York: Council on Foreign Relations, 1956.

Goulden, Joseph C. *Korea: The Untold Story of the War*. New York: Times Books, 1982.

Ha, Tae-Hung. *A Trip through Historic Korea*. Seoul: Yonsei University Press, 1958.

Hahm, Pyong-Choon. *The Korean Political Tradition and Law: Essays in*

Korean Law and Legal History. Seoul: Royal Asiatic Society, Korea Branch, 1967.

Han, Woo-Keun. *The History of Korea*. Translated by Kyong-shik Lee, edited by Grafton K. Mintz. Honolulu: University Press of Hawaii, 1971.

Han, Sung-Joo. *The Failure of Democracy in South Korea*. Berkeley. University of California Press, 1974.

Harrington, Fred Harvey. *God, Mammon, and the Japanese: Dr. Horace N. Allen and Korean-American Relations, 1884–1905*. Madison: University of Wisconsin Press, 1944.

Henderson, Gregory. *Korea: The Politics of the Vortex*. Cambridge, Mass.: Harvard University Press, 1968.

Henthorn, William E. *A History of Korea*. New York: Free Press, 1971.

———. *Korea: The Mongol Invasions*. Leiden: Brill, 1963.

Hulbert, Homer B. *The History of Korea*. 2 vols. 1905. Edited by Clarence N. Weems. New York: Hilary House, 1962.

———. *The Passing Korea*. New York: Doubleday Page, 1906. Reprint, Seoul: Yonsei University Press, 1969.

Hyun, Peter. *Darkness at Dawn: A North Korean Diary*. Seoul: Hanjin, 1981.

———. *Koreana*. Seoul: Korea Britannica, 1984.

Hyun, Peter. *Man Sei! The Making of a Korean American*. Honolulu: University of Hawaii Press, 1986.

Hwang, Sun-Won. *Shadows of a Sound*. Edited by Holman, J. Martin. San Francisco: Mercury House, 1990.

Iryon. *Samguk Yusa: Legends and History of the Three Kingdoms of Ancient Korea*. Translated by Tae-Hung Ha and Grafton K. Mintz. Seoul: Yonsei University Press, 1972.

Jin, Tak, Gang-Il Kim, and Hong-Je Pak. *Great Leader: Kim Jong Il*. Tokyo: Sorinsha, 1986.

Joe, Wanne J. *Traditional Korea: A Cultural History*. Seoul: Chungang University Press, 1972.

Juche! Towards a United Independent Korea. Melbourne: New Democratic Publications, 1973.

Kang, Hugh H. W., ed. *The Traditional Culture and Society of Korea: Thought and Institutions.* Honolulu: Center for Korean Studies, University of Hawaii, 1975.

Kang, Younghill. *The Grass Roof.* New York: Scribner's, 1931. Reprint, Chicago: Follett, 1966.

————.*East Goes West.* New York: Scribner's, 1937.

Kho, Songmoo. *Koreans in Soviet Central Asia.* Helsinki: Finnish Oriental Society, 1987.

Kim, Chi-Ha. *Cry of the People and Other Poems.* Tokyo: Autumn Press, 1974.

Kim, C. I. Eugene, and Han-Kyo Kim. *Korea and the Politics of Imperialism, 1876–1910.* Berkeley: University of California Press, 1967.

Kim, Jeong-Hak. *The Prehistory of Korea.* Translated by Richard J. Pearson and Kazue Pearson. Honolulu: University Press of Hawaii, 1979.

Kim, Key-Hiuk. *The Last Phase of the East Asian World Order: Korea, Japan, and the Chinese Empire, 1860–1882.* Berkeley: University of California Press, 1980.

Kim, Kwan-Bong. *The Korea-Japan Treaty Crisis and the Instability of the Korean Political System.* New York: Praeger, 1971.

Kim, Richard. *Lost Names: Scenes from a Korean Boyhood.* New York: Praeger, 1970.

Kim, Quee-Young. *The Fall of Syngman Rhee.* Berkeley: Institute of East Asian Studies, University of California, 1983.

Kim, Se-Jin. *The Politics of Military Revolution in Korea.* Chapel Hill: University of North Carolina Press, 1971.

Kim, Yung-Chung, ed. and trans. *Women of Korea: A History from Ancient Times to 1945.* Seoul: Ewha Womans University Press, 1976.

Ko, Won. *Some Other Times.* Los Angeles: Bombshelter Press, 1990.

Koh, Byung-Chul. *The Foreign Policy of North Korea.* New York: Praeger, 1960.

Kwak, Tae-Hwan, and Seong Hyong Lee, eds. *The Korean-American Community: Present and Future.* Pusan: Kyungnam University Press, 1991.

Ledyard, Gari. *The Dutch Come to Korea.* Seoul: Royal Asiatic Society, Korea Branch, 1971.

Lee, Chong-Sik. *The Politics of Korean Nationalism.* Berkeley: University of California Press, 1965.

Lee, Ki-Baik. *A New History of Korea.* Translated by Edward W. Wagner, with Edward J. Shultz. Cambridge, Mass: Harvard University Press, 1984.

Li, Mirok. *The Yalu Flows: A Korean Childhood.* East Lansing: Michigan State University Press, 1956.

Liem, Channing. *Philip Jaisohn: The First Korean American—A Forgotten Hero.* Seoul: Kyujang, 1984.

McCune, George M. *Korea Today.* Cambridge, Mass: Harvard University Press, 1950.

McGrane, George A. *Korea's Tragic Hours: The Closing of the Yi Dynasty.* Edited by Harold F. Cook and Alan M. MacDougall. Seoul: Taewon, 1973.

McKenzie, Frederick A. *Korea's Fight for Freedom.* New York: Revell, 1920. Reprint, Seoul: Yonsei University Press, 1969.

———. *The Tragedy of Korea.* London: Hodder & Strongton, 1908. Reprint, Seoul: Yonsei University Press, 1969.

Meade, E. Grant. *American Military Government in Korea.* New York: King's Crown Press, 1951.

Oliver, Robert T. *Syngman Rhee: The Man behind the Myth.* New York: Dodd Mead, 1954.

———. *Syngman Rhee and American Involvement in Korea, 1942–1960: A Personal Narrative.* Seoul: Panmun Book Company, 1978.

O'Rourke, Kevin, trans. *A Washed-Out Dream.* Larchmont, N.Y.: Larchwood Publications, 1973.

Osgood, Cornelius. *The Koreans and Their Culture.* New York: Ronald Press, 1951.

Paige, Glenn D. *The Korean Decision, June 24–30, 1950.* New York: Free Press, 1968.

Palais, James B. *Politics and Policy in Traditional Korea.* Cambridge, Mass.: Harvard University Press, 1975.

Park, Yune-Hee. *Admiral Yi Sun-Sin and His Turtleboat Armada.* Rev. ed. Seoul: Hanjin, 1978.

Patterson, Wayne. *The Korean Frontier in America: Immigration to Hawaii, 1896–1910*. Honolulu: University of Hawaii Press, 1988.

Patterson, Wayne, and Hyung-Chan Kim, *Koreans in America*. Minneapolis: Lerner, 1992.

Rees, David. *Korea: The Limited War*. New York: St. Martin's Press, 1964.

Ridgway, Matthew B. *The Korean War*. New York: Da Capo Press, 1967.

Rutt, Richard. *The Bamboo Grove: An Introduction to Sijo*. Berkeley: University of California Press, 1971.

————.*James Scarth Gale's History of the Korean People*. Seoul: Royal Asiatic Society, Korea Branch, 1975.

————.*Korean Works and Days: Notes from the Diary of a Country Priest*. 2nd ed. Seoul: Royal Asiatic Society, Korea Branch, 1964, (reprinted 1978).

Rutt, Richard, and Chong-Un Kim, trans. *Virtuous Women: Three Masterpieces of Korean Fiction*. Seoul: Korea National Commission for UNESCO, 1974.

Scalapino, Robert A. ed. *North Korea Today*. New York: Praeger, 1963.

Scalapino, Robert A., and Chong-Sik Lee. *Communism in Korea*. 2 vols. Berkeley: University of California Press, 1972.

Schaeffer, Robert. *Warpaths: The Politics of Partition*. New York: Hill & Wang, 1990.

Sohn, Pow-Key, Chol-Choon Kim, and Yi-Sup Hong. *The History of Korea*. Seoul: Korean National Commission for UNESCO, 1970.

Solzhenitsyn, Aleksandr I. *The Gulag Archipelago*. New York: Harper & Row, 1973.

Solberg, S. E. *The Land and People of Korea*. New York: HarperCollins, 1991.

Stone, I. F. *The Hidden History of the Korean War*. New York: Monthly Review Press, 1952.

Suh, Dae-Sook. *The Korean Communist Movement, 1918–1948*. Princeton University Press, 1967.

Suh, Dae-Sook, ed. *Koreans in the Soviet Union,* Papers of the Center for Korean Studies, University of Hawaii, 1986.

Takaki, Ronald. *Strangers from a Different Shore: A History of Asian Americans.* Boston: Little, Brown, 1989.

Voorhees, Melvin B. *Korean Tales.* New York: Simon & Schuster, 1952.

Wales, Nym, and San Kim. *Song of Ariran: A Korean Communist in the Chinese Revolution.* San Francisco: Ramparts Press, revised edition, 1972.

Weems, Benjamin B. *Reform, Rebellion and the Heavenly Way.* Tucson: University of Arizona Press, 1964.

Wilson, Jim. *Retreat, Hell! We're Just Attacking in Another Direction.* New York: William Morrow, 1988.

Yi, Pangja. *The World Is One: Princess Yi Pangja's Autobiography.* Translated by Sukkyu Kim. Seoul: Taewon, 1973.

Yu, Eui-Young. *Korean Community Profile.* Los Angeles: Korea Times/Hankook Ilbo, 1990.

Yu, Eui-Young, ed. *Black-Korean Encounter: Toward Understanding and Alliance.* Los Angeles: Institute for Asian American and Pacific Asian Studies, California State University, 1994.

PERMISSION ACKNOWLEDGMENTS

Grateful acknowledgment is made to the following writers for permission to reprint their previously published and unpublished material:

Peter Hyun: Translation of Chin-I Hwang's sijo and Byong-Hwa Cho's "Sqeezed between City and Civilization," from Hyun's book, *Koreana*.

Sung-Won Ko (Ko Won): "Panmunjom" from his book of poetry, *Some Other Time*.

K. W. Lee: Excerpts from one of numerous interviews with the author about Korean Independence.

Sung-Il Lee: His late father, In-Soo Lee's translation of Sang-Hwa Yi's "Does Spring Come Also to These Stolen Fields?" and Yook-Sa Yi's "The Vertex," from *Korean Verses*.

S. E. Solberg: Translation of Nam-Son Choe's "We Have Nothing" from Solberg's latest book, *The Land and People of Korea*, and his soon-to-be published translation of Young-Nang Kim's "Until the Peony Blooms," which Solberg has so generously allowed the author to publish first.